STANDARDS PRACTICE
FOR HOME OR SCHOOL
Grade 3

INCLUDES:

- Home or School Practice
- Lesson Practice and Test Preparation
- English and Spanish School-Home Letters
- Dig Deeper and Connect Lessons
- Getting Ready for Grade 4 Lessons

HOUGHTON MIFFLIN HARCOURT

Printed in the U.S.A.

ISBN 978-0-547-39263-9

9 10 0928 15 14

4500496016   ^ B C D E

Number and Operations

1

1 Place Value

School-Home Letter (English) **P1**
School-Home Letter (Spanish) **P2**
1.1 **Algebra:** Number Patterns **P3**
1.2 **Problem Solving:** Make a List • Place Value **P5**
1.3 Numbers Through Hundreds **P7**
1.4 Numbers Through Thousands **P9**
1.5 Read and Write Numbers Through Thousands . . . **P11**
1.6 Compare and Order Numbers **P13**
1.7 Round to the Nearest Ten, Hundred, or Thousand . . **P15**
Extra Practice **P17**

2 Addition and Subtraction

School-Home Letter (English) **P19**
School-Home Letter (Spanish) **P20**
2.1 Estimate Sums **P21**
2.2 Add 3-Digit Numbers **P23**
2.3 Add 4-Digit Numbers **P25**
2.4 Estimate Differences **P27**
2.5 Subtract 3-Digit Numbers **P29**
2.6 Subtract 4-Digit Numbers **P31**
2.7 **Problem Solving:**
Draw a Diagram • Addition and Subtraction **P33**
Extra Practice **P35**

3 **Time and Money**

School-Home Letter (English) **P37**
School-Home Letter (Spanish) **P38**
3.1 Tell Time **P39**
3.2 Time to the Minute **P41**
3.3 A.M. and P.M. **P43**
3.4 Elapsed Time **P45**
3.5 **Problem Solving:** Act It Out • Elapsed Time **P47**
3.6 Count Coins and Bills **P49**
3.7 Compare Amounts of Money **P51**
3.8 **Problem Solving:** Make a Table • Money **P53**
3.9 Make Change **P55**
3.10 Add and Subtract Money Amounts **P57**
Extra Practice **P59**

4 **Collect and Analyze Data**

School-Home Letter (English) **P61**
School-Home Letter (Spanish) **P62**
4.1 Collect Data **P63**
4.2 **Problem Solving:** Make a Table • Data **P65**
4.3 Use Pictographs **P67**
4.4 Make Pictographs **P69**
4.5 Use Bar Graphs **P71**
4.6 Make Bar Graphs **P73**
4.6A CONNECT Solve Data Problems **P74a**
4.7 Understand Line Plots **P75**
Extra Practice **P77**

© Houghton Mifflin Harcourt Publishing Company

5 Understand Multiplication

School-Home Letter (English) **P79**
School-Home Letter (Spanish) **P80**
5.1 Count Equal Groups **P81**
5.2 Algebra: Relate Addition and Multiplication **P83**
5.3 Multiply with 2 . . . . **P85**
5.4 Multiply with 4 . . . . **P87**
5.5 Multiply with 5 and 10 . . . . **P89**
5.6 Problem Solving:
Draw a Diagram • Multiplication **P91**
5.7 Algebra: Model with Arrays **P93**
5.8 Algebra: Commutative Property of Multiplication **P95**
5.9 Algebra: Multiply with 1 and 0 . . . . **P97**
Extra Practice **P99**

6 Multiplication Facts and Strategies

School-Home Letter (English) **P101**
School-Home Letter (Spanish) **P102**
6.1 Multiply with 3 . . . . **P103**
6.2 Multiply with 6 . . . . **P105**
6.3 Algebra: Associative Property of Multiplication **P107**
6.4 Algebra: Distributive Property **P109**
6.5 Multiply with 8 . . . . **P111**
6.6 Problem Solving: Make a Table • Multiplication **P113**
6.7 Multiply with 9 . . . . **P115**
6.8 Multiply with 7 . . . . **P117**
6.9 Algebra: Find a Rule **P119**
6.10 Algebra: Missing Factors **P121**
Extra Practice **P123**

7 Understand Division

School-Home Letter (English) **P125**
School-Home Letter (Spanish) **P126**
7.1 Size of Equal Groups **P127**
7.2 Number of Equal Groups **P129**
7.3 Divide by 2 . . . . **P131**
7.4 Divide by 5 . . . . **P133**
7.5 **Algebra:** Relate Division and Subtraction **P135**
7.6 **Investigate:** Model with Arrays **P137**
7.7 **Problem Solving:** Act It Out • Division **P139**
7.8 **Algebra:** Relate Multiplication and Division . . . **P141**
7.9 **Algebra:** Fact Families **P143**
7.10 Divide by 10 . . . . **P145**
Extra Practice **P147**

8 Division Facts and Strategies

School-Home Letter (English) **P149**
School-Home Letter (Spanish) **P150**
8.1 Divide by 3 . . . . **P151**
8.2 Divide by 4 . . . . **P153**
8.3 **Algebra:** Division Rules for 1 and 0 . . . . **P155**
8.4 Divide by 6 . . . . **P157**
8.5 Divide by 7 . . . . **P159**
8.6 Divide by 8 . . . . **P161**
8.7 Divide by 9 . . . . **P163**
8.8 **Problem Solving:** Act It Out • Division **P165**
8.9 **Algebra:** Expressions and Equations **P167**
Extra Practice **P169**

Fractions

9 Understand Fractions

School-Home Letter (English) **P171**
School-Home Letter (Spanish) **P172**
9.1 Equal Parts of a Whole **P173**
9.2 Equal Shares **P175**
9.3 Unit Fractions of a Whole **P177**
9.4 Fractions of a Whole **P179**
9.5 Fractions Greater Than 1 . . . . **P181**
9.6 Fractions of a Group **P183**
9.7 Find Part of a Group **P185**
9.8 **Problem Solving:** Draw a Diagram • Fractions **P187**
Extra Practice **P189**

10 Compare and Order Fractions

School-Home Letter (English) **P191**
School-Home Letter (Spanish) **P192**
10.1 **Problem Solving:**
Act It Out • Compare Fractions **P193**
10.2 Compare Fractions Using Benchmarks **P195**
10.3 Compare Fractions with the Same Numerator **P197**
10.4 Compare Fractions **P199**
10.5 Order Fractions **P201**
10.6 **Investigate:** Model Equivalent Fractions **P203**
10.7 Equivalent Fractions **P205**
Extra Practice **P207**

11 Two-Dimensional Shapes

School-Home Letter (English) **P209**
School-Home Letter (Spanish) **P210**
11.1 Describe Plane Shapes **P211**
11.2 Classify Angles **P213**
11.3 Identify Polygons **P215**
11.4 Describe Lines **P217**
11.5 Classify Quadrilaterals **P219**
11.6 Classify Triangles **P221**
11.7 Combine and Separate Shapes **P223**
11.8 Identify Congruent Shapes **P225**
11.9 Identify Symmetry **P227**
11.10 Draw Lines of Symmetry **P229**
11.11 **Problem Solving:**
Draw a Diagram • Plane Shapes **P231**
11.12 Slides, Flips, and Turns **P233**
Extra Practice **P235**

12 Three-Dimensional Shapes and Geometric Patterns

School-Home Letter (English) **P237**
School-Home Letter (Spanish) **P238**
12.1 Identify Solid Shapes **P239**
12.2 Model Solid Shapes **P241**
12.3 Combine Solid Shapes **P243**
12.4 Identify Relationships **P245**
12.5 **Algebra:** Patterns with Shapes **P247**
12.6 **Algebra:** Make a Pattern **P249**
12.7 **Problem Solving:**
Find a Pattern • Plane Shapes **P251**
Extra Practice **P253**

13 Measurement

School-Home Letter (English) **P255**

School-Home Letter (Spanish) **P256**

13.1   Customary Units for Length **P257**

13.2   Measure to the Nearest Half Inch **P259**

    13.2A DIG DEEPER Measure to the Nearest Fourth Inch **P260a**

13.3   Metric Units for Length **P261**

13.4   Centimeters, Decimeters, and Meters **P263**

13.5   **Investigate:** Model Perimeter **P265**

13.6   Measure Perimeter **P267**

    13.6A DIG DEEPER Change Customary Units for Length **P268a**

13.7   **Problem Solving:** Find a Pattern • Perimeter **P269**

13.8   **Investigate:** Find Area **P271**

13.9   Relate Perimeter and Area **P273**

    13.9A DIG DEEPER Solve Perimeter and Area **P274a**

13.10 Investigate: Customary Units for Capacity **P275**

    13.10A DIG DEEPER Change Customary Units for Capacity . . **P276a**

13.11 Customary Units for Weight **P277**

    13.11A DIG DEEPER Change Customary Units for Weight . . . **P278a**

13.12 Metric Units for Capacity and Mass **P279**

    Extra Practice **P281**

End-of-Year Resources

Getting Ready for Grade 4

These lessons review important skills and prepare you for Grade 4.

Lesson 1 Read and Write Numbers Through Ten Thousands **P283**

Lesson 2 Compare 4- and 5-Digit Numbers . . **P285**

Lesson 3 Add More than Two Addends **P287**

Lesson 4 **Algebra:** Addition and Subtraction Expressions **P289**

Lesson 5 **Algebra:** Addition and Subtraction Equations **P291**

Checkpoint **P293**

Lesson 6 Multiplication with 11 and 12 . . . . **P295**

Lesson 7 Division with 11 and 12 . . . . **P297**

Lesson 8 **Algebra:** Multiplication and Division Relationships **P299**

Lesson 9 **Algebra:** Multiplication and Division Expressions and Equations **P301**

Lesson 10 Use Multiplication Patterns **P303**

Checkpoint **P305**

Lesson 11 Use Models to Multiply Tens and Ones **P307**

Lesson 12 **Algebra:** Use Multiplication Properties **P309**

Lesson 13 Model Division with Remainders . . . **P311**

Lesson 14 Model and Record Division **P313**

Lesson 15 Use Division Patterns **P315**

Checkpoint **P317**

Lesson 16 Fahrenheit Temperature **P319**

Lesson 17 Celsius Temperature **P321**

Lesson 18 Change Units for Length **P323**

Lesson 19 Change Units for Capacity **P325**

Lesson 20 Change Units for Weight and Mass **P327**

Checkpoint **P329**

School-Home Letter

Dear Family,

During the next few weeks, our math class will be learning about place value and numbers through thousands.

You can expect to see homework that provides practice with writing numbers, number patterns, comparing and ordering numbers, and rounding.

Here is a sample of one way your child will be taught to compare numbers.

Vocabulary

equal to =

greater than >

less than <

round To find a number that tells you *about how much* or *about how many*

🔑 MODEL Compare numbers.

Compare digits in the same place value position from left to right. Compare 314 and 342.

Hundreds	Tens	Ones
3	1	4
3	4	2

Both numbers have 3 hundreds. Look at the tens digit. 4 is greater than 1, so, 4 tens is greater than 1 ten.

342 > 314

So, 342 is greater than 314.

Tips

Comparing Numbers by the Number of Digits

A whole number with more digits is always greater than a whole number with fewer digits. For example, any 4-digit number is greater than any 3-digit number.

Activity

Have your child use everyday situations to compare numbers. For example: "We are traveling on Route 527. What number can you think of that is greater than 527? What number is less than 527?"

Carta para la casa

© Houghton Mifflin Harcourt Publishing Company

Vocabulario

igual a =

mayor que >

menor que <

redondear Hallar el número que dice *aproximadamente cuánto* o *aproximadamente cuántos*

Querida familia,

Durante las próximas semanas, en la clase de matemáticas estudiaremos el valor de posición y los números hasta los millares.

Llevaré a la casa tareas con actividades que incluyen escribir números, patrones de números, comparar y ordenar números, y redondear.

Este es un ejemplo de la manera como aprenderemos a comparar números.

🔑 MODELO Comparar números.

Compara dígitos con el mismo valor de posición de izquierda a derecha. Compara 314 y 342.

Centenas	Decenas	Unidades
3	1	4
3	4	2

Ambos números tienen 3 centenas. Observa el dígito de las decenas. 4 es mayor que 1. 4 decenas es mayor que 1 decena.

342 > 314

Por tanto, 342 es mayor que 314.

Pistas

Comparar números por el número de dígitos

Un número entero con más dígitos es siempre mayor que un número entero con menos dígitos. Por ejemplo, cualquier número de 4 dígitos es mayor que cualquier número de 3 dígitos.

Actividad

Pida a su hijo que compare números en situaciones de la vida diaria. Por ejemplo: "Vamos por la Ruta 527. Piensa en un número que sea mayor que 527. ¿Cuál es? ¿Qué número es menor que 527?"

Name _____

Number Patterns

Write a rule for the pattern. Then write the missing number.

1. 32, 37, 42, 47, __52__   Rule: __Add 5.__

2. 75, 65, 55, 45, __35__   Rule: __Subd 10__

3. 66, 69, 72, 75, __78__   Rule: __Add 3__

4. 90, 88, 86, 84, __82__   Rule: __Sub 2__

5. 12, 16, 20, 24, __28__   Rule: __Add 4__

6. 53, 59, 65, 71, __77__   Rule: __Add 6__

Write each number in the correct group.

7. 25   47   34   80   61   14   77

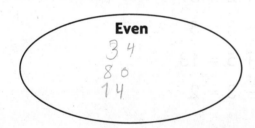

Even
34
80
14

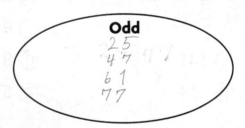

Odd
25
47
61
77

Problem Solving REAL WORLD

8. Kerry has 25 pennies. She saves 3 pennies every day for 4 days. How many pennies does Kerry have now?

___37 pennies___

9. Sean has 20¢. He saves 5¢ every day for 5 days. How much money does Sean have now? Write a rule to show his saving pattern.

___25¢___

Lesson Check

1. Dan writes this number pattern. If he continues the pattern, what will the next number be?

   52, 55, 58, 61, ⬜

   (A) 62   (C) 64
   (B) 63   (D) 65

2. Sue writes this number pattern. Which rule best describes the pattern?

   76, 72, 68, 64, 60

   (A) Add 2.   (C) Subtract 2.
   (B) Add 4.   (D) Subtract 4.

Spiral Review

3. What number do the blocks show? (Grade 2)

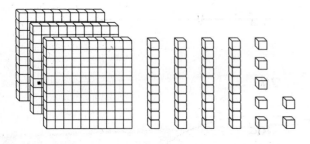

   (A) 347   (C) 147
   (B) 311   (D) 14

4. Which number sentence completes this fact family? (Grade 2)

   $5 + 3 = 8$ $8 - 5 = 3$

   $3 + 5 = 8$ $8 - 3 = 5$

   (A) $3 + 2 = 5$
   (B) $8 - 3 = 5$
   (C) $8 + 5 = 13$
   (D) $5 - 3 = 2$

5. What is the difference? (Grade 2)

   7 3
   − 3 8
   ─────
   3 5

   (A) 35
   (B) 45
   (C) 46
   (D) 111

6. What is the total value of the coins?

   (Grade 2)

   (A) 6¢
   (B) 15¢
   (C) 24¢
   (D) 28¢

Name _____

Make a List · Place Value

Solve.

1. Robert's number is between 20 and 32. The sum of the digits is 10. What is his number?

   Think: 2 + 8 = 10

   _____ **28**

2. Grant thinks of an odd number between 48 and 64. The tens digit is greater than the ones digit. The difference between the two digits is 4. What is Grant's number?

   _____

3. Emily has an even number between 70 and 85. The sum of the digits is an even number less than 10. What is her number?

   _____

4. Lauren made up a riddle about a number between 50 and 70. The tens and ones digits are the same. The number is closer to 70 than 50. What is Lauren's number?

   _____

5. Jacob thinks of an odd number between 402 and 418. The sum of the tens digit and ones digit is equal to the hundreds digit. What is Jacob's number?

   _____

6. The prize-winning number is an even number between 110 and 130. The digit 2 is in the tens place and the sum of the hundreds and ones digits equals 5. What is the winning number?

   _____

Lesson Check

1. Amanda thinks of a number between 35 and 48. The sum of the digits is 7. What is Amanda's number?

   Ⓐ 38
   Ⓑ 41
   Ⓒ 43
   Ⓓ 47

2. Josh thinks of an odd number between 268 and 282. The sum of the hundreds digit and ones digit is equal to the tens digit. What is Josh's number?

   Ⓐ 269　　Ⓒ 275
   Ⓑ 273　　Ⓓ 281

Spiral Review

3. How many numbers between 10 and 30 have digits whose sum is 5? (Grade 2)

   Ⓐ 1
   Ⓑ 2
   Ⓒ 3
   Ⓓ 4

4. Which of the following lists all the even numbers between 50 and 64? (Lesson 1.1)

   Ⓐ 51, 53, 54, 56, 58, 60, 62, 64
   Ⓑ 52, 54, 56, 58, 60, 62
   Ⓒ 54, 58, 62
   Ⓓ 51, 53, 55, 57, 59, 61

5. Jeff's puppy gains 3 pounds each month. How many pounds will the puppy gain in 5 months? (Grade 2)

   Ⓐ 8 pounds
   Ⓑ 12 pounds
   Ⓒ 15 pounds
   Ⓓ 18 pounds

6. Ms. Smith's classroom has 5 rows of desks with 5 seats in each row. How many seats are there in all? (Grade 2)

   Ⓐ 10
   Ⓑ 15
   Ⓒ 20
   Ⓓ 25

Name _____

Numbers Through Hundreds

Write the number the quick picture shows. Draw a quick picture to show the number another way.

1.

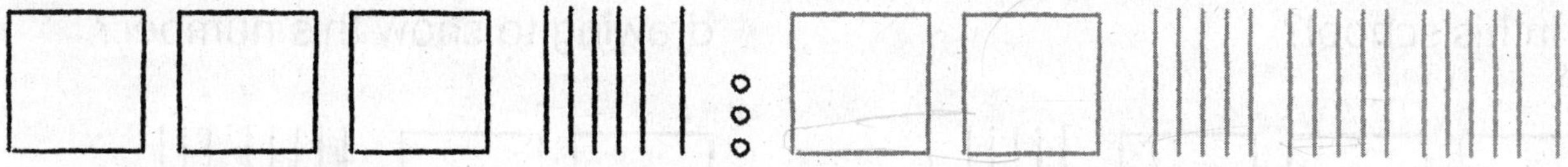

363

2.

182

3.

219

Problem Solving REAL WORLD

4. Kyle wants to use the fewest base-ten blocks possible to model the number 437. Draw a quick picture to show the blocks he should use.

5. Andrea has 12 tens blocks. What base-ten blocks does she need to add to show 198?

_____

_____

Lesson Check

1. The quick picture shows the number of students in Pedro's school. How many students are in his school?

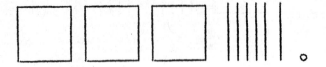

Ⓐ 163 Ⓒ 631

Ⓑ 361 Ⓓ 641

2. Hannah wants to draw a quick picture to show the number 482. Which could she add to her drawing to show this number?

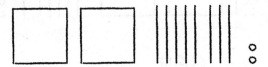

Ⓐ 2 ones

Ⓑ 2 tens

Ⓒ 2 hundreds

Ⓓ 2 thousands

Spiral Review

3. What will the next number in this pattern be? (Lesson 1.1)

15, 18, 21, 24, 27, ■

Ⓐ 24 Ⓒ 28

Ⓑ 29 Ⓓ 30

4. Emma used 4 red blocks, 6 blue blocks, and 2 green blocks to build a fort. How many blocks did she use? (Grade 2)

Ⓐ 4 Ⓒ 12

Ⓑ 10 Ⓓ 14

5. Which is one way to model 37?
(Grade 2)

Ⓐ 3 tens 7 ones

Ⓑ 7 tens 3 ones

Ⓒ 37 tens

Ⓓ 73 ones

6. How many tens are in 360?
(Grade 2)

Ⓐ 360

Ⓑ 36

Ⓒ 30

Ⓓ 3

Name _____

Numbers Through Thousands

Complete the packing chart. Use the fewest packages possible.

	Number of Blocks Ordered	Crates (Thousands)	Boxes (Hundreds)	Stacks (Tens)	Single Blocks (Ones)
1.	1,492	1	4	9	2
2.	3,016	3	0	1	6
3.	2,804	2	8	0	4
4.	4,675	4	6	7	5

Complete the packing chart. When there is a zero, use the next smaller size package.

	Number of Blocks Ordered	Crates (Thousands)	Boxes (Hundreds)	Stacks (Tens)	Single Blocks (Ones)
5.	1,727	0	72	2	7
6.	2,351	1	35	0	1
7.	5,008	0	00	0	8
8.	4,976	4	29	0	6

Problem Solving REAL WORLD

9. A worker at the block factory packed blocks in 3 crates of 1,000, 4 boxes of 100, and 9 single blocks. How many blocks did the worker pack?

_____

10. Matt needs to pack an order for 1,816 blocks. How can Matt pack the blocks without using crates of 1,000?

_____

_____

_____

Lesson Check

1. Which could be added to show 2,237?

Ⓐ 1 one Ⓒ 1 hundred

Ⓑ 1 ten Ⓓ 1 thousand

2. What number does the quick picture show?

Ⓐ 1,140 Ⓒ 1,014

Ⓑ 1,114 Ⓓ 114

Spiral Review

3. Which number is NOT even? (Lesson 1.1)

Ⓐ 35
Ⓑ 36
Ⓒ 42
Ⓓ 78

4. Tom thinks of an odd number between 15 and 30. The sum of the digits is 7. What is Tom's number? (Lesson 1.2)

Ⓐ 16 Ⓒ 25

Ⓑ 17 Ⓓ 27

5. Which is another way to show the number? (Lesson 1.3)

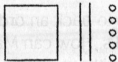

Ⓐ 128 ones
Ⓑ 128 tens
Ⓒ 11 tens 8 ones
Ⓓ 10 tens 18 ones

6. Which addition fact can help you find the difference? (Grade 2)

$16 - 7 = \blacksquare$

Ⓐ $7 + 8 = 15$

Ⓑ $9 + 0 = 9$

Ⓒ $9 + 7 = 16$

Ⓓ $16 + 7 = 23$

P10

Name _____

Read and Write Numbers Through Thousands

Write the number in standard form.

1. 2,000 + 600 + 30 + 5

   2,635
   _____

2. five thousand, three hundred sixty

   _____

3. 8,000 + 800 + 90 + 9

   _____

4. one thousand, fifty-one

   _____

Complete the chart to show three forms of the number.

Standard Form	Expanded Form	Word Form
5. 4,906		_____ thousand, _____ hundred _____
6.	7,000 + 20 + 3	_____ thousand, _____
7.		nine thousand, one hundred eighty-five

Write the value of the underlined digit.

8. 5,<u>8</u>96   9. 4,4<u>9</u>2   10. <u>1</u>,350   11. 3,41<u>3</u>

_____   _____   _____   _____

Problem Solving REAL WORLD

12. The population of a town is 4,951 people. What is the value of the digit 4 in the number?

    _____

13. The number of tourists who visited a national park in one day was nine thousand, twelve. Write this number in two other ways.

    _____

Lesson Check

1. What is the value of the underlined digit?

3,2<u>9</u>7

Ⓐ 9,000
Ⓑ 900
Ⓒ 90
Ⓓ 9

2. Which shows the following number written in standard form?

8,000 + 200 + 80 + 9

Ⓐ 8,089
Ⓑ 8,280
Ⓒ 8,289
Ⓓ 9,089

Spiral Review

3. Which is a way to show the number 582? **(Lesson 1.3)**

Ⓐ 582 hundreds
Ⓑ 58 tens 2 ones
Ⓒ 5 hundreds 82 tens
Ⓓ 582 tens

4. Juanita drew a quick picture to show 31 tens. Which could she add to her drawing to show 347? **(Lesson 1.3)**

Ⓐ 4 tens
Ⓑ 7 ones
Ⓒ 37 tens
Ⓓ 3 tens 7 ones

5. Which is a way to show 4,700? **(Lesson 1.4)**

Ⓐ 47 tens
Ⓑ 470 tens
Ⓒ 470 hundreds
Ⓓ 47 thousands

6. Ava writes an even number between 24 and 34. The sum of the digits is odd. Which number could Ava have written? **(Lesson 1.2)**

Ⓐ 26
Ⓑ 27
Ⓒ 32
Ⓓ 41

TEST PREP

© Houghton Mifflin Harcourt Publishing Company

P12

Name _____

Compare and Order Numbers

Compare the numbers. Write <, >, or = in the ○.

1. 835 ⬤ 853   **2.** 5,154 ○ 5,154   **3.** 1,837 ○ 837

4. 560 ○ 56   **5.** 2,517 ○ 2,715   **6.** 7,483 ○ 7,834

7. 219 ○ 2,119   **8.** 809 ○ 890   **9.** 5,107 ○ 5,105

Write the numbers in order from greatest to least.

10. 652, 650, 655   **11.** 4,038; 4,533; 4,179

_____, _____, _____   _____; _____; _____

Write the numbers in order from least to greatest.

12. 4,282; 4,281; 4,218   **13.** 1,789; 1,987; 1,787

_____; _____; _____   _____; _____; _____

Problem Solving  REAL WORLD

14. The CN Tower in Canada is 1,815 feet tall. The KFVS TV Tower in the United States is 1,677 feet tall. Which tower is taller?

15. There are 3,145 people living in Hopewell. There are 2,951 people in Pearl River and 2,541 people in Greenville. Which town has the fewest people?

_____   _____

Lesson Check

1. Which number is less than 4,078?

Ⓐ 4,807
Ⓑ 4,707
Ⓒ 4,087
Ⓓ 4,076

2. Which number is greater than 398 but less than 427?

Ⓐ 389
Ⓑ 411
Ⓒ 429
Ⓓ 472

Spiral Review

3. What is $6,000 + 40 + 7$ written in standard form? (Lesson 1.5)

Ⓐ 6,470
Ⓑ 6,407
Ⓒ 6,047
Ⓓ 647

4. Daniel thinks of an odd number between 13 and 28. The difference between the digits is 6. What is the number? (Lesson 1.2)

Ⓐ 28
Ⓑ 17
Ⓒ 16
Ⓓ 15

5. What is the value of the underlined digit? (Lesson 1.5)

8,4̲63

Ⓐ 4
Ⓑ 40
Ⓒ 400
Ⓓ 4,000

6. A factory worker packed blocks in 3 crates, 5 boxes, and 9 stacks. How many blocks were packed in all? (Remember: 1 crate = 1,000 blocks, 1 box = 100 blocks, 1 stack = 10 blocks) (Lesson 1.4)

Ⓐ 359
Ⓑ 3,059
Ⓒ 3,509
Ⓓ 3,590

Name _____

Round to the Nearest Ten, Hundred, or Thousand

Use the number line for 1–2. Locate 748 on the number line.

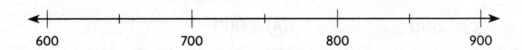

1. Between which two hundreds is 748? _____

2. To which hundred is 748 closer? _____

Round to the nearest ten.

3. 27 _____   4. 81 _____   5. 44 _____

Round to the nearest hundred.

6. 360 _____   7. 829 _____   8. 572 _____

9. 209 _____   10. 663 _____   11. 949 _____

Round to the nearest thousand.

12. 4,762 _____   13. 7,399 _____   14. 1,499 _____

15. 6,087 _____   16. 5,623 _____   17. 8,190 _____

Problem Solving REAL WORLD

18. The baby elephant weighs 435 pounds. What is its weight rounded to the nearest hundred pounds?

19. On Saturday, 2,479 people visited the zoo. What is this number rounded to the nearest thousand?

_____   _____

Lesson Check

1. One day 758 people visited the Monkey House at the zoo. What is 758 rounded to the nearest hundred?

Ⓐ 700   Ⓒ 800
Ⓑ 760   Ⓓ 1,000

2. What is 2,370 rounded to the nearest thousand?

Ⓐ 3,000   Ⓒ 2,300
Ⓑ 2,400   Ⓓ 2,000

Spiral Review

3. What is the value of the underlined digit? (Lesson 1.5)

3,571

Ⓐ 3,000
Ⓑ 300
Ⓒ 30
Ⓓ 3

4. Which list shows the numbers in order from least to greatest? (Lesson 1.6)

Ⓐ 580, 609, 598, 589
Ⓑ 609, 598, 589, 580
Ⓒ 598, 589, 580, 609
Ⓓ 580, 589, 598, 609

5. Miguel writes this number pattern. If he continues the pattern, what will the next number be? (Lesson 1.1)

67, 71, 75, 79, ■

Ⓐ 80
Ⓑ 81
Ⓒ 83
Ⓓ 84

6. What is nine thousand, three hundred eight written in standard form? (Lesson 1.5)

Ⓐ 9,380
Ⓑ 9,308
Ⓒ 9,038
Ⓓ 938

TEST PREP

© Houghton Mifflin Harcourt Publishing Company

P16

Name _____

Chapter 1 Extra Practice

Lesson 1.1

Write a rule for the pattern. Then write the missing number.

1. 28, 32, 36, _____, 44, 48   **Rule:** _____

2. 55, 45, 35, 25, _____, 5   **Rule:** _____

Lesson 1.2

Solve.

1. Lexi thinks of a number between 405 and 415. The ones digit is the difference between the hundreds and tens digits. What is Lexi's number?

_____

2. Max thinks of an odd number between 41 and 64. The difference between the digits is the same as the ones digit. What is Max's number?

_____

Lesson 1.3

Write the number the quick picture shows. Draw a quick picture that shows the number another way.

1.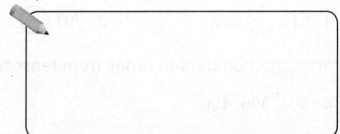

_____

Lesson 1.4

Complete the packing chart. Use the fewest packages possible.

	Number of Blocks Ordered	Crates (Thousands)	Boxes (Hundreds)	Stacks (Tens)	Single Blocks (Ones)
1.	1,364	1			
2.	2,709		7		

Lesson 1.5

Write the number in standard form.

1. eight thousand, four hundred sixteen

2. 4,000 + 10 + 2

_____

_____

Complete the chart to show three forms of the number.

Standard Form	Expanded Form	Word Form
3. 9,408		_____ thousand, _____ hundred _____
4.	2,000 + 600 + 50	_____ thousand, _____ hundred _____
5.		four thousand, three hundred seventeen

Lesson 1.6

Compare the numbers. Write <, >, or = in the ◯.

1. 610 ◯ 513

2. 791 ◯ 1,502

3. 5,008 ◯ 8,005

Write the numbers in order from least to greatest.

4. 504, 396, 400

5. 6,980; 7,004; 6,091

_____, _____, _____

_____; _____; _____

Lesson 1.7

Round to the nearest hundred.

1. 539 _____

2. 809 _____

3. 755 _____

Round to the nearest thousand.

4. 7,641 _____

5. 4,487 _____

6. 1,099 _____

School-Home Letter

Vocabulary

estimate A number close to an exact amount

compatible numbers Numbers that are easy to compute mentally and are close to the real numbers

Dear Family,

During the next few weeks, our math class will be learning to estimate and solve addition and subtraction problems using numbers through thousands.

You can expect to see homework that provides practice with adding and subtracting numbers as well as estimating sums and differences.

Here is a sample of how your child will be taught to estimate sums.

🔒 MODEL Estimate Sums

These are two methods we will be using to estimate sums.

$367 + 512 = \blacksquare$

Use rounding.		Use compatible numbers.	
STEP 1	**STEP 2**	**STEP 1**	**STEP 2**
Round each number to the nearest hundred.	Add the rounded numbers.	Find a compatible number for each addend.	Add the numbers mentally.
$367 \rightarrow 400$ $+512 \rightarrow 500$	400 $+500$ $\overline{900}$	$2{,}105 \rightarrow 2{,}100$ $+\ 362 \rightarrow\ \ 400$	$2{,}100$ $+\ \ 400$ $\overline{2{,}500}$

Tips

Choosing Compatible Numbers to Estimate Sums and Differences

A number may have more than one compatible number. For example, a compatible number for 362 could be 350 or 400. Whichever numbers are easiest to add or subtract mentally are the best ones to use for estimations.

Activity

Provide books with large numbers of pages (3-digit and 4-digit numbers). Have your child use rounding and compatible numbers to estimate the total number of pages in the two books and compare how many more pages one book has than the other.

Carta para la casa

Vocabulario

estimación Un número que se aproxima a una cantidad exacta

números compatibles Números que son fáciles de calcular mentalmente y se aproximan a los números reales

Querida familia,

Durante las próximas semanas, en la clase de matemáticas aprenderemos a estimar y resolver problemas de suma y resta usando números hasta los millares.

Llévare a la casa tareas con actividades para practicar la suma y la resta, y para estimar la suma y la diferencia.

Este es un ejemplo de la manera como aprenderemos a estimar sumas.

🔑 MODELO Estimar sumas

Estos son dos métodos que usaremos para estimar sumas.
$$376 + 512 = \blacksquare$$

Usar el redondeo.

PASO 1	PASO 2
Redondea cada número a la centena más cercana.	Suma los números que hallaste.
$367 \rightarrow 400$ $+\,512 \rightarrow 500$	400 $+\,500$ 900

Usar números compatibles.

PASO 1	PASO 2
Halla en un número compatible para cada sumando.	Suma los números mentalmente.
$2,105 \rightarrow 2,100$ $+\ \ 362 \rightarrow \ \ 400$	$2,100$ $+\ \ 400$ $2,500$

Pistas

Elegir números compatibles para estimar sumas y restas

Un número puede tener más de un número compatible. Por ejemplo, un número compatible para 362 puede ser 350 o 400. Cualquiera de los números que sea más fácil de sumar y restar mentalmente sirve para hacer estimaciones.

Actividad

Dé a su hijo dos libros que tengan bastantes páginas (con números de 3 y 4 dígitos). Pídale que use el redondeo y los números compatibles para estimar el total de páginas de los dos libros y para averiguar cuántas más páginas tiene un libro que el otro.

Name _____

Estimate Sums

Use rounding or compatible numbers to estimate the sum.

1. $\begin{array}{r} 198 \rightarrow \\ +\,727 \rightarrow \end{array}$ $\begin{array}{r} \mathbf{200} \\ +\,\mathbf{725} \\ \hline \mathbf{925} \end{array}$

2. $\begin{array}{r} 87 \rightarrow \\ +\,34 \rightarrow \end{array}$ $\begin{array}{r} \underline{} \\ +\,\underline{} \end{array}$

3. $\begin{array}{r} 2{,}202 \rightarrow \\ +\,5{,}031 \rightarrow \end{array}$ $\begin{array}{r} \underline{} \\ +\,\underline{} \end{array}$

4. $\begin{array}{r} 52 \rightarrow \\ +\,39 \rightarrow \end{array}$ $\begin{array}{r} \underline{} \\ +\,\underline{} \end{array}$

5. $\begin{array}{r} 256 \rightarrow \\ +\,321 \rightarrow \end{array}$ $\begin{array}{r} \underline{} \\ +\,\underline{} \end{array}$

6. $\begin{array}{r} 2{,}027 \rightarrow \\ +\,4{,}127 \rightarrow \end{array}$ $\begin{array}{r} \underline{} \\ +\,\underline{} \end{array}$

7. $\begin{array}{r} 519 \rightarrow \\ +\,124 \rightarrow \end{array}$ $\begin{array}{r} \underline{} \\ +\,\underline{} \end{array}$

8. $\begin{array}{r} 890 \rightarrow \\ +\,112 \rightarrow \end{array}$ $\begin{array}{r} \underline{} \\ +\,\underline{} \end{array}$

9. $\begin{array}{r} 5{,}407 \rightarrow \\ +\,3{,}794 \rightarrow \end{array}$ $\begin{array}{r} \underline{} \\ +\,\underline{} \end{array}$

10. 2,325 + 458

_____ + _____ = _____

11. 6,238 + 561

_____ + _____ = _____

Problem Solving REAL WORLD

12. Stephanie's class read an article about weights of cars. They found that two medium-sized cars weighed 3,640 and 3,800 pounds. About how many pounds in all did the cars weigh?

13. The attendance at the school fair was 1,234 on Saturday, and 967 on Sunday. About how many people attended the fair that weekend?

_____

_____

Lesson Check

1. Estimate the sum.

$$\begin{array}{r} 2,980 \\ +\ 3,023 \end{array}$$

- (A) 2,900
- (B) 3,000
- (C) 5,000
- (D) 6,000

2. Estimate the sum.

$$\begin{array}{r} 789 \\ +\ 302 \end{array}$$

- (A) 300
- (B) 700
- (C) 900
- (D) 1,100

Spiral Review

3. Bill wrote an odd number between 27 and 45. The sum of the digits is 8. Which number did Bill write?

(Lesson 1.2)

- (A) 35
- (B) 38
- (C) 43
- (D) 44

4. Which is NOT a way to model 492 with base-ten blocks? **(Lesson 1.4)**

- (A) 4 hundreds 9 tens 2 ones
- (B) 4 hundreds 92 ones
- (C) 49 hundreds 2 ones
- (D) 49 tens 2 ones

5. Which numbers are in order from least to greatest? **(Lesson 1.6)**

- (A) 946; 1,248; 1,394; 1490
- (B) 946; 1,248, 1,490; 1,394
- (C) 1,490; 1,394; 1,248; 946
- (D) 1,490; 1,248; 1,394; 946

6. What is 4,645 rounded to the nearest thousand? **(Lesson 1.7)**

- (A) 4,000
- (B) 4,600
- (C) 5,000
- (D) 6,000

Name _____

Add 3-Digit Numbers

Estimate. Then find the sum.

1. Estimate: **600**

$$\begin{array}{r} \overset{1}{3}24 \\ +\ 285 \\ \hline \mathbf{609} \end{array}$$

2. Estimate: _____

$$\begin{array}{r} 519 \\ +\ 347 \\ \hline \end{array}$$

3. Estimate: _____

$$\begin{array}{r} 323 \\ +\ 151 \\ \hline \end{array}$$

4. Estimate: _____

$$\begin{array}{r} 169 \\ +\ 354 \\ \hline \end{array}$$

5. Estimate: _____

$$\begin{array}{r} 148 \\ +\ 285 \\ \hline \end{array}$$

6. Estimate: _____

$$\begin{array}{r} 270 \\ +\ 453 \\ \hline \end{array}$$

7. Estimate: _____

$$\begin{array}{r} 275 \\ +\ 116 \\ \hline \end{array}$$

8. Estimate: _____

$$\begin{array}{r} 157 \\ +\ 141 \\ \hline \end{array}$$

9. Estimate: _____

$$\begin{array}{r} 127 \\ +\ 290 \\ \hline \end{array}$$

10. Estimate: _____

$$\begin{array}{r} 258 \\ +\ 665 \\ \hline \end{array}$$

11. Estimate: _____

$$\begin{array}{r} 311 \\ +\ 298 \\ \hline \end{array}$$

12. Estimate: _____

$$\begin{array}{r} 534 \\ +\ 256 \\ \hline \end{array}$$

Problem Solving  REAL WORLD

13. Mark has 215 baseball cards. Emily has twice as many baseball cards as Mark. How many baseball cards does Emily have?

14. Jason has 330 pennies. Richie has 268 pennies. Rachel has 381 pennies. Which two students have more than 700 pennies combined?

_____

_____

Lesson Check

1. There are 167 students in the third grade. The same number of students is in the fourth grade. How many students are in both grades?

   Ⓐ 224
   Ⓑ 234
   Ⓒ 324
   Ⓓ 334

2. Paco read a book with 128 pages. Then he read a book with 179 pages. How many pages did he read in all?

   Ⓐ 397
   Ⓑ 307
   Ⓒ 297
   Ⓓ 207

Spiral Review

3. Adam travels 248 miles on Monday. He travels 167 miles on Tuesday. Which is the best estimate for the total number of miles Adam travels? (Lesson 2.1)

   Ⓐ 200
   Ⓑ 300
   Ⓒ 400
   Ⓓ 500

4. Suri writes this number pattern. Which rule describes her pattern? (Lesson 1.1)

   53, 50, 47, 44, 41

   Ⓐ Add 2.
   Ⓑ Add 3.
   Ⓒ Subtract 2.
   Ⓓ Subtract 3.

5. What is the value of the underlined digit in the number 4,637? (Lesson 1.5)

   Ⓐ 6,000
   Ⓑ 600
   Ⓒ 60
   Ⓓ 6

6. There were 3,475 people at the baseball game on Sunday. What is 3,475 rounded to the nearest thousand? (Lesson 1.7)

   Ⓐ 3,000
   Ⓑ 3,400
   Ⓒ 3,500
   Ⓓ 4,000

Name _____

Add 4-Digit Numbers

Estimate. Then find the sum.

1. Estimate: __8,000__

$$
\begin{array}{r}
{\scriptstyle 1 \quad 1}\\
6,756\\
+\;1,417\\
\hline
8,173
\end{array}
$$

2. Estimate: _____

$$
\begin{array}{r}
4,280\\
+\;3,998\\
\hline
\end{array}
$$

3. Estimate: _____

$$
\begin{array}{r}
1,200\\
+\quad304\\
\hline
\end{array}
$$

4. Estimate: _____

$$
\begin{array}{r}
2,434\\
+\;3,602\\
\hline
\end{array}
$$

5. Estimate: _____

$$
\begin{array}{r}
5,234\\
+\;1,450\\
\hline
\end{array}
$$

6. Estimate: _____

$$
\begin{array}{r}
1,295\\
+\;2,844\\
\hline
\end{array}
$$

7. Estimate: _____

$$
\begin{array}{r}
4,591\\
+\;2,310\\
\hline
\end{array}
$$

8. Estimate: _____

$$
\begin{array}{r}
5,438\\
+\;1,281\\
\hline
\end{array}
$$

9. Estimate: _____

$$
\begin{array}{r}
2,659\\
+\;4,813\\
\hline
\end{array}
$$

Problem Solving REAL WORLD

10. The attendance the first night of the school play was 1,285 people. The next night 1,324 people attended. How many people in all attended the school play?

11. The third graders collected 4,736 bottles for recycling. The fourth graders collected 3,982 bottles. How many bottles were collected altogether?

_____   _____

Lesson Check

1. Find the sum.

$$3,895$$
$$+ \ 4,459$$

Ⓐ 7,354   Ⓒ 8,354

Ⓑ 7,544   Ⓓ 8,454

2. Find the sum.

$$7,402$$
$$+ \ 1,839$$

Ⓐ 8,241   Ⓒ 9,231

Ⓑ 8,341   Ⓓ 9,241

Spiral Review

3. Which is 7,034 in word form? (Lesson 1.5)

Ⓐ seven hundred thirty-four

Ⓑ seven thousand, thirty-four

Ⓒ seven thousand, three hundred four

Ⓓ seven thousand, three hundred forty

4. What is the value of the underlined digit? (Lesson 1.5)

3,760

Ⓐ 7,000

Ⓑ 700

Ⓒ 70

Ⓓ 7

5. Which shows the numbers in order from greatest to least? (Lesson 1.6)

Ⓐ 429, 567, 708, 720

Ⓑ 429, 567, 720, 708

Ⓒ 708, 720, 567, 429

Ⓓ 720, 708, 567, 429

6. Dara collects stickers. She has 426 stickers in one sticker book and 342 stickers in another book. How many stickers does she have in all? (Lesson 2.2)

Ⓐ 124

Ⓑ 724

Ⓒ 768

Ⓓ 868

Name _____

Estimate Differences

Use rounding or compatible numbers to estimate the difference.

1. $\begin{array}{r} 40 \to \\ -13 \to \end{array}$ $\begin{array}{r} 40 \\ -\ 10 \\ \hline 30 \end{array}$

2. $\begin{array}{r} 762 \to \\ -332 \to \end{array}$ $\begin{array}{r} 800 \\ -\ 300 \\ \hline 500 \end{array}$

3. $\begin{array}{r} 4{,}923 \to \\ -2{,}421 \to \end{array}$ $-\ \underline{}$

4. $\begin{array}{r} 98 \to \\ -49 \to \end{array}$ $-\ \underline{}$

5. $\begin{array}{r} 287 \to \\ -162 \to \end{array}$ $-\ \underline{}$

6. $\begin{array}{r} 8{,}973 \to \\ -7{,}304 \to \end{array}$ $-\ \underline{}$

7. $\begin{array}{r} 68 \to \\ -31 \to \end{array}$ $-\ \underline{}$

8. $\begin{array}{r} 476 \to \\ -155 \to \end{array}$ $-\ \underline{}$

9. $\begin{array}{r} 7{,}987 \to \\ -\ 989 \to \end{array}$ $-\ \underline{}$

10. $6{,}254 - 531$

_____ − _____ = _____

11. $3{,}179 - 160$

_____ − _____ = _____

Problem Solving REAL WORLD

12. Ben has a collection of 1,965 stamps. He gives his brother 245 stamps. About how many stamps does Ben have left?

13. The population of Chester in 1990 was 4,950. During the next ten years, 280 people moved away. About how many people remained in Chester?

_____

Lesson Check

1. Estimate the difference.

$$4,972$$
$$- \ 1,035$$

(A) 5,000

(B) 4,000

(C) 3,000

(D) 2,000

2. Estimate the difference.

$$601$$
$$- \ 285$$

(A) 200

(B) 250

(C) 300

(D) 400

Spiral Review

3. What is 3,276 rounded to the nearest thousand? (Lesson 1.7)

(A) 3,000

(B) 3,200

(C) 3,300

(D) 4,000

4. Which rule best describes this pattern? (Lesson 1.1)

82, 78, 74, 70, 66

(A) Add 3.

(B) Add 4.

(C) Subtract 3.

(D) Subtract 4.

5. Find the sum. (Lesson 2.3)

$$5,852$$
$$+ \ 2,341$$

(A) 7,193

(B) 8,193

(C) 8,293

(D) 9,193

6. Which number is less than 742 but greater than 698? (Lesson 1.6)

(A) 681

(B) 692

(C) 701

(D) 759

Name _____

Subtract 3-Digit Numbers

Estimate. Then find the difference.

1. Estimate: _500_

$$\begin{array}{r} {\scriptstyle 7\ \ 15}\\ 58\!\!\!\!/\,5 \\ -\ 119 \\ \hline 466 \end{array}$$

2. Estimate: _____

$$\begin{array}{r} 738 \\ -\ 227 \\ \hline \end{array}$$

3. Estimate: _____

$$\begin{array}{r} 651 \\ -\ 376 \\ \hline \end{array}$$

4. Estimate: _____

$$\begin{array}{r} 815 \\ -\ 281 \\ \hline \end{array}$$

5. Estimate: _____

$$\begin{array}{r} 487 \\ -\ 290 \\ \hline \end{array}$$

6. Estimate: _____

$$\begin{array}{r} 936 \\ -\ 329 \\ \hline \end{array}$$

7. Estimate: _____

$$\begin{array}{r} 270 \\ -\ 128 \\ \hline \end{array}$$

8. Estimate: _____

$$\begin{array}{r} 364 \\ -\ 177 \\ \hline \end{array}$$

9. Estimate: _____

$$\begin{array}{r} 627 \\ -\ 253 \\ \hline \end{array}$$

10. Estimate: _____

$$\begin{array}{r} 862 \\ -\ 419 \\ \hline \end{array}$$

11. Estimate: _____

$$\begin{array}{r} 726 \\ -\ 148 \\ \hline \end{array}$$

12. Estimate: _____

$$\begin{array}{r} 543 \\ -\ 358 \\ \hline \end{array}$$

Problem Solving  REAL WORLD

13. Mrs. Cohen has 427 buttons. She uses 195 buttons to make puppets. How many buttons does Mrs. Cohen have left?

_____

14. There were 425 ears of corn and 247 tomatoes sold at a farm stand. How many more ears of corn were sold than tomatoes?

_____

Lesson Check

1. On Saturday, 453 people go to a school play. On Sunday, 294 people go to the play. How many more people go to the play on Saturday?

   Ⓐ 159
   Ⓑ 169
   Ⓒ 259
   Ⓓ 747

2. Corey has 430 marbles. He fills one jar with 265 marbles. How many of Corey's marbles are NOT in the jar?

   Ⓐ 695
   Ⓑ 275
   Ⓒ 175
   Ⓓ 165

Spiral Review

3. Shane writes a number sentence to compare 3,067 and 3,607. Which number sentence should he write?
   (Lesson 1.6)

   Ⓐ $3,067 > 3,607$
   Ⓑ $3,067 < 3,607$
   Ⓒ $3,067 = 3,607$
   Ⓓ $3,607 < 3,067$

4. An airplane flies 617 miles in the morning. Then it flies 385 miles in the afternoon. About how many more miles did the airplane fly in the morning? (Lesson 2.4)

   Ⓐ about 100 miles
   Ⓑ about 200 miles
   Ⓒ about 300 miles
   Ⓓ about 900 miles

5. There are 3,727 adults at a soccer game. There are 1,678 children at the game. How many people in all are at the soccer game? (Lesson 2.3)

   Ⓐ 2,049
   Ⓑ 4,395
   Ⓒ 5,405
   Ⓓ 5,504

6. Jamal has 128 shells. He needs 283 more shells for his art project. How many shells will he use for his art project? (Lesson 2.2)

   Ⓐ 155
   Ⓑ 165
   Ⓒ 401
   Ⓓ 411

TEST PREP

© Houghton Mifflin Harcourt Publishing Company

P30

Name _____

Subtract 4-Digit Numbers

Estimate. Then subtract.

1. Estimate: _3,000_

$$\begin{array}{r} \overset{\scriptstyle 12}{\overset{\scriptstyle 8\,\cancel{9}\,14}{8,9\cancel{3}4}} \\ -\ 5,697 \\ \hline 3,237 \end{array}$$

2. Estimate: _____

$$\begin{array}{r} 2,112 \\ -\ 1,003 \\ \hline \end{array}$$

3. Estimate: _____

$$\begin{array}{r} 3,849 \\ -\ 1,210 \\ \hline \end{array}$$

4. Estimate: _____

$$\begin{array}{r} 8,724 \\ -\ 6,493 \\ \hline \end{array}$$

5. Estimate: _____

$$\begin{array}{r} 3,410 \\ -\ 2,890 \\ \hline \end{array}$$

6. Estimate: _____

$$\begin{array}{r} 8,007 \\ -\ 6,620 \\ \hline \end{array}$$

7. Estimate: _____

$$\begin{array}{r} 4,061 \\ -\ 3,965 \\ \hline \end{array}$$

8. Estimate: _____

$$\begin{array}{r} 5,892 \\ -\ 3,963 \\ \hline \end{array}$$

9. Estimate: _____

$$\begin{array}{r} 1,000 \\ -\ \ \ 895 \\ \hline \end{array}$$

Problem Solving REAL WORLD

10. There are 1,960 visitors to the museum on Monday. On Tuesday, there are 465 fewer visitors. How many more vistors are there on Monday than on Tuesday?

11. Mr. Perez is buying a computer on sale. The computer costs $1,700. The store is taking $395 off that price. How much does the computer cost on sale?

_____

_____

Lesson Check

1. Subtract.

$$8{,}720$$
$$- \ 6{,}962$$

Ⓐ 2,102

Ⓑ 2,062

Ⓒ 1,758

Ⓓ 1,748

2. Subtract.

$$4{,}297$$
$$- \ 3{,}879$$

Ⓐ 402

Ⓑ 410

Ⓒ 418

Ⓓ 422

Spiral Review

3. What number do the blocks show?

(Lesson 1.3)

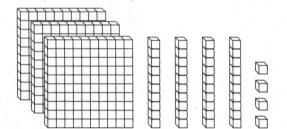

Ⓐ 300

Ⓑ 324

Ⓒ 340

Ⓓ 344

4. Which base-ten blocks do you need to add to show 262? (Lesson 1.3)

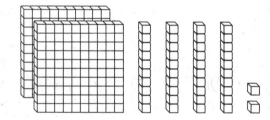

Ⓐ 2 tens 6 ones

Ⓑ 2 tens 2 ones

Ⓒ 8 ones

Ⓓ 2 tens

5. Estimate the difference. (Lesson 2.4)

$$527$$
$$- \ 392$$

Ⓐ 50

Ⓑ 75

Ⓒ 100

Ⓓ 300

6. Find the difference. (Lesson 2.5)

$$607$$
$$- \ 185$$

Ⓐ 525

Ⓑ 422

Ⓒ 420

Ⓓ 418

Draw a Diagram · Addition and Subtraction

Complete the bar model to solve the problem.

1. Elena went bowling. Elena's score in the first game was 127. Her score in the second game was 143. What was her total score?

127	143

270

270

2. In a basketball game, the Bobcats scored 41 points in the first half. The team scored 29 points in the second half. What is the total number of points the team scored?

_____ points	_____ points

_____ points

_____

3. The Panthers scored 82 points in a basketball game. If the Bobcats scored 57 points, how many more points did the Panthers score?

Panthers | _____ points |

Bobcats | _____ points |

_____ points

_____

4. Jack scored 216 points in a computer game. Marco scored 165 points. How many more points did Jack score than Marco?

Jack | _____ points |

Marco | _____ points |

_____ points

_____

Lesson Check

1. Ms. Golan picked 46 tomatoes from her garden on Friday. On Saturday, she picked 17 tomatoes. How many tomatoes did she pick in all?

  Ⓐ 109   Ⓒ 53

  Ⓑ 63   Ⓓ 29

2. Rosa read 57 pages of a book in the morning. She read 13 fewer pages in the afternoon. How many pages did Rosa read in the afternoon?

  Ⓐ 44   Ⓒ 70

  Ⓑ 60   Ⓓ 83

Spiral Review

3. A factory made 1,946 action figures on Monday. On Tuesday, the factory made 3,078 action figures. How many action figures did the factory make in all? (Lesson 2.3)

  Ⓐ 5,024

  Ⓑ 4,954

  Ⓒ 4,024

  Ⓓ 1,132

4. Tammy writes this number pattern. If she continues the pattern, what will be the next number? (Lesson 1.1)

28, 31, 34, 37, ▪

  Ⓐ 38

  Ⓑ 39

  Ⓒ 40

  Ⓓ 41

5. There were 5,241 visitors to the science museum in May. There were 4,098 visitors in June. How many more people visited the museum in May? (Lesson 2.6)

  Ⓐ 1,043

  Ⓑ 1,143

  Ⓒ 2,143

  Ⓓ 9,339

6. Ravi scores 3,287 points in a video game. How many more points does he need to score a total of 5,250? (Lesson 2.6)

  Ⓐ 8,537

  Ⓑ 2,063

  Ⓒ 1,973

  Ⓓ 1,963

Name _____

Chapter 2 Extra Practice

Lesson 2.1

Use rounding or compatible numbers to estimate the sum.

1. $52 \rightarrow$ _____
    $+\ 39 \rightarrow +$ _____

2. $513 \rightarrow$ _____
    $+\ 326 \rightarrow +$ _____

3. $1{,}492 \rightarrow$ _____
    $+\ \ 447 \rightarrow +$ _____

Lesson 2.2

Estimate. Then find the sum.

1. Estimate: _____
    526
    $+\ 281$

2. Estimate: _____
    408
    $+\ 390$

3. Estimate: _____
    812
    $+\ 149$

4. Estimate: _____
    376
    $+\ 175$

Lesson 2.3

Estimate. Then find the sum.

1. Estimate: _____
    $2{,}549$
    $+\ 1{,}702$

2. Estimate: _____
    $5{,}250$
    $+\ 2{,}402$

3. Estimate: _____
    $7{,}290$
    $+\ 2{,}326$

Lesson 2.4

Estimate the difference.

1. $54 \rightarrow$ _____
    $-\ 22 \rightarrow -$ _____

2. $690 \rightarrow$ _____
    $-\ 278 \rightarrow -$ _____

3. $6{,}123 \rightarrow$ _____
    $-\ 2{,}854 \rightarrow -$ _____

Lesson 2.5

Estimate. Then find the difference.

1. Estimate: _____

$$
\begin{array}{r}
639 \\
- 325 \\
\hline
\end{array}
$$

2. Estimate: _____

$$
\begin{array}{r}
891 \\
- 124 \\
\hline
\end{array}
$$

3. Estimate: _____

$$
\begin{array}{r}
502 \\
- 231 \\
\hline
\end{array}
$$

4. Estimate: _____

$$
\begin{array}{r}
725 \\
- 297 \\
\hline
\end{array}
$$

Lesson 2.6

Estimate. Then subtract.

1. Estimate: _____

$$
\begin{array}{r}
7,893 \\
- 4,921 \\
\hline
\end{array}
$$

2. Estimate: _____

$$
\begin{array}{r}
5,673 \\
- 4,786 \\
\hline
\end{array}
$$

3. Estimate: _____

$$
\begin{array}{r}
6,402 \\
- 2,542 \\
\hline
\end{array}
$$

4. Last summer, the Oritz family traveled 2,528 miles on a family trip. Last winter, they traveled 2,857 miles on another trip. How many more miles did they travel last winter?

_____

5. Beth and her family are planning a trip that is 1,160 miles. The first day they will drive 235 miles. How many more miles will they need to travel?

_____

Lesson 2.7

Solve.

1. There were 765 runners in a town race last year. This year there are 47 fewer runners than last year. How many runners are in the race this year?

_____

2. This year 2,462 people watched the race. This is 128 fewer people than the number of people who watched last year. How many people watched the race last year?

_____

Chapter 3
School-Home Letter

Vocabulary

change The money you get back if you have paid for an item with coins or bills that have a value greater than the cost of the item

elapsed time The amount of time that passes from the start of an activity to the end of the activity

Dear Family,

During the next few weeks, our math class will be learning about time and money.

You can expect to see homework that provides practice with telling time, finding elapsed time, making change, and adding and subtracting money amounts.

Here is a sample of how your child will be taught to make change.

🔑 MODEL Make Change

This is one way we will be learning to make change.

STEP 1

Start with the cost of the item.

Count up with coins to the amount paid.

cost of item

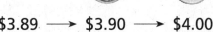

$3.89 ⟶ $3.90 ⟶ $4.00

                amount paid

STEP 2

Count the value of the coins received.

$0.10 ⟶ $0.11

Tips

Other Ways to Make Change

Another way to find the amount of change is to use a number line.

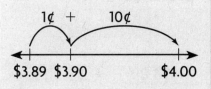

So, if an item costs $3.89, and you pay with $4.00, your change will be $0.11.

Activity

Have your child practice making change. Price items with costs between $3.00 and $5.00. Pay for each item with a $5 bill and have your child count out the correct change.

Carta
para la casa

Vocabulario

cambio El dinero que recibes después de pagar por un artículo con monedas o billetes cuyo valor es mayor al del precio del artículo

tiempo transcurrido El periodo de tiempo que transcurre desde el inicio hasta el final de una actividad

Querida familia,

Durante las próximas semanas, en la clase de matemáticas aprenderemos sobre el tiempo y el dinero.

Llevaré a la casa tareas con actividades que incluyen decir la hora, hallar el tiempo transcurrido, dar cambio, y sumar y restar cantidades de dinero.

Este es un ejemplo de la manera como aprenderemos a dar cambio.

🔑 MODELO Dar cambio

Esta es una manera de dar cambio.

PASO 1

Comienza con el precio del artículo.

Cuenta con la monedas hasta la cantidad que pagaste.

precio del artículo

$3.89 ⟶ $3.90 ⟶ $4.00

cantidad pagada

PASO 2

Cuenta el valor de las monedas que recibiste.

$0.10 ⟶ $0.11

Pistas

Otras Maneras de Dar Cambio

Otra manera de hallar la cantidad de cambio es usar una recta numérica.

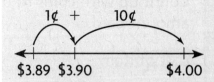

Por tanto, si un artículo cuesta $3.89 y pagamos con $4.00, el cambio es $0.11.

Actividad

Pida a su hijo que practique cómo dar cambio. Ponga precios de entre $3.00 y $5.00 a algunos artículos. Pague cada artículo con un billete de $5 y pida a su hijo que le dé el cambio correcto.

Name _____

Tell Time

Draw the hour hand and the minute hand.

1. 1:30

2. six o'clock

3. 10:45

Write the time.

4.

_____

5.

_____

6.

_____

7.

_____

8.

_____

9.

_____

Problem Solving REAL WORLD

10. Roxanne sees that the hour hand on her watch is on the eleven and the minute hand is on the twelve. What time is it?

11. Pete leaves his house for school at 7:15. What is one way to read this time?

_____

_____

_____

Lesson Check

1. Mrs. Carter's class began at thirty minutes after eight. What is another way to write this time?

- Ⓐ 7:30
- Ⓑ 8:00
- Ⓒ 8:30
- Ⓓ 8:45

2. What time does the clock show?

- Ⓐ 9:15
- Ⓒ 10:15
- Ⓑ 9:45
- Ⓓ 10:45

Spiral Review

3. Mr. Baker has an even number of students in his class. The number of students is between 24 and 36. The sum of the digits is 7. How many students are in Mr. Baker's class? **(Lesson 1.2)**

- Ⓐ 25
- Ⓒ 34
- Ⓑ 26
- Ⓓ 35

4. What is a rule for this pattern?
(Lesson 1.1)

48, 52, 56, 60, 64

- Ⓐ Add 4.
- Ⓑ Add 10.
- Ⓒ Subtract 4.
- Ⓓ Subtract 6.

5. Northside Library collected 2,628 fiction books and 5,098 nonfiction books for their used book sale. About how many books did Northside Library collect? **(Lesson 2.1)**

- Ⓐ 6,000
- Ⓑ 7,000
- Ⓒ 8,000
- Ⓓ 9,000

6. Nora exercised for 109 minutes last week. This week she exercised for 116 minutes. How many more minutes did Nora exercise this week than last week? **(Lesson 2.5)**

- Ⓐ 3 minutes
- Ⓑ 7 minutes
- Ⓒ 13 minutes
- Ⓓ 25 minutes

Name _____

Time to the Minute

Write the time. Write one way you can read the time.

1.

1:16; sixteen minutes after one

2.

_____

_____

_____

3.

_____

_____

_____

4.

_____

_____

5.

_____

_____

6.

_____

_____

Write the time another way.

7. 23 minutes after 4

_____

8. 18 minutes before 11

_____

9. 10 minutes before 9

_____

10. 7 minutes after 1

_____

Problem Solving REAL WORLD

11. What time is it when the hour hand is a little past the 3 and the minute hand is pointing to the 3?

_____

12. Pete began practicing at twenty-five minutes before eight. What is another way to write this time?

_____

Lesson Check

1. Which is another way to write 13 minutes before 10?

- (A) 9:47
- (B) 10:13
- (C) 10:47
- (D) 11:13

2. What time does the clock show?

- (A) 2:20
- (C) 3:20
- (B) 2:40
- (D) 4:10

Spiral Review

3. What is 569 rounded to the nearest hundred? **(Lesson 1.7)**

- (A) 500
- (B) 560
- (C) 570
- (D) 600

4. Which numbers are in order from least to greatest? **(Lesson 1.6)**

- (A) 101, 110, 120, 121
- (B) 121, 120, 110, 101
- (C) 110, 101, 121, 120
- (D) 120, 121, 101, 110

5. Dion drew a quick picture to record the number of books on the shelf.

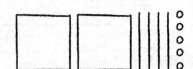

How many books are on the shelf?

(Lesson 1.3)

- (A) 29
- (C) 542
- (B) 245
- (D) 2,045

6. Add. **(Lesson 2.3)**

$$
\begin{array}{r}
4{,}583 \\
+3{,}925 \\
\end{array}
$$

- (A) 7,468
- (B) 7,502
- (C) 8,402
- (D) 8,508

Name _____

A.M. and P.M.

Write the time for the activity. Use A.M. or P.M.

1. eat lunch

12:20 P.M.

2. go home after school

_____

3. see the sunrise

_____

4. go for a walk

_____

5. go to school

_____

6. get ready for art class

_____

Write the time. Use A.M. or P.M.

7. 13 minutes after 5 in the morning

_____

8. 19 minutes before 9 in the evening

_____

9. quarter before midnight

_____

10. one half hour after 4 in the morning

_____

Problem Solving REAL WORLD

11. Jaime is in math class. What time is it? Write A.M. or P.M.

_____

12. Pete began practicing his trumpet at fifteen minutes past three. Write this time using A.M. or P.M.

_____

Lesson Check

1. Steven is doing his homework. What time is it?

Ⓐ 4:15 P.M.

Ⓑ 4:25 A.M.

Ⓒ 4:35 P.M.

Ⓓ 4:35 A.M.

2. When he finished breakfast, Mr. Edwards left for work at fifteen minutes after seven. What time is this?

Ⓐ 6:15 A.M.

Ⓑ 7:15 A.M.

Ⓒ 6:45 P.M.

Ⓓ 7:30 P.M.

Spiral Review

3. If the pattern continues, what will the next number be? (Lesson 1.1)

80, 83, 86, 89, 92

Ⓐ 91

Ⓑ 93

Ⓒ 94

Ⓓ 95

4. Mrs. Johnson saved 2,790 pennies. Which is a way to write 2,790? (Lesson 1.5)

Ⓐ two thousand, seven hundred ninety

Ⓑ two hundred seventy-nine

Ⓒ two thousand, seven hundred nine

Ⓓ two thousand, seventy-nine

5. There were 145 bags of beef flavored dog food and 263 bags of cheese flavored dog food sold at a pet store. How many bags of dog food were sold? (Lesson 2.2)

Ⓐ 118

Ⓑ 308

Ⓒ 408

Ⓓ 422

6. Mr. Benson ordered 2,391 red bricks and 4,280 brown bricks to build a wall. About how many more brown bricks did he order? (Lesson 2.4)

Ⓐ 5,000

Ⓑ 2,000

Ⓒ 1,000

Ⓓ 500

Elapsed Time

Find the elapsed time.

1. Start: 8:10 A.M.   End: 11:20 A.M.

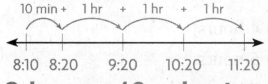

3 hours 10 minutes

2. Start: 6:45 P.M.   End: 8:30 P.M.

3. Start: 3:00 P.M.   End: 6:25 P.M.

4. Start: 10:05 A.M.   End: 2:15 P.M.

5. Start: 7:30 A.M.   End: 9:00 A.M.

6. Start: 5:55 A.M.   End: 11:00 A.M.

Problem Solving

7. A movie starts at 7:40 P.M. and ends at 9:55 P.M. How long is the movie?

8. The first train leaves the station at 6:15 A.M. The second train leaves 1 hour 30 minutes later. At what time does the second train leave the station?

Lesson Check

TEST PREP

1. Marcus began playing basketball at 3:30 P.M. and stopped playing at 4:15 P.M. For how many minutes did he play basketball?

Ⓐ 30 minutes
Ⓑ 35 minutes
Ⓒ 40 minutes
Ⓓ 45 minutes

2. The school day begins at 8:30 A.M. and ends at 2:30 P.M. For how long are the students in school?

Ⓐ 4 hours
Ⓑ 5 hours
Ⓒ 6 hours
Ⓓ 7 hours

Spiral Review

3. Subtract. (Lesson 2.6)

6,784
−3,345

Ⓐ 3,459
Ⓑ 3,439
Ⓒ 3,349
Ⓓ 3,129

4. Which is a way to write 5,081?
(Lesson 1.5)

Ⓐ 5,000 + 800 + 10
Ⓑ 5,000 + 800 + 1
Ⓒ 5,000 + 80 + 1
Ⓓ 500 + 80 + 1

5. Sara used 6 hundreds blocks and 7 tens blocks to model a number. What number did Sara model?

(Lesson 1.3)

Ⓐ 67
Ⓑ 76
Ⓒ 607
Ⓓ 670

6. Mr. Martin drove 290 miles last week. This week he drove 125 miles more than last week. How many miles did Mr. Martin drive this week? (Lesson 2.2)

Ⓐ 125 miles
Ⓑ 165 miles
Ⓒ 315 miles
Ⓓ 415 miles

Act It Out · Elapsed Time

Solve each problem. Show your work.

1. Hannah wants to meet her friends downtown on Saturday. Before she leaves, she does 1 hour of homework and eats lunch for 20 minutes. The walk downtown takes 15 minutes. She starts her homework at 11:45 A.M. At what time does Hannah meet her friends?

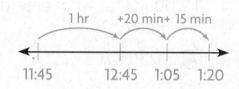

1:20 P.M.

2. Katie practiced the flute for 45 minutes. Then she ate a snack for 15 minutes. Next, she watched television for 1 hour, until 6:00 P.M. At what time did Katie start practicing the flute?

_____

3. Nick got out of school at 2:25 P.M. He had a 15-minute ride home on the bus. He spent 30 minutes riding his bike. Then he spent 1 hour 15 minutes doing homework. At what time did Nick finish his homework?

_____

4. The third-grade class went on a field trip by bus to the museum. The bus left the school at 9:45 A.M. The bus ride took 1 hour 30 minutes. At what time did the bus arrive at the museum?

_____

Lesson Check

1. Gloria and her sister went shopping at the mall for 50 minutes. Then they took 30 minutes to eat lunch. If they began shopping at 11:00 A.M., at what time did they finish lunch?

- Ⓐ 11:30 A.M.
- Ⓑ 11:50 A.M.
- Ⓒ 12:20 P.M.
- Ⓓ 12:30 P.M.

2. The ball game begins at 2:00 P.M. It takes 30 minutes to get to the ballpark. At what time should Ying leave to get to the game 30 minutes before it starts?

- Ⓐ 12:30 P.M.
- Ⓑ 1:00 P.M.
- Ⓒ 1:30 P.M.
- Ⓓ 3:00 P.M.

Spiral Review

3. Rama wants to model 1,235 using base-ten blocks. Which blocks can Rama use for her model? (Lesson 1.4)

- Ⓐ 1 thousand 23 hundreds 5 ones
- Ⓑ 12 thousands 3 tens 5 ones
- Ⓒ 12 hundreds 35 ones
- Ⓓ 1 thousand 2 tens 35 ones

4. On Saturday, 868 people saw the new movie. On Sunday, 2,921 people saw the new movie. How many people saw the new movie during the weekend? (Lesson 2.3)

- Ⓐ 3,899
- Ⓒ 2,889
- Ⓑ 3,789
- Ⓓ 2,147

5. There were 405 books on the library shelf. Some books were checked out. Now there are 215 books left on the shelf. How many books were checked out? (Lesson 2.5)

- Ⓐ 620
- Ⓑ 220
- Ⓒ 210
- Ⓓ 190

6. Aaron writes the number 5,263. Beth writes a number 1,500 less than Aaron's number. What number does Beth write? (Lesson 2.6)

- Ⓐ 4,763
- Ⓑ 4,363
- Ⓒ 3,763
- Ⓓ 3,363

Name _____

Count Coins and Bills

Write the amount.

1.

$1.77

2.

_____

Find two equivalent sets for each. List the coins and bills.

3. 52¢

_____

_____

4. 80¢

_____

_____

5. $1.45

_____

_____

6. $2.25

_____

_____

Problem Solving

7. Maya has three $1 bills, 1 nickel, and 3 pennies. How much money does Maya have in all?

_____

8. Suresh has only nickels. She has 35¢. How many coins does Suresh have?

_____

Lesson Check

1. Adam has only dimes. He has more than 65¢. Which amount could Adam have?

   Ⓐ 60¢   Ⓒ 75¢

   Ⓑ 70¢   Ⓓ 85¢

2. Harry has two $1 bills, 5 quarters, 3 nickels, and 1 penny. How much money does Harry have in all?

   Ⓐ $1.53   Ⓒ $3.16

   Ⓑ $2.41   Ⓓ $3.41

Spiral Review

3. What time is shown on the clock? (Lesson 3.1)

   Ⓐ 1:35

   Ⓑ 2:35

   Ⓒ 3:30

   Ⓓ 7:12

4. The talent show starts at 10:10 A.M. and ends at 11:45 A.M. How long is the talent show? (Lesson 3.4)

   Ⓐ 55 minutes

   Ⓑ 1 hour 35 minutes

   Ⓒ 1 hour 45 minutes

   Ⓓ 2 hours 35 minutes

5. There are 2,694 people signed up to run in the marathon next weekend. What is the number of people rounded to the nearest thousand? (Lesson 1.7)

   Ⓐ 3,000

   Ⓑ 2,700

   Ⓒ 2,600

   Ⓓ 2,000

6. Last year, the third graders sold 2,474 tickets to the talent show. This year, the third graders sold 4,039 tickets. How many tickets did the third graders sell in the last 2 years? (Lesson 2.3)

   Ⓐ 6,513

   Ⓑ 6,503

   Ⓒ 6,413

   Ⓓ 6,403

Compare Amounts of Money

Count to compare the amounts of money. Use <, >, or =.

1.

$$\underline{\$3.55} \gtrdot \underline{\$2.52}$$

2.

_____ ◯ _____

Use place value to compare the amounts of money.
Circle the greater amount.

3. $1.45 or $1.40   **4.** $2.05 or $2.50   **5.** $3.98 or $4.13

Problem Solving

6. Lauren has 2 quarters, 2 dimes, and 1 penny. Aiden has 4 dimes and 3 nickels. Who has more money?

_____

7. Eli has $2.80 in his pocket. Megan has two $1 bills, 2 quarters, 1 dime, and 3 nickels. Who has more money?

_____

Lesson Check

1. Jason has 5 quarters and 2 nickels. Which amount of money is greater than Jason's amount?

Ⓐ 2 quarters, 5 nickels

Ⓑ 2 quarters, 3 dimes

Ⓒ 5 quarters, 2 dimes

Ⓓ 5 quarters, 10 pennies

2. Hannah has $4.78 saved in her coin bank. Which amount of money is less than Hannah's amount?

Ⓐ $5.07

Ⓑ $4.78

Ⓒ $4.87

Ⓓ $4.75

Spiral Review

3. What time is shown on the clock? (Lesson 3.2)

Ⓐ 2:42

Ⓑ 3:42

Ⓒ 8:12

Ⓓ 9:12

4. There were 6,187 visitors at a museum in April; 6,278 visitors in May; 5,982 visitors in June; and 6,099 visitors in July. In which month did the museum have the greatest number of visitors? (Lesson 1.6)

Ⓐ April

Ⓑ May

Ⓒ June

Ⓓ July

5. Malik has one $1 bill, 3 quarters, 1 dime, and 2 pennies. How much money does Malik have? (Lesson 3.6)

Ⓐ $1.87

Ⓑ $1.75

Ⓒ $1.37

Ⓓ $1.12

6. Shawn has 359 baseball cards. Midori has 116 baseball cards. How many more cards does Shawn have? (Lesson 2.7)

Ⓐ 243

Ⓑ 263

Ⓒ 465

Ⓓ 475

Make a Table · Money

Solve each problem. Show your work.

1. Sheldon has three $1 bills, 3 quarters, 4 dimes, and 5 nickels. He wants to buy a CD for $3.55. How many different ways can Sheldon make $3.55?

$1 Bills	Quarters	Dimes	Nickels	Total Value
3	2	0	1	$3.55

So, there are _____ ways Sheldon can make $3.55.

2. Abigail has 6 quarters, 5 dimes, and 3 nickels. She pays for a toy that costs $1.80 using the fewest coins possible. How many coins does Abigail use? **Explain.**

_____

_____

3. Emily has 1 quarter, 2 dimes, and 3 nickels in her pocket. How many different ways can Emily make 40¢? **Explain.**

_____

_____

TEST PREP

Lesson Check

1. Ramon has 3 quarters, 5 dimes, and 5 nickels. He buys juice that costs 65¢ using the greatest number of coins possible. How many coins does Ramon use to pay for the juice?

   (A) 4   (C) 9

   (B) 6   (D) 13

2. Cheryl has 2 quarters, 2 dimes, and 5 nickels. How many different ways can Cheryl make 45¢?

   (A) 5   (C) 3

   (B) 4   (D) 2

Spiral Review

3. Neil eats lunch 15 minutes before noon. Which shows the time Neil eats lunch? (Lesson 3.3)

   (A) 11:15 A.M.

   (B) 11:45 A.M.

   (C) 11:45 P.M.

   (D) 12:15 P.M.

4. Diane has 1 quarter, 2 dimes, and 2 pennies. Which amount of money is greater than Diane's amount? (Lesson 3.7)

   (A) 1 quarter, 5 nickels

   (B) 1 quarter, 2 nickels

   (C) 3 dimes, 2 nickels

   (D) 2 dimes, 3 nickels

5. A ferry is carrying 517 people. If 159 people get off, how many people are still on the ferry? (Lesson 2.5)

   (A) 458

   (B) 442

   (C) 368

   (D) 358

6. On Saturday, 489 people attended a soccer game. What is this number rounded to the nearest hundred? (Lesson 1.7)

   (A) 400

   (B) 480

   (C) 490

   (D) 500

Name _____

Make Change

Find the amount of change.

1. Riley buys a notepad for $1.59. She pays with two $1 bills.

$$\$0.41$$
_____

2. Mario buys a bag of peanuts for $3.45. He pays with a $5 bill.

_____

3. Zach buys a comic book for $2.17. He pays with three $1 bills.

_____

4. Liam buys a bottle of water for $1.55. He pays with two $1 bills.

_____

5. Latrell buys an action figure for $4.39. He pays with a $5 bill.

_____

6. Lu Chen buys a calendar for $3.14. She pays with a $5 bill.

_____

Problem Solving  REAL WORLD

Use the pictures for 7–8.

$1.39

$2.74

$3.30

7. Sonya buys a bag of popcorn. She pays with three $1 bills and 2 quarters. How much change should Sonya receive?

_____

8. Keesha buys a sandwich. Her change is 1 quarter and 1 penny. How much money did Keesha give the cashier?

_____

Lesson Check

1. Alicia buys a baseball for $4.27. She pays with a $5 bill. How much change should Alicia receive?

   (A) $1.83

   (B) $1.73

   (C) $0.83

   (D) $0.73

2. Harry buys yogurt for $1.64. He pays with two $1 bills. How much change should Harry receive?

   (A) $0.26

   (B) $0.36

   (C) $0.46

   (D) $1.36

Spiral Review

3. What time is 3 hours 25 minutes after 4:30 P.M.? (Lesson 3.4)

   (A) 1:05 P.M.   (C) 7:55 P.M.

   (B) 4:55 P.M.   (D) 8:05 P.M.

4. Which number is greater than 789 but less than 815? (Lesson 1.6)

   (A) 816

   (B) 799

   (C) 786

   (D) 715

5. Moira has 247 pennies in a jar. Latifa has 168 pennies. How many pennies do the two girls have in all?

   (Lesson 2.2)

   (A) 415

   (B) 405

   (C) 315

   (D) 305

6. Ricardo has 2 quarters, 4 dimes, and 2 nickels. He buys a pen that costs 75¢ using the fewest coins possible. How many coins does Ricardo use to pay for the pen? (Lesson 3.8)

   (A) 3

   (B) 4

   (C) 5

   (D) 6

Name _____

Add and Subtract Money Amounts

Use the number line to find the sum or difference.

1. 65¢ − 27¢ _____38¢_____

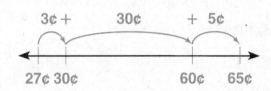

2. $1.29 + $3.70 _____

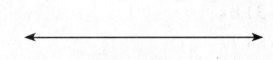

Estimate. Then find the sum or difference.

3. Estimate: _____
$1.23
+ $0.45

4. Estimate: _____
$2.80
− $1.20

5. Estimate: _____
$3.25
+ $1.34

6. Estimate: _____
$1.84
+ $1.11

7. Estimate: _____
$0.96
− $0.37

8. Estimate: _____
$0.15
+ $0.95

9. Estimate: _____
$3.67
− $0.55

10. Estimate: _____
$0.87
− $0.29

Problem Solving REAL WORLD

Use the pictures for 11–12.

$2.35

$4.14

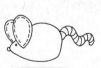
$3.55

11. Caitlin buys a toy mouse. Brandon buys a toy cat. How much more does Caitlin spend than Brandon?

12. Jake buys a toy cat and a toy dog. How much does Jake spend on the two toy animals?

_____

_____

Lesson Check

1. Ben bought a marker for $1.27 and a pen for $0.50. How much money did Ben spend?

   Ⓐ $1.87
   Ⓑ $1.77
   Ⓒ $0.87
   Ⓓ $0.77

2. Karim has $2.55. He spends $1.30 on a postcard. How much money does Karim have left?

   Ⓐ $3.85
   Ⓑ $3.15
   Ⓒ $1.25
   Ⓓ $1.15

Spiral Review

3. Kara gets on the bus at 3:15 P.M. Her bus ride takes 50 minutes. What time does Kara get off the bus? (Lesson 3.5)

   Ⓐ 3:50 P.M.   Ⓒ 4:05 P.M.
   Ⓑ 3:55 P.M.   Ⓓ 4:15 P.M.

4. Wayne buys a T-shirt for $3.68. He pays with a $5 bill. How much change should he receive? (Lesson 3.9)

   Ⓐ $1.32
   Ⓑ $1.42
   Ⓒ $2.32
   Ⓓ $2.68

5. What is 7,000 + 600 + 4 written in standard form? (Lesson 1.5)

   Ⓐ 764
   Ⓑ 7,064
   Ⓒ 7,604
   Ⓓ 7,640

6. Giselle writes this number pattern. Which rule best describes her pattern? (Lesson 1.1)

   48, 45, 42, 39, 36

   Ⓐ Add 2.
   Ⓑ Subtract 2.
   Ⓒ Add 3.
   Ⓓ Subtract 3.

© Houghton Mifflin Harcourt Publishing Company

Chapter 3 Extra Practice

Lessons 3.1 – 3.2

Write the time.

1.

```
6:30
```

2.

3.

_____   _____   _____

Lesson 3.3

Write the time. Use A.M. or P.M.

1. 30 minutes past noon

2. 14 minutes before 7 in the morning

_____   _____

Lesson 3.4

Find the elapsed time.

1. Start: 10:50 P.M. End: 11:35 P.M.

2. Start: 7:00 A.M.   End: 10:30 A.M.

←————————————→

_____   _____

Lesson 3.5

1. Lucas volunteers at the recycling center after school.
He leaves school at 3:05 P.M. The bus ride home
takes 25 minutes. Then it takes 15 minutes for his
mom to drive him to the center. At what time does
Lucas arrive at the recycling center?   _____

Lessons 3.6–3.7

Write the amount. Circle the greater amount.

1.

_____   _____

Lesson 3.8

1. Lamar has three $1 bills, 4 quarters, 3 dimes, and 4 nickels. He wants to pay the $3.50 zoo entrance fee. How many different ways can Lamar make $3.50?

_____

Lesson 3.9

Find the amount of change.

1. Liz buys a snack for $1.09. She pays with two $1 bills.

2. Antonio buys breakfast for $3.17. He pays with a $5 bill.

_____   _____

Lesson 3.10

Estimate. Then find the sum or difference.

1. Estimate: _____

$0.85
+ $0.64

2. Estimate: _____

$1.37
+ $3.61

3. Estimate: _____

$0.72
− $0.46

4. Estimate: _____

$4.96
− $2.23

School-Home Letter

Chapter 4

Dear Family,

During the next few weeks, our math class will be learning about collecting and analyzing data.

You can expect to see homework that provides practice with tally tables, frequency tables, pictographs, bar graphs, and line plots.

Here is a sample of how your child will be taught to collect and organize data in a tally table and a frequency table.

Vocabulary

data Information that is collected about people or things

tally table A table in which you can make tally marks to record data that you collect. You make 1 tally mark | to stand for 1 thing. You make 5 tally marks ||||| to stand for 5 things.

frequency table A table in which you can write the number of tally marks to make the data easier to read. For example, you would write the number 3 to show |||.

🔑 MODEL Make a Tally Table and a Frequency Table

This is one way we will be collecting and organizing data.

STEP 1

Find things to count.

Shapes:
   squares
   circles
   rectangles
   triangles

STEP 2

Draw a table and make 1 tally mark for each kind of shape you count.

Shapes	
Kind	**Tally**
square	||||
circle	|||
rectangle	|||||
triangle	||

STEP 3

Put the data in a frequency table by writing numbers for the tally marks.

Shapes	
Kind	**Number**
square	4
circle	3
rectangle	5
triangle	2

Tips

Other Ways to Collect Data

Another way to collect data is to ask people a question, such as what their favorite color is. Data can also be collected about an experiment, such as tossing a number cube to find out how many times each number is tossed.

Activity

Have your child find several objects to count, such as four types of toys. Help your child make a tally table and a frequency table to show data about these objects.

Carta para la casa

Estimada familia,

Durante la próximas semanas, en la clase de matemáticas aprenderemos acerca de la recolección y análisis de datos.

Llevaré a la casa tareas que sirven para poner en práctica las tablas de conteo, las tablas de frecuencia, las gráficas de barras y los diagramas de puntos.

Este es un ejemplo de la manera como aprenderemos a recolectar y organizar datos en una tabla de conteo y en una tabla de frecuencia.

Vocabulario

datos La información que se recolecta sobre las personas o cosas

tabla de conteo Una tabla en la que se pueden hacer marcas de conteo para registrar los datos recolectados. Se hace 1 marca de conteo | para representar 1 cosa. Se hacen 5 marcas de conteo ||||| para representar 5 cosas.

tabla de frecuencia Una tabla en la que se puede anotar la cantidad de marcas de conteo para que los datos sean más fáciles de leer. Por ejemplo, se anota el número 3 para mostrar |||.

🔑 MODELO Hacer una tabla de conteo y una tabla de frecuencia

De esta manera recolectaremos y organizaremos datos.

PASO 1

Encuentra cosas para contar.

Figuras:

cuadrados
círculos
rectángulos
triángulos

PASO 2

Dibuja una tabla y haz 1 marca de conteo para cada tipo de figura que cuentes.

Figuras	
Tipo de figuras	Conteo
cuadrado	||||
círculo	|||
rectángulo	||||
triángulo	||

PASO 3

Anota los datos en la tabla de frecuencia escribiendo números en vez de las marcas de conteo.

Figuras	
Tipo de figuras	Frecuencia
cuadrado	4
círculo	3
rectángulo	5
triángulo	2

Pistas

Otras formas de recolectar datos

Otra forma de recolectar datos es haciendo una pregunta a la gente, como cuál es su color favorito. También se pueden recolectar datos de un experimento, por ejemplo, lanzando un cubo numerado para averiguar cuántas veces cae cada número.

Actividad

Pida a su hijo que encuentre varios objetos que se puedan contar, como cuatro tipos de juguetes. Ayúdelo a hacer una tabla de conteo y una tabla de frecuencia para mostrar los datos de estos objetos.

Name _____

Collect Data

Use the Favorite School Subjects data for 1–4.

Joe asked his friends about their favorite subjects in school.

He made a list of the results of his survey.

Show the data in a tally table and in a frequency table.

Favorite School Subjects			
		Ben	Science
Grace	Math	Lauren	Math
Sean	Science	Carlos	Science
Hannah	Science	Mary	Social Studies
Patrick	Social Studies	Jeremy	Reading
Manuel	Math	Matthew	Science

Favorite School Subjects	
Subject	Tally
Math	|||
Science	
Social Studies	
Reading	

Favorite School Subjects	
Subject	Number
Math	3
Science	
Social Studies	
Reading	

1. Which subject did the most students choose as their favorite?

_____

2. How many more students chose math than reading?

_____

Problem Solving REAL WORLD

3. How would the results of Joe's survey change if Jeremy was not asked about his favorite subject?

4. How many more votes would social studies need to have the same number as math?

_____

Lesson Check

TEST PREP

Favorite Winter Sports	
Sport	Number
Ice Skating	8
Hockey	4
Sledding	12
Snowboarding	15

1. In the table of Favorite Winter Sports, how many people chose snowboarding or hockey as favorite winter sports?

Ⓐ 8   Ⓒ 16

Ⓑ 12   Ⓓ 19

Spiral Review

2. What is one way to model 1,297 without a thousands block?
(Lesson 1.4)

Ⓐ 12 tens 97 ones

Ⓑ 129 hundreds 7 ones

Ⓒ 12 hundreds 97 ones

Ⓓ 129 tens 97 ones

3. What is this number in standard form? **(Lesson 1.5)**

$7,000 + 500 + 90 + 9$

Ⓐ 7,099

Ⓑ 7,509

Ⓒ 7,590

Ⓓ 7,599

4. Scott made breakfast at a quarter after seven. What is one way to write that time? **(Lesson 3.1)**

Ⓐ 6:45 A.M.

Ⓑ 7:15 A.M.

Ⓒ 6:45 P.M.

Ⓓ 7:15 P.M.

5. Count by tens. What is the next number? **(Lesson 1.1)**

20, 30, 40, 50, _____

Ⓐ 51

Ⓑ 55

Ⓒ 60

Ⓓ 70

Name _____

Make a Table • Data

Use the information below for 1–5.

Carlos lives in Ohio. He asked students in his school which states they have recently visited. Seventy-two students completed the survey. The most students said California. Missouri was visited by the fewest students. Ten more students said Arizona than Pennsylvania. Fourteen students said Pennsylvania. Twice as many students said Pennsylvania as Missouri.

States Recently Visited	
State	**Number**
Pennsylvania	14
Arizona	
Missouri	
California	

1. Complete the frequency table at the right.

_____

2. How did you find the number of students who visited Missouri?

_____

_____

3. How did you find the number of students who visited Arizona?

4. How did you find the number of students who visited California?

_____   _____

5. List the states in the order that you found the number who visited each one. Could you have found the number for each state in a different order? **Explain**.

_____

_____

_____

_____

Lesson Check

1. If the pattern below continues, how many wheels will 6 wagons have?

Wagons	1	2	3	4	5
Number of Wheels	4	8		16	

Ⓐ 6

Ⓑ 12

Ⓒ 20

Ⓓ 24

2. Sue used a pattern to choose flowers for her garden. If the pattern continues in the table below, how many roses would Sue choose?

Sue's Flowers	
Flower	Number
Daisy	2
Sunflower	4
Orchid	8
Rose	

Ⓐ 16   Ⓑ 12   Ⓒ 10   Ⓓ 6

Spiral Review

3. Find the difference. (Lesson 2.5)

$$805 - 697$$

Ⓐ 1,502   Ⓒ 118

Ⓑ 292   Ⓓ 108

4. Estimate the sum. (Lesson 2.1)

$$1,492 + 675$$

Ⓐ 3,000   Ⓒ 1,900

Ⓑ 2,200   Ⓓ 800

5. Megan buys 2 cartons of yogurt that cost $0.99 each. She pays with a $5 bill. How much change should she get? (Lesson 3.9)

Ⓐ $1.98   Ⓒ $3.99

Ⓑ $3.02   Ⓓ $4.12

6. Compare the numbers. Which symbol makes the sentence true?

(Lesson 1.6)

8,039 ⬤ 8,061

Ⓐ >   Ⓒ =

Ⓑ <   Ⓓ +

Name _____

Use Pictographs

Use the pictograph for 1–7.

Mrs. Perez made a pictograph of her students' scores on a math test.

Math Test Scores	
100	★★★★★
95	★★★
90	★★★★
85	★
Key: Each ★ = 4 students.	

1. How many students made 100? How can you find the answer?

   To find the number of students who made 100, count each star as 4 students. So, 20 students made 100.

   _____

2. What does the ★ mean?

   _____

   _____

3. How many students in all made 100 or 95?

   _____

   _____

4. How many more students made 90 than 85?

   _____

   _____

5. How many students in all took the test?

   _____

   _____

Problem Solving REAL WORLD

6. Suppose the students who made 85 and 90 on the math test take the test again and make 95. How many stars would you have to add to the pictograph next to 95?

   _____

   _____

7. If 2 more students took the math test and both made a score of 80, what would the pictograph look like?

   _____

   _____

Lesson Check

1. Karen asked her friends to name their favorite type of dog.

Favorite Dogs

Retriever	🦴 🦴 🦴 🦴 🦴 🦴
Poodle	🦴 🦴 🦴
Terrier	🦴 🦴

Key: Each 🦴 = 2 People.

How many people chose poodles?

Ⓐ 10   Ⓒ 4

Ⓑ 6   Ⓓ 3

2. Henry made a pictograph to show what topping people like on their pizza. This is his key.

Each 🍕 = 6 people.

How many people do 🍕 ◖ stand for?

Ⓐ $1\frac{1}{2}$ Ⓒ 9

Ⓑ 2   Ⓓ 12

Spiral Review

3. Estimate the sum. (Lesson 2.1)

$$\begin{array}{r} 823 \\ + 295 \\ \hline \end{array}$$

Ⓐ 1,100   Ⓒ 700

Ⓑ 900   Ⓓ 300

4. Ben bought a whistle for $1.79 and book for $3.98. How much did he spend in all? (Lesson 3.10)

Ⓐ $2.19   Ⓒ $4.77

Ⓑ $4.67   Ⓓ $5.77

5. What is 4,871 rounded to the nearest thousand? (Lesson 1.7)

Ⓐ 5,000

Ⓑ 4,900

Ⓒ 4,870

Ⓓ 4,000

6. What is 2,473 rounded to the nearest hundred? (Lesson 1.7)

Ⓐ 2,570

Ⓑ 2,500

Ⓒ 2,400

Ⓓ 2,000

Name _____

Make Pictographs

Ben asked his classmates about their favorite kind of TV show. He recorded their responses in a frequency table. Use the data in the table to make a pictograph.

Favorite TV Shows	
Type	Number
Cartoons	9
Sports	6
Movies	3

Follow the steps to make a pictograph.

Step 1 Write the title at the top of the graph.

Step 2 Look at the numbers in the table. Choose a key that tells how many each picture represents.

Step 3 Draw the correct number of pictures for each kind of show.

Cartoons	▨ ▨ ▨
Sports	
Movies	

Key: Each ▨ =

1. What title did you give the graph?

   _____
   _____

2. What key did you use?

   _____
   _____

3. How many pictures did you use to show sports?

   _____

Problem Solving REAL WORLD

4. How many pictures would you draw if 12 students chose game shows as their favorite kind of TV show?

   _____

5. What key would you use if 10 students chose cartoons?

   _____

Lesson Check

1. Sandy made a pictograph to show the sports her classmates like to play. How many more students chose soccer than baseball?

Favorite Sports

Basketball	○○○○○○○○
Soccer	○○○○○○○○○◖
Baseball	○○○○○○

Key: Each ○ = 2 students.

Ⓐ $15\frac{1}{2}$ Ⓒ 8

Ⓑ $9\frac{1}{2}$ Ⓓ 7

2. Tommy is making a pictograph to show his friends' favorite kinds of music. He plans to use one musical note to represent 2 people. How many notes will he use to show that 4 people chose country music?

Ⓐ 2

Ⓑ 4

Ⓒ 6

Ⓓ 8

Spiral Review

3. Find the sum. (Lesson 2.3)

$$5,480$$
$$+\ 2,954$$

Ⓐ 7,334   Ⓒ 8,334

Ⓑ 7,434   Ⓓ 8,434

4. Count by fives. What is the next number? (Lesson 1.1)

25, 30, 35, 40, 45, 50, ____

Ⓐ 50   Ⓒ 60

Ⓑ 55   Ⓓ 70

5. Alex goes to soccer practice after school. Which time shows when soccer practice might be? (Lesson 3.3)

Ⓐ 3:45 A.M.

Ⓑ 9:00 A.M.

Ⓒ 11:30 A.M.

Ⓓ 4:15 P.M.

6. James and Marie bought plants at a nursery. James spent $7.47. Marie spent $8.90. Which correctly compares the amounts? (Lesson 3.7)

Ⓐ $8.90 = $7.47

Ⓑ $7.47 > $8.90

Ⓒ $7.47 < $8.90

Ⓓ $8.90 < $7.47

Name _____

Use Bar Graphs

Use the bar graph for 1–6.

The students at Case Elementary School were asked what they spend the most time doing after dinner. The results are shown in the bar graph at the right.

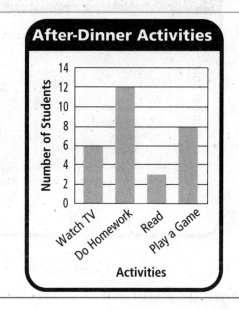

1. How many students watch TV after dinner?

   _____ 6 students _____

2. Which activity do the most students do?

   _____

3. How many students in all do homework or read?

   _____

4. Which activity do 8 students do?

   _____

5. How many more students do homework than play a game?

   _____

Problem Solving REAL WORLD

6. Suppose 3 students changed their answers to reading instead of doing homework. Where would the bar for reading end?

   _____

Lesson Check

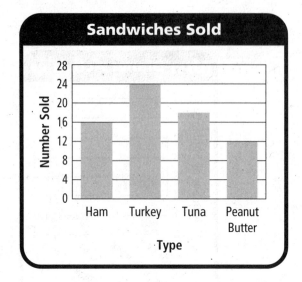

Sandwiches Sold

1. The bar graph shows the number of sandwiches sold at Lisa's shop yesterday. How many tuna sandwiches were sold?

   (A) 12

   (B) 16

   (C) 18

   (D) 20

Spiral Review

2. Which is NOT a way to model 4,821? **(Lesson 1.5)**

   (A) 48 hundreds 21 ones

   (B) 4 thousands 821 tens

   (C) 4 thousands 82 tens 1 one

   (D) 482 tens 1 one

3. Grant has saved $89. How much more money does he need to buy a bike that costs $135? **(Lesson 2.7)**

   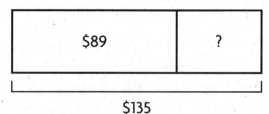

   | $89 | ? |

   $135

   (A) $223   (C) $54

   (B) $56   (D) $46

4. Jonah ate dinner at a quarter to seven. Which shows his dinner time? **(Lesson 3.2)**

   (A) 6:45 A.M.   (C) 6:45 P.M.

   (B) 7:15 A.M.   (D) 7:45 P.M.

5. Cory's soccer practice lasted 90 minutes. It ended at 5:15 P.M. At what time did it start? **(Lesson 3.4)**

   (A) 6:45 P.M.   (C) 4:15 P.M.

   (B) 4:45 P.M.   (D) 3:45 P.M.

Make Bar Graphs

Use the data in the table to complete the bar graph.

Ben asked some friends to name their favorite breakfast foods. He recorded their choices in the frequency table at the right.

Favorite Breakfast Foods	
Food	Number of Friends
Waffles	8
Cereal	14
Pancakes	12
Oatmeal	4

1. Complete the bar graph by shading in the bars for pancakes and oatmeal.

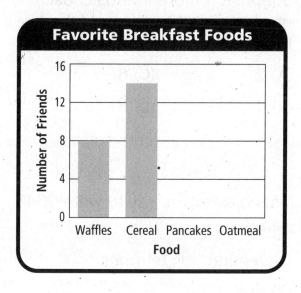

2. Which food did the most people choose as their favorite breakfast food?

   _____

3. How many people chose waffles as their favorite breakfast food?

   _____

4. How did you know how high to draw the bar for pancakes?

   _____

   _____

   _____

5. Suppose 5 people chose oatmeal as their favorite breakfast food. How would you change the bar graph?

   _____

   _____

   _____

   _____

Lesson Check

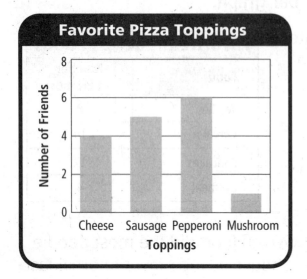

Favorite Pizza Toppings

1. Gary asked his friends to name their favorite pizza toppings. He recorded the results in a bar graph. How many people chose pepperoni?

   Ⓐ 6   Ⓒ 4
   Ⓑ 5   Ⓓ 1

2. Suppose 3 more friends chose mushrooms. Where would the bar for mushrooms end?

   Ⓐ 2   Ⓒ 6
   Ⓑ 4   Ⓓ 8

Spiral Review

3. Estimate the difference. (Lesson 2.4)

   $$\begin{array}{r} 2{,}683 \\ -\ 1{,}547 \end{array}$$

   Ⓐ 4,000   Ⓒ 1,000
   Ⓑ 1,500   Ⓓ 500

4. Which is NOT a way to write 564?
   (Lesson 1.3)

   Ⓐ 5 hundreds 64 ones

   Ⓑ 564 ones

   Ⓒ 56 tens 4 ones

   Ⓓ 5 hundreds 64 tens

5. As soon as Tracy got home from school, she spent 45 minutes doing homework. Then she spent 20 minutes giving her dog a bath. She finished at 5:40 P.M. At what time did Tracy get home from school? (Lesson 3.5)

   Ⓐ 4:15 P.M.   Ⓒ 4:30 P.M.
   Ⓑ 4:35 P.M.   Ⓓ 5:20 P.M.

6. Jeff has a $1 bill and some coins. He has a total of $2.83. Which coins could he have? (Lesson 3.8)

   Ⓐ 7 quarters 8 pennies

   Ⓑ 6 quarters 3 dimes

   Ⓒ 5 quarters 6 dimes 8 pennies

   Ⓓ 4 quarters 8 nickels 3 pennies

Name _____

Solve Data Problems

Essential Question How can you use data to solve problems?

Real World Derek's class voted on a topic for the school bulletin board. The bar graph at the right shows the results. How many more votes did computers receive than space?

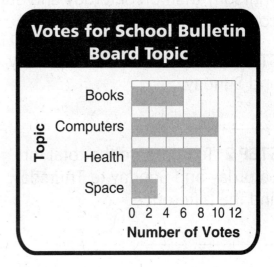

Votes for School Bulletin Board Topic

One Way Count back along the scale to find the difference between the bars.

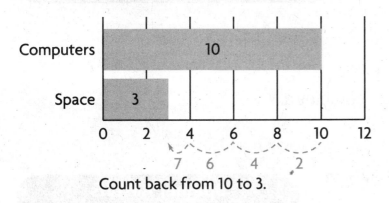

Count back from 10 to 3.

The difference is _____ votes.

Another Way Write a number sentence to find the difference.

Think: There are 10 votes for computers. There are 3 votes for space. Subtract to compare the number of votes.

_____

So, computers received _____ more votes than space.

 Answering questions about data helps you better understand the information.

Remember

When you need to compare or find how many more or fewer, subtract.

Math Talk **Explain** another way you can skip count to find the difference.

© Houghton Mifflin Harcourt Publishing Company

More Comparisons

Use the pictograph at the right. How many fewer students volunteered on Thursday than on Saturday and Sunday combined?

STEP 1 Find the total for Saturday and Sunday.

_____

STEP 2 To compare the total for Saturday and Sunday to Thursday, find the difference.

_____

So, _____ fewer students volunteered on Thursday than on Saturday and Sunday combined.

Volunteers for the Food Drive	
Thursday	☺ ☺ ☺ ◖
Friday	☺ ☺ ☺ ☺
Saturday	☺ ☺ ☺ ☺ ☺ ☺
Sunday	☺ ☺ ☺ ☺ ☺ ☺ ◖

Key: Each ☺ = 4 students.

Think About It

Use the Spinner Results bar graph for 1–3.

1. **Explain** how you can find how many fewer times the pointer stopped on red than on green.

_____

_____

_____

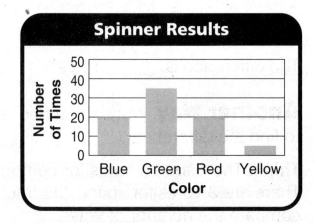

2. **Apply** How many fewer times did the pointer stop on yellow than on blue and red combined?

_____ fewer times

3. **Apply** On which three colors did the pointer stop a total of 60 times?

_____

Math Talk **Explain** how the length of the bars in a bar graph can help you check your comparisons.

Name _____

Practice

Use the November Weather bar graph for 4–6.

4. Which two kinds of weather occurred on 17 days combined?

   Think: Find two bars that represent 17 days.

   _____

5. How many more rainy days than sunny days were there?

   _____

6. **What if** there had been one more snowy day and one fewer rainy day? How many fewer snowy days than rainy days would there have been?

   _____

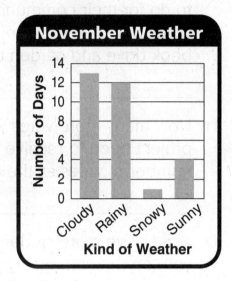

Use the Favorite Science Project pictograph for 7–9.

7. How many fewer votes did the least popular project receive than the most popular project?

   _____

8. How many more votes would rocks need to receive to have the same number of votes as electricity?

   _____

9. Is the number of votes for animals greater than or less than the combined votes for all of the other projects?

   Explain. _____

   _____

   _____

Problem Solving • Real World

Use the Community Project bar graph for 10–12.

10. The third-grade students voted for a project to do for their community. How many fewer votes did the mural project receive than the book drive and garden projects combined?

_____

11. How many more votes would the tutor project need to receive to have the same number of votes as the book drive?

_____

12. 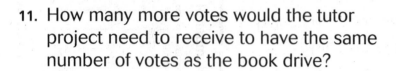 Five more students are asked to vote on the community project. Three students vote for the clean park, one votes for the garden, and one votes for the mural. **Explain** how the order of the projects would be different if you listed them from the most to fewest votes received.

_____

_____

_____

Use the Library Computer Center bar graph for 13–14.

13. ⭐ **Test Prep** How many fewer students used a computer for games than for homework?

Ⓐ 5   Ⓑ 15   Ⓒ 20   Ⓓ 40

14. ⭐ **Test Prep** How many more students used a computer for homework and email combined than for projects and games combined?

Ⓐ 5   Ⓑ 10   Ⓒ 30   Ⓓ 80

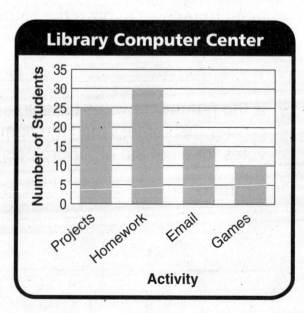

Name _____

Understand Line Plots

Use the Shirt Prices line plot for 1–6.

Erin made this line plot to record the number of shirts that sold for each price.

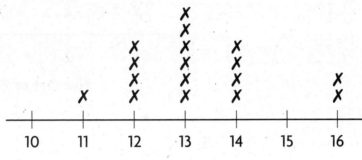

Shirt Prices (in Dollars)

1. How many shirts sold for $12?

   4 shirts

   _____

2. At which price were the most shirts sold?

   _____

3. How many shirts in all did Erin record?

   _____

4. How many shirts were sold for $13 or more?

   _____

Problem Solving REAL WORLD

5. Were more shirts sold for less than $13 or greater than $13? **Explain**.

   _____

6. Write a sentence to describe the data.

   _____

   _____

   _____

Lesson Check

1. Pedro made a line plot to show the number of pets his friends have. How many friends have fewer than 3 pets?

   Ⓐ 4   Ⓒ 10
   Ⓑ 5   Ⓓ 16

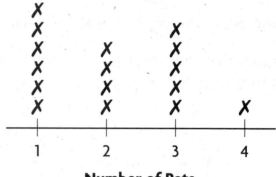

Number of Pets

Spiral Review

2. There were 2,049 runners in a road race. What is 2,049 in expanded form? (Lesson 1.5)

   Ⓐ 2 + 4 + 9
   Ⓑ 20 + 49
   Ⓒ 2,000 + 40 + 9
   Ⓓ 2,000 + 400 + 9

3. Which is one way you could model the number 421 if you had no hundreds? (Lesson 1.3)

   Ⓐ 40 tens 21 ones
   Ⓑ 421 tens
   Ⓒ 4 tens 21 ones
   Ⓓ 41 tens 10 ones

4. Rebecca buys lunch for $3.96. She pays with a $5 bill. How much change should she get? (Lesson 3.9)

   Ⓐ $2.14
   Ⓑ $2.04
   Ⓒ $1.14
   Ⓓ $1.04

5. What time does the clock show? (Lesson 3.1)

   Ⓐ 12:40   Ⓒ 2:40
   Ⓑ 1:40   Ⓓ 8:10

Name _____

Chapter 4 Extra Practice

Lessons 4.1 - 4.2

Use the Pets list for 1–2.

1. Manny made this list of pets owned by students in his class. Complete the tally table and frequency table to organize his data.

Pets

Pam	cat	Julio	bird
Dwayne	dog	Grace	fish
Rhonda	dog	Chen	cat
Stacy	cat	Mark	cat

Pets	Tally		
cat			4
dog			2
bird			1
fish			1

2. How many more students have cats than have dogs or birds?

_____

Lessons 4.3 - 4.4

Use the Seashells pictograph for 1–2.

1. Maggie and her sister put the seashells they collected in a box. How many seashells are in the box?

_____

2. How many more cockle shells were collected than lightning whelks?

_____

3. What if the key was Each 🐚 = 5 shells? How many pictures would there be for conch?

_____

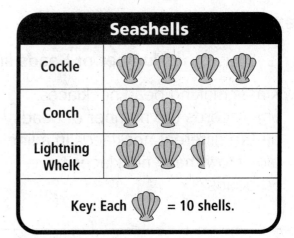

Lessons 4.5 - 4.6

Use the Bicycle Rides table for 1–2.

Bicycle Rides	
Day	**Number of Miles**
Monday	4
Wednesday	9
Saturday	12

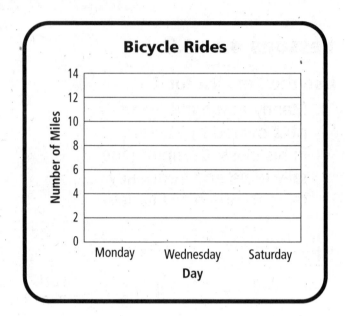

1. The table shows the number of miles Sean rode on his bicycle. Use the data to complete the bar graph.

2. How many more miles did Sean ride on Saturday than on Monday?

_____

3. How many miles in all did Sean ride?

_____

Lesson 4.7

For 1–2, use the Number of Beads line plot.

1. Kim is making bead necklaces. She records the number of beads on the different necklaces in a line plot. How many necklaces have 50 beads?

_____

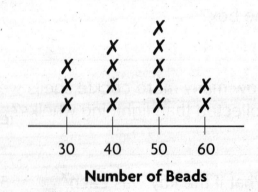

2. How many necklaces have fewer than 40 beads?

_____

3. How many necklaces have 50 or more beads?

_____

School-Home Letter

Dear Family,

During the next few weeks, our math class will be learning about multiplication. We will learn how addition is related to multiplication and how to multiply with the factors 0, 1, 2, 4, 5, and 10.

You can expect to see homework that provides practice with multiplication.

Here is a sample of how your child will be shown the relationship between addition and multiplication.

🔑 MODEL Relate Addition and Multiplication

This is how we will add or multiply to solve problems about equal groups.

Add.

STEP 1

Draw 2 counters in each rectangle to show 4 equal groups.

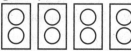

STEP 2

Write an addition sentence to find how many counters in all.

$2 + 2 + 2 + 2 = 8$

Multiply.

STEP 1

Draw 2 counters in each rectangle to show 4 equal groups.

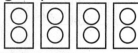

STEP 2

Write a multiplication sentence to find how many counters in all.

$4 \times 2 = 8$

> **Tips**
>
> **Skip Counting**
>
> Skip counting is another way to find how many objects in all. For example, there are 4 groups with 2 counters in each group, so skip counting by 2s can be used: 2, 4, 6, 8. There are 8 counters in all.

Activity

Help your child arrange 3 equal groups of like objects (no more than 10 objects in each group). Then have him or her write an addition sentence and a multiplication sentence to find how many objects in all.

Capítulo 5

Carta
para la casa

Vocabulary

grupos iguales Grupos que tienen la misma cantidad de objetos

multiplicar Cuando uno multiplica, combina grupos iguales para hallar cuántos hay en total.

Durante las próximas semanas, en la clase de matemáticas aprenderemos sobre la multiplicación. Aprenderemos cómo la suma se relaciona con la multiplicación y cómo multiplicar por los factores 0, 1, 2, 4, 5, y 10.

Llevaré a la casa tareas que sirven para practicar la multiplicación.

Este es un ejemplo de la manera como aprenderemos la relación entre la suma y la multiplicación.

🔑 MODELO Relacionar la suma y multiplicación

Así es como vamos a sumar y multiplicar para resolver problemas de grupos iguales.

Sumar.

PASO 1

Dibuja 2 fichas en cada rectángulo para mostrar 4 grupos iguales.

PASO 2

Escribe un enunciado de suma para hallar cuántas fichas hay en total.

$2 + 2 + 2 + 2 = 8$

Multiplicar.

PASO 1

Dibuja 2 fichas en cada rectángulo para mostrar 4 grupos iguales.

PASO 2

Escribe un enunciado de multiplicación para hallar cuántas fichas hay en total.

$4 \times 2 = 8$

Pistas

Contar salteado
Contar salteado es otra manera de hallar cuántos objetos hay en total. Por ejemplo, hay 4 grupos con 2 fichas cada uno, por lo tanto puedes contar salteado de 2 en 2: 2, 4, 6, 8. Hay 8 fichas en total.

Actividad

Ayude a su hijo a formar 3 grupos iguales de objetos parecidos (no más de 10 objetos en cada grupo). Después, pídale que escriba un enunciado de suma y uno de multiplicación para hallar cuántos objetos hay en total.

© Houghton Mifflin Harcourt Publishing Company

Name *Ariana H, Thomas 03/20/15*

Count Equal Groups

Draw equal groups. Skip count to find how many in all.

1. 4 groups of 3

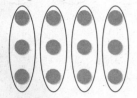

Think:

3, 6, 9, 12

__12__

2. 4 groups of 2

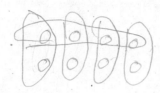

__8__

3. 3 groups of 5

__15__

4. 6 groups of 3

__18__

5. 4 groups of 4

__16__

6. 2 groups of 6

__12__

Problem Solving REAL WORLD

7. Allie is baking muffins for students in her class. There are 6 muffins in each baking tray. She bakes 2 trays of muffins. How many muffins is she making in all?

__12__

8. A snack package has 4 cheese sticks. How many cheese sticks are in 5 packages?

__20__

Lesson Check

1. Skip count to find how many in all.

  (A) 3

  (B) 6

  (C) 9

  (D) 12

2. Skip count to find how many in all.

  (A) 6

  (B) 12

  (C) 18

  (D) 24

Spiral Review

3. Which number is 1,000 more than 2,487? **(Lesson 1.5)**

  (A) 2,488

  (B) 2,497

  (C) 2,587

  (D) 3,487

4. Which number would you put in a frequency table to show a tally of 卌 ||| ? **(Lesson 4.1)**

  (A) 5

  (B) 6

  (C) 7

  (D) 8

5. Brian and his friends went to a movie that started at 2:15. The movie lasted 1 hour 35 minutes. At what time was the movie over? **(Lesson 3.4)**

  (A) 3:15

  (B) 3:35

  (C) 3:50

  (D) 4:00

6. Jillian had $5.50. She bought a set of jacks for $3.25. How much money does she have left? **(Lesson 3.10)**

  (A) $1.75

  (B) $2.00

  (C) $2.25

  (D) $3.25

Name _Ariana H. Thomas 03/20/15_

Relate Addition and Multiplication

Write related addition and multiplication sentences.

1. 3 groups of 5

$$\underline{5} + \underline{5} + \underline{5} = \underline{15}$$
$$\underline{3} \times \underline{5} = \underline{15}$$

2. 4 groups of 2

$$\underline{2} + \underline{2} + \underline{2} + \underline{2} = \underline{8}$$
$$\underline{4} \times \underline{2} = \underline{8}$$

3. 3 groups of 4

$$\underline{4} + \underline{4} + \underline{4} = \underline{12}$$
$$\underline{3} \times \underline{4} = \underline{12}$$

4. 2 groups of 7

$$\underline{7} + \underline{7} = \underline{14}$$
$$\underline{2} \times \underline{7} = \underline{14}$$

5. 4 groups of 3

$$\underline{3} + \underline{3} + \underline{3} + \underline{3} = \underline{12}$$
$$\underline{4} \times \underline{3} = \underline{12}$$

6. 3 groups of 7

$$\underline{7} + \underline{7} + \underline{7} = \underline{21}$$
$$\underline{3} \times \underline{7} = \underline{21}$$

7. 4 groups of 4

$$\underline{4} + \underline{4} + \underline{4} + \underline{4} = \underline{16}$$
$$\underline{4} \times \underline{4} = \underline{16}$$

8. 2 groups of 6

$$\underline{6} + \underline{6} = \underline{12}$$
$$\underline{2} \times \underline{6} = \underline{12}$$

9. 5 groups of 2

$$\underline{2} + \underline{2} + \underline{2} + \underline{2} + \underline{2} = \underline{10}$$
$$\underline{5} \times \underline{2} = \underline{10}$$

10. 4 groups of 6

$$\underline{6} + \underline{6} + \underline{6} + \underline{6} = \underline{24}$$
$$\underline{4} \times \underline{6} = \underline{24}$$

Problem Solving REAL WORLD

11. There are 6 jars of pickles in a box. Ed has 4 boxes of pickles. How many jars of pickles does he have in all? Write a multiplication sentence to find the answer.

$$\underline{6} \times \underline{4} = \underline{24} \text{ jars}$$

12. Each day, Jared rides his bike 5 miles. How many miles does Jared ride in all in 4 days? Write a multiplication sentence to find the answer.

$$\underline{5} \times \underline{4} = \underline{20} \text{ miles}$$

Lesson Check

1. What is another way to show

3 + 3 + 3 + 3 + 3 + 3?

Ⓐ 5 × 3

Ⓑ 4 × 3

Ⓒ 8 × 3

Ⓓ 6 × 3

2. Use the model. How many counters in all?

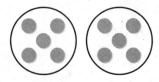

Ⓐ 8   Ⓒ 12

Ⓑ 10   Ⓓ 14

Spiral Review

3. What is the number in standard form. (Lesson 1.5)

1,000 + 200 + 80 + 7

Ⓐ 1,000   Ⓒ 1,287

Ⓑ 1,200   Ⓓ 1,807

4. Find the difference. (Lesson 2.6)

$$\begin{array}{r} 2,968 \\ -524 \\ \hline \end{array}$$

Ⓐ   444   Ⓒ 2,444

Ⓑ 2,434   Ⓓ 2,532

5. The line plot below shows how many points Trevor scored in 20 games. (Lesson 4.7)

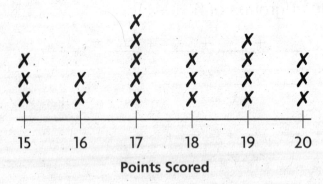

Points Scored

In how many games did Trevor score at least 18 points?

Ⓐ 3   Ⓒ 6

Ⓑ 5   Ⓓ 10

6. Derek wants to buy a snow globe for $2.17. What is one way to use coins and bills to make $2.17?

(Lesson 3.6)

Ⓐ 2 $1 bills, 2 nickels

Ⓑ 1 $1 bill, 3 quarters, 1 dime

Ⓒ 2 $1 bills, 1 dime, 1 nickel, 2 pennies

Ⓓ 2 $1 bills, 1 dime, 1 nickel, 6 pennies

Name Ariana H.Thomas 03/20/15

Multiply with 2

Find the product.

1. $\begin{array}{r} 4 \\ \times\, 2 \\ \hline 8 \end{array}$

2. $\begin{array}{r} 2 \\ \times\, 6 \\ \hline 3 \end{array}$

3. $\begin{array}{r} 2 \\ \times\, 7 \\ \hline 14 \end{array}$

4. $\begin{array}{r} 9 \\ \times\, 2 \\ \hline 18 \end{array}$

5. $\begin{array}{r} 3 \\ \times\, 2 \\ \hline 6 \end{array}$

6. $\begin{array}{r} 2 \\ \times\, 1 \\ \hline 2 \end{array}$

7. $\begin{array}{r} 5 \\ \times\, 2 \\ \hline 10 \end{array}$

8. $\begin{array}{r} 2 \\ \times\, 2 \\ \hline 4 \end{array}$

Complete.

9. $\underline{8} \times 2 = 16$

10. $\underline{6} \times 2 = 12$

11. $9 \times \underline{2} = 18$

12. $\underline{3} \times 2 = 6$

13. $\underline{2} \times 2 = 4$

14. $\underline{5} \times 2 = 10$

15. $1 \times \underline{2} = 2$

16. $\underline{4} \times 2 = 8$

17. $12 = \underline{6} \times 2$

18. $16 = \underline{8} \times 2$

19. $\underline{10} = 5 \times 2$

20. $\underline{18} = 9 \times 2$

Problem Solving REAL WORLD

21. Jamie plans to give everyone at her party 2 gift certificates to the local ice cream shop. There will be 8 friends at her party. How many gift certificates will she give in all?

$\underline{2 \times 8 = 16}$

22. On Monday, Steven read 9 pages of his new book. To finish the first chapter on Tuesday, he needs to read twice as many pages as he read on Monday. How many pages does he need to read on Tuesday?

$\underline{9 \times 12 = 6}$

Lesson Check

1. What multiplication sentence matches the model?

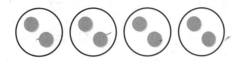

- (A) $3 \times 2 = 6$
- (B) $4 \times 2 = 8$
- (C) $5 \times 2 = 10$
- (D) $6 \times 2 = 12$

2. Find the product.

$$\begin{array}{r} 2 \\ \times\ 9 \\ \hline \end{array}$$

- (A) 9
- (B) 11
- (C) 18
- (D) 20

Spiral Review

3. Which number do the blocks show? **(Lesson 1.4)**

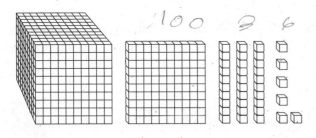

- (A) 1,136
- (C) 1,130
- (B) 1,236
- (D) 136

4. Meagan ate lunch at quarter to one. Which shows her lunch time?

(Lesson 3.2)

- (A) 12:15
- (B) 12:45
- (C) 1:15
- (D) 1:45

5. What is one way to make $7.53 using bills and coins? **(Lesson 3.6)**

- (A) 1 $5 bill, 1 $1 bill, 2 quarters, 3 pennies
- (B) 1 $5 bill, 2 $1 bill, 1 quarter, 3 pennies
- (C) 7 $1 bills, 2 quarters, 3 pennies
- (D) 7 $1 bills, 2 dimes, 1 nickel, 3 pennies

6. Sean made a pictograph to show how many friends like blue. This is his key.

Each ⬤ = 2 friends.

How many friends does 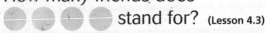 stand for? **(Lesson 4.3)**

- (A) 4
- (C) 8
- (B) 6
- (D) 10

Multiply with 4

Find the product.

1.
$$\begin{array}{r} 3 \\ \times\ 4 \\ \hline 12 \end{array}$$

2.
$$\begin{array}{r} 8 \\ \times\ 4 \\ \hline \end{array}$$

3.
$$\begin{array}{r} 7 \\ \times\ 4 \\ \hline \end{array}$$

4.
$$\begin{array}{r} 6 \\ \times\ 4 \\ \hline \end{array}$$

5.
$$\begin{array}{r} 4 \\ \times\ 4 \\ \hline \end{array}$$

6.
$$\begin{array}{r} 9 \\ \times\ 4 \\ \hline \end{array}$$

7.
$$\begin{array}{r} 5 \\ \times\ 4 \\ \hline \end{array}$$

8.
$$\begin{array}{r} 2 \\ \times\ 4 \\ \hline \end{array}$$

Complete.

9. $4 + 4 = \underline{8} \times 4$

10. $4 \times 6 = \underline{\hspace{1cm}}$

11. $4 \times 7 = \underline{\hspace{1cm}}$

12. $3 \times 4 = 4 + 4 + \underline{\hspace{1cm}}$

13. $8 \times 4 = \underline{\hspace{1cm}}$

14. $6 \times 4 = \underline{\hspace{1cm}} \times 6$

15. $4 + 4 + 4 + 4 = \underline{\hspace{1cm}} \times 4$

16. $9 \times 4 = \underline{\hspace{1cm}}$

Problem Solving  REAL WORLD

17. Courtney's school is having a family game night. Each table has 4 players. There are 7 tables in all. How many players are at the game night?

_____

18. Matthew is in a reading contest at school. He plans to read 4 books each month. How many books will he read in 9 months?

_____

Lesson Check

1. Which multiplication sentence matches the model?

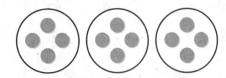

(A) $3 \times 4 = 12$ (C) $1 \times 4 = 4$
(B) $2 \times 4 = 8$ (D) $0 \times 4 = 0$

2. Find the product.

$$7 \times 4$$

(A) 11   (C) 21
(B) 14   (D) 28

Spiral Review

3. Riley has 1 $5 bill, 7 quarters, and 3 dimes. She wants to buy a kite for $7.99. How much more money does she need? **(Lesson 3.10)**

(A) $0.59   (C) $0.94
(B) $0.75   (D) $1.00

4. In Jane's pictograph, the symbol ☺ is equal to two students. One row has 8 symbols. How many students does that row represent?
(Lesson 4.3)

(A) 8   (C) 24
(B) 16   (D) 36

5. Use the pictograph below to answer the question.

Color of Eyes	
Blue	● ● ●
Green	● ● ● ●
Brown	● ● ● ● ●

Key: Each ● = 4 students.

How many students have green eyes? **(Lesson 4.4)**

(A) 3   (C) 12
(B) 4   (D) 16

6. The table below shows the lengths of some bicycle trails.

Bicycle Trails	
Name	Length (in feet)
N. Mountain Trail, AZ	8,448
Warrensburg Trail, MO	7,920
Harmony Trail, PA	5,280

How much longer is N. Mountain Trail than Harmony Trail? **(Lesson 2.6)**

(A) 528 feet   (C) 3,168 feet
(B) 2,640 feet   (D) 5,280 feet

© Houghton Mifflin Harcourt Publishing Company

P88

Name _____

Multiply with 5 and 10

Find the product.

1.
$$
\begin{array}{r}
5 \\
\times\ 6 \\
\hline
30
\end{array}
$$

2.
$$
\begin{array}{r}
10 \\
\times\ 7 \\
\hline
70
\end{array}
$$

3.
$$
\begin{array}{r}
5 \\
\times\ 3 \\
\hline
15
\end{array}
$$

4.
$$
\begin{array}{r}
10 \\
\times\ 4 \\
\hline
40
\end{array}
$$

5.
$$
\begin{array}{r}
5 \\
\times\ 0 \\
\hline
0
\end{array}
$$

6.
$$
\begin{array}{r}
10 \\
\times\ 8 \\
\hline
80
\end{array}
$$

7.
$$
\begin{array}{r}
5 \\
\times\ 2\ . \\
\hline
10
\end{array}
$$

8.
$$
\begin{array}{r}
10 \\
\times\ 6 \\
\hline
60
\end{array}
$$

9. $5 \times 7 = 35$

10. $5 \times 1 = 5$

11. $2 \times 10 = 20$

12. $8 \times 5 = 40$

13. $1 \times 10 = 10$

14. $4 \times 5 = $ _____

15. $5 \times 10 = 50$

16. $7 \times 5 = 35$

17. $5 \times 5 = 25$

18. $5 \times 8 = 40$

19. $5 \times 9 = 45$

20. $10 \times 3 = 30$

Problem Solving 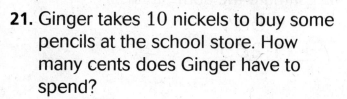 REAL WORLD

21. Ginger takes 10 nickels to buy some pencils at the school store. How many cents does Ginger have to spend?

_____50_____

22. The gym at Evergreen School has three basketball courts. There are 5 players playing on each of the courts. How many players are there in all?

_____

Lesson Check

1. Which multiplication sentence does the array show?

○ ○ ○ ○ ○
○ ○ ○ ○ ○
○ ○ ○ ○ ○

(A) $0 \times 5 = 0$ (C) $1 \times 5 = 5$
(B) $2 \times 5 = 10$ (D) $3 \times 5 = 15$

2. Find the product.

$$\begin{array}{r} 5 \\ \times\ 8 \\ \hline \end{array}$$

(A) 8   (C) 35
(B) 16   (D) 40

Spiral Review

3. Mr. Miller's class voted on where to go for a field trip. Use the pictograph to find which choice had the most votes. **(Lesson 4.3)**

Field Trip Choices	
Science Center	★★
Aquarium	★★★⋆
Zoo	★★★★
Museum	★★
Key: Each ★ = 2.	

(A) Science Center   (C) Zoo
(B) Aquarium   (D) Museum

4. Zack made this table for his survey.

Favorite Juice	
Flavor	Votes
Grape	16
Orange	10
Berry	9
Apple	12

How many students voted for their favorite juice in this survey? **(Lesson 4.1)**

(A) 38
(B) 43
(C) 47
(D) 49

5. At which time are most third graders asleep? **(Lesson 3.3)**

(A) 10:00 A.M.   (C) 7:00 P.M.
(B) 1:00 P.M.   (D) 2:00 A.M.

6. Estimate the sum. **(Lesson 2.1)**

$$\begin{array}{r} 9{,}881 \\ +\ 1{,}235 \\ \hline \end{array}$$

(A) 10,000   (C) 12,000
(B) 11,000   (D) 13,000

Draw a Diagram · Multiplication

Draw a diagram to solve each problem.

1. Robert put some toy blocks into 3 rows. There are 5 blocks in each row. How many blocks are there in all?

    15 blocks

2. Mr. Fernandez is putting tiles on his kitchen floor. There are 2 rows with 9 tiles in each row. How many tiles are there in all?

3. In Jillian's garden, there are 3 rows of carrots, 2 rows of string beans, and 1 row of peas. There are 8 plants in each row. How many plants are there in all?

4. In Sorhab's classroom, there are 3 rows with 7 desks in each row. How many desks are there in all?

5. Maya visits the movie rental store. On one wall, there are 6 DVDs on each of 5 shelves. On another wall, there are 4 DVDs on each of 4 shelves. How many DVDs are there in all?

6. The media center at Josh's school has a computer area. The first 4 rows have 6 computers. The fifth row has 4 computers. How many computers are there in all?

Lesson Check

1. Part of a sidewalk has 2 rows of red bricks with 4 bricks in each row. Another part has 2 rows of brown bricks with 4 bricks in each row. How many red and brown bricks are there in all?

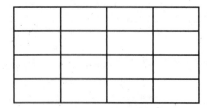

 Ⓐ 8   Ⓒ 16

 Ⓑ 12   Ⓓ 20

2. Ken watches the marching band in a parade. He sees 2 rows of flute players. Six people are in each row. How many flute players are there?

○ ○ ○ ○ ○ ○
○ ○ ○ ○ ○ ○

 Ⓐ 2

 Ⓑ 6

 Ⓒ 12

 Ⓓ 14

Spiral Review

3. What is the sum of 438 and 382? (Lesson 2.2)

 Ⓐ 720   Ⓒ 820

 Ⓑ 810   Ⓓ 910

4. What is this number in standard form? (Lesson 1.4)

$$3,000 + 300 + 60 + 4$$

 Ⓐ 3,064   Ⓒ 3,360

 Ⓑ 3,300   Ⓓ 3,364

5. Francis buys a tube of glue for $3.95. She gives the cashier a $5 bill. What change should Francis receive? (Lesson 3.9)

 Ⓐ $.05

 Ⓑ $.55

 Ⓒ $1.05

 Ⓓ $2.00

6. Caitlen has only quarters. She has more than 75¢. Which amount could Caitlen have? (Lesson 3.6)

 Ⓐ $0.85

 Ⓑ $1.05

 Ⓒ $1.50

 Ⓓ $1.70

Model with Arrays

Draw an array to find the product.

1. $2 \times 5 =$ __10__

○ ○ ○ ○ ○
○ ○ ○ ○ ○

2. $3 \times 6 =$ _____

3. $4 \times 2 =$ _____

4. $4 \times 4 =$ _____

5. $3 \times 2 =$ _____

6. $2 \times 8 =$ _____

Problem Solving REAL WORLD

7. Lenny is moving tables in the school cafeteria. He places all the tables in a 7×4 array. How many tables are in the cafeteria?

_____

8. Ms. DiMeo directs the school choir. She has the singers stand in 3 rows. There are 8 singers in each row. How many singers are there in all?

_____

Lesson Check

1. Which multiplication sentence does the array show?

Ⓐ $2 \times 3 = 6$ Ⓒ $3 \times 4 = 12$

Ⓑ $6 \times 3 = 18$ Ⓓ $3 \times 5 = 15$

2. Which multiplication sentence does the array show?

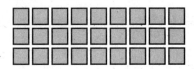

Ⓐ $3 \times 9 = 27$ Ⓒ $3 \times 7 = 21$

Ⓑ $3 \times 8 = 24$ Ⓓ $4 \times 5 = 20$

Spiral Review

3. Use the table to find who traveled 750 miles farther than Paul during summer vacation. (Lesson 2.3)

Summer Vacations	
Name	**Distance in Miles**
Paul	2,330
Andrew	3,080
Bonnie	2,790
Tara	2,930
Susan	2,850

Ⓐ Andrew   Ⓒ Tara

Ⓑ Bonnie   Ⓓ Susan

4. Use the bar graph to find what hair color most students have. (Lesson 4.5)

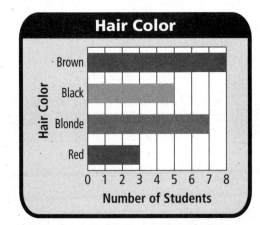

Ⓐ Brown   Ⓒ Blonde

Ⓑ Black   Ⓓ Red

5. Spencer has 3 quarters. Sam has 2 quarters and 4 dimes. Meg has 2 quarters, 2 dimes, and 1 nickel. David has 1 quarter, 4 dimes, and 4 nickels. Who has the most money? (Lesson 3.7)

Ⓐ Spencer   Ⓒ Meg

Ⓑ Sam   Ⓓ David

6. Which bar would be the longest on a bar graph for this data? (Lesson 4.6)

Favorite Pizza Toppings	
Topping	**Votes**
Cheese	5
Pepperoni	4
Vegetable	1
Sausage	3

Ⓐ Cheese   Ⓒ Vegetable

Ⓑ Pepperoni   Ⓓ Sausage

Name _____

Commutative Property of Multiplication

Write a multiplication sentence for the array.
Then use the Commutative Property of Multiplication
to write another multiplication sentence.

1.

$5 \times 2 = 10$
$2 \times 5 = 10$

2.

_____

_____

3.

_____

_____

4.

_____

_____

Write the missing factor.

5. $7 \times 2 = \underline{\hspace{1cm}} \times 7$

6. $9 \times 4 = \underline{\hspace{1cm}} \times 9$

Problem Solving REAL WORLD

7. A garden store sells trays of plants.
Each tray holds 2 rows of 8 plants.
How many plants are in one tray?

8. Jeff collects toy cars. They are
displayed in a case that has 4 rows.
There are 6 cars in each row. How
many cars does Jeff have?

_____

_____

Lesson Check

1. Which shows the Commutative
Property of Multiplication for
$2 \times 4 = 8$?

Ⓐ $8 \times 4 = 32$

Ⓑ $4 \times 2 = 8$

Ⓒ $2 \times 8 = 16$

Ⓓ $2 + 4 = 6$

2. What is the missing factor?

$$7 \times 4 = \underline{} \times 7$$

Ⓐ 2

Ⓑ 4

Ⓒ 7

Ⓓ 28

Spiral Review

3. How many thousands are in
23,459? (Lesson 1.4)

Ⓐ 59

Ⓑ 45

Ⓒ 34

Ⓓ 23

4. Find the difference. (Lesson 2.6)

$$\begin{array}{r} 7{,}835 \\ -\ 2{,}094 \end{array}$$

Ⓐ 4,741   Ⓒ 5,841

Ⓑ 5,741   Ⓓ 5,861

5. Becky had $23.47. She spent
$4.16 to buy a toy. How much
does she have left? (Lesson 3.10)

Ⓐ $19.31

Ⓑ $19.33

Ⓒ $21.31

Ⓓ $27.63

6. Jeremy made a tally table to record
how his friends voted for their
favorite pets. His chart shows
Ⅲ Ⅲ Ⅱ next to dog. How many
voted for dog? (Lesson 4.1)

Ⓐ 6

Ⓑ 8

Ⓒ 10

Ⓓ 12

Name _____

Multiply with 1 and 0

Find the product.

1.　4
　×1
　——
　4

2.　8
　×0
　——

3.　4
　×0
　——

4.　6
　×1
　——

5.　0
　×3
　——

6.　9
　×0
　——

7.　8
　×1
　——

8.　2
　×1
　——

9. $0 \times 6 =$ ____

10. $0 \times 4 =$ ____

11. $7 \times 1 =$ ____

12. $1 \times 5 =$ ____

13. $3 \times$ ____ $= 3$

14. ____ $\times 7 = 0$

15. $1 \times 9 =$ ____

16. $5 \times$ ____ $= 0$

Problem Solving REAL WORLD

17. Peter is in the school play. His teacher gave 1 copy of the play to each of 6 students. How many copies did the teacher hand out?

_____

18. There are 4 egg cartons on the table. There are 0 eggs in each carton. How many eggs are there in all?

_____

Lesson Check

1. What multiplication sentence does the array show?

(A) $1 \times 6 = 6$ (C) $2 \times 6 = 12$

(B) $1 \times 0 = 0$ (D) $0 \times 6 = 0$

2. What is the product?

$$1 \times 0 = \underline{\quad}$$

(A) 0

(B) 1

(C) 10

(D) 11

Spiral Review

3. Tonya wrote an even number between 440 and 452. The sum of the digits is 12. What is the number? **(Lesson 1.2)**

(A) 440   (C) 444

(B) 442   (D) 452

4. Find the difference. **(Lesson 2.6)**

$$8,817$$
$$- 2,462$$

(A) 6,345   (C) 6,445

(B) 6,355   (D) 6,455

Use the table for 5–6.

Rachel's Earnings	
Day	Amount
Friday	$2.75
Saturday	$5.58
Sunday	$6.30

5. How much money did Rachel earn in all on Friday and Saturday?

(Lesson 3.10)

(A) $7.23

(B) $7.33

(C) $8.23

(D) $8.33

6. Rachel earned 2 bills and 6 coins on Sunday. What bills and coins did she earn? **(Lesson 3.8)**

(A) 1 $5 bill, 1 $1 bill, 6 nickels

(B) 1 $5 bill, 1 $1 bill, 1 nickel, 5 pennies

(C) 1 $5 bill, 1 $1 bill, 2 dimes, 4 nickels

(D) 1 $5 bill, 1 $1 bill, 1 dime, 5 pennies

Name _____

Chapter 5 Extra Practice

Lessons 5.1 - 5.2

Draw equal groups. Skip count to find how many in all.

1. 2 groups of 4

2. 4 groups of 3

_____   _____

Write a multiplication sentence for each.

3. 4 + 4 + 4 + 4 = 16

4. 5 + 5 + 5 = 15

_____ × _____ = _____   _____ × _____ = _____

Lessons 5.3 - 5.5

Find the product.

1. 5
     × 4

2. 2
     × 5

3. 4
     × 3

4. 10
     × 2

5. 4
     × 6

6. 10
     × 5

7. 7
     × 5

8. 2
     × 3

9. 10
     × 6

10. 2
      × 7

11. 5
      × 9

12. 4
      × 8

13. 5 × 5 = _____

14. 2 × 6 = _____

15. 4 × 2 = _____

16. 10 × 3 = _____

17. Aaron has 5 stacks of cards with 7 cards in each stack. How many cards does he have in all?

_____

18. Noah has 5 sisters. He gave 2 balloons to each sister. How many balloons did Noah give away in all?

_____

Lesson 5.6

Draw a diagram to solve.

1. Tyler has 4 stickers. Camile has 4 times as many. How many stickers does Camile have?

_____

2. There are 5 cars with 4 wheels on each. How many wheels in all?

_____

Lesson 5.7

Draw an array to find the product.

1. $2 \times 8 =$ _____

2. $3 \times 6 =$ _____

Lesson 5.8

Write a multiplication sentence for the model. Then use the Commutative Property to write a related multiplication sentence.

1.

_____ × _____ = _____

_____ × _____ = _____

2.

_____ × _____ = _____

_____ × _____ = _____

Lesson 5.9

Find the product.

1. 6
   × 0
   ____

2. 5
   × 1
   ____

3. 0
   × 9
   ____

4. 1
   × 8
   ____

5. $1 \times 4 =$ _____

6. $9 \times 1 =$ _____

7. $1 \times 0 =$ _____

8. $7 \times 0 =$ _____

9. $0 \times 5 =$ _____

10. $1 \times 10 =$ _____

11. $1 \times 7 =$ _____

12. $2 \times 0 =$ _____

Vocabulary

factor A number that is multiplied by another number to find a product

product The answer to a multiplication problem

multiple A multiple of a number is any product that has that number as one of its factors

Dear Family,

During the next few weeks, our math class will be learning more about multiplication. We will learn how to multiply with the factors 3, 6, 7, 8, and 9.

You can expect to see homework that provides practice with multiplication facts and strategies.

Here is a sample of how your child will be taught to multiply with 3 as a factor.

🔑 MODEL Multiply with 3

This is one way we will be multiplying with 3 to solve problems.

Teddy made a face on 1 cookie, using 3 raisins. How many raisins will he need for 4 cookies?

Drawing a picture is a way to solve this problem.

3,   6,   9,   12

Skip count by 3s to find the number of raisins in all.

3, 6, 9, 12

4 groups of 3 is 12.   4 × 3 = 12

So, he will need 12 raisins for 4 cookies.

Tips

Another Way to Solve Multiplication Problems

Making an array is another way to solve the problem. Use tiles to make an array of 4 rows with 3 tiles in each row.

Count all the tiles.

4 groups of 3 is 12
4 × 3 = 12

Activity

Have your child draw more groups of 3 for 5, 6, 7, 8, and 9 cookies. Then have your child answer questions such as "How many raisins would be on 8 cookies? What do you multiply to find out?"

Capítulo 6

Carta para la casa

Vocabulario

factor Un número que se multiplica por otro para hallar un producto

producto El resultado de un problema de multiplicación

múltiplo Un múltiplo de un número es cualquier producto que tiene ese número como uno de sus factores

Querida familia,

Durante las próximas semanas, en la clase de matemáticas aprenderemos más sobre la multiplicación. Aprenderemos cómo multiplicar con los factores 3, 6, 7, 8 y 9.

Llevaré a la casa tareas que sirven para practicar las operaciones de multiplicación y sus estrategias.

Este es un ejemplo de la manera como aprenderemos a multiplicar por el factor 3.

🔑 MODELO Multiplicar por 3

Esta es una manera de multiplicar por 3 para resolver problemas.

Teddy hizo una cara en 1 galleta, con 3 pasas.
¿Cuántas pasas necesitará para hacer caras en 4 galletas?

Una manera de resolver el problema es hacer un dibujo.

  3,   6,   9,   12

Cuenta salteado de 3 en 3 para hallar el número total de pasas.

                3, 6, 9, 12

4 grupos de 3 son 12.   4 × 3 = 12

Por tanto, él necesitará 12 pasas para 4 galletas.

Pistas

Otra manera de resolver problemas de multiplicación

Hacer una matriz es otra manera de resolver el problema. Usa fichas para hacer una matriz de 4 filas con 3 fichas en cada fila.

Cuenta todas las fichas.

4 grupos de 3 son 12
      4 × 3 = 12

Actividad

Pida a su hijo que dibuje más grupos de 3 para 5, 6, 7, 8 y 9 galletas. Después, pídale que conteste preguntas como "¿Cuántas pasas se necesitan para 8 galletas? ¿Qué factores debes multiplicar para hallar la respuesta?"

© Houghton Mifflin Harcourt Publishing Company

Name _____

Multiply with 3

Find the product.

1. 3
    × 5
    ___
    15

2. 3
    × 7
    ___

3. 4
    × 3
    ___

4. 3
    × 3
    ___

5. 3
    × 0
    ___

6. 1
    × 3
    ___

7. 9
    × 3
    ___

8. 6
    × 3
    ___

9. 3
    × 8
    ___

10. 2
    × 3
    ___

Complete.

11. $3 + 3 =$ _____ $\times 3$

12. $8 \times 3 =$ _____

13. $7 \times 3 =$ _____

14. $3 \times 3 = 3 + 3 +$ _____

15. $20 - 2 =$ _____ $\times 3$

16. _____ $+ 3 = 5 \times 3$

Problem Solving  REAL WORLD

17. Lexi has 1 can of tennis balls. There are 3 tennis balls in each can. She buys 2 more cans. How many tennis balls does she now have in all?

    _____

18. James got 3 hits in his baseball game. If he gets 3 hits in the next game, how many hits will he have for the 2 games?

    _____

Lesson Check

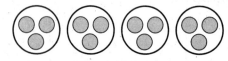

1. Find the product.

9×3

- (A) 18
- (B) 24
- (C) 27
- (D) 36

2. How many counters are there in all?

- (A) 6
- (B) 9
- (C) 12
- (D) 15

Spiral Review

3. What is this number in standard form? (Lesson 1.5)

$4,000 + 800 + 90 + 2$

- (A) 4,000
- (B) 4,800
- (C) 4,890
- (D) 4,892

4. Find the difference. (Lesson 2.6)

$$\begin{array}{r} 3,568 \\ -\ 1,280 \\ \hline \end{array}$$

- (A) 2,280
- (B) 2,288
- (C) 2,300
- (D) 2,968

5. The line plot shows the number of brothers and sisters the students in Ms. Cade's class have. How many students have 2 brothers and sisters? (Lesson 4.7)

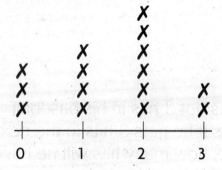

Number of Brothers and Sisters

- (A) 2
- (B) 3
- (C) 4
- (D) 6

6. Find the product. (Lesson 5.5)

$$\begin{array}{r} 10 \\ \times\ \ 5 \\ \hline \end{array}$$

- (A) 5
- (B) 15
- (C) 50
- (D) 60

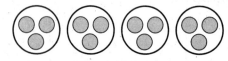

Name _____

Multiply with 6

Find the product.

1.	6 × 3 18	2.	6 × 4	3.	2 × 6	4.	6 × 5	5.	1 × 6

6.	6 × 8	7.	9 × 6	8.	6 × 6	9.	7 × 6	10.	6 × 0

11. $6 \times 6 =$ _____

12. $7 \times 6 =$ _____

13. $0 \times 6 =$ _____

14. $3 \times 6 =$ _____

15. $5 \times 6 =$ _____

16. _____ $= 8 \times 6$

Problem Solving REAL WORLD

17. Paco buys a carton of eggs. The carton has 2 rows of eggs. There are 6 eggs in each row. How many eggs are in the carton?

_____

18. Mrs. Burns is buying muffins at the store. There are 6 muffins in each box. If she buys 5 boxes, how many muffins will she buy?

_____

Lesson Check

1. Use the number line to find how many in 3 groups of 6.

0 2 4 6 8 10 12 14 16 18 20 22 24

- (A) 24
- (B) 20
- (C) 18
- (D) 12

2. Use the array to find 5×6.

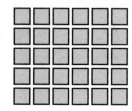

- (A) 24
- (B) 30
- (C) 36
- (D) 42

Spiral Review

3. Find the sum. (Lesson 2.2)

$$219$$
$$+\ 763$$

- (A) 972
- (C) 982
- (B) 976
- (D) 992

4. Sasha bought 2 boxes of pencils. If each box has 6 pencils, how many pencils does she have in all?

(Lesson 5.1)

- (A) 8
- (C) 12
- (B) 10
- (D) 18

5. In a survey, sports books received 9 votes. If the scale counts by twos, where should the bar end for the sports books? (Lesson 4.5)

- (A) between 6 and 8
- (B) on 8
- (C) between 8 and 10
- (D) on 10

6. Dwight made twice as many baskets in the second half of the basketball game than in the first half. He made 5 baskets in the first half. How many baskets did he make in the second half? (Lesson 5.3)

- (A) 8
- (C) 15
- (B) 10
- (D) 18

Name _____

Associative Property of Multiplication

**Write another way to group the factors.
Then find the product.**

1. (3 × 2) × 5

$$3 × (2 × 5)$$

$$\underline{30}$$

2. (4 × 3) × 2

____ × ____ × ____

____

3. 2 × (2 × 8)

____ × ____ × ____

____

4. 9 × (2 × 1)

____ × ____ × ____

____

5. 2 × (3 × 6)

____ × ____ × ____

____

6. (4 × 2) × 5

____ × ____ × ____

____

**Use parentheses and multiplication properties.
Find the product.**

7. 9 × 1 × 5 = ____

8. 3 × 3 × 2 = ____

9. 2 × 4 × 3 = ____

10. 5 × 2 × 3 = ____

11. 7 × 1 × 5 = ____

12. 8 × 2 × 3 = ____

13. 7 × 2 × 3 = ____

14. 4 × 1 × 3 = ____

15. 10 × 2 × 4 = ____

Problem Solving REAL WORLD

16. Beth and Maria are going to the county fair. It costs $4 per person for each day. They plan to go for 3 days. How much will the girls pay in all?

_____

17. Randy's garden has 3 rows of carrots with 3 plants in each row. Next year he plans to plant 4 times as many rows of 3 plants. How many plants will he have next year?

_____

Lesson Check

1. There are 2 benches in each car of a train ride. Two people ride on each bench. If a train has 5 cars, how many people in all can be on a train?

(A) 4

(B) 9

(C) 10

(D) 20

2. What is the product of 3, 2, and 6?

(A) 6

(B) 12

(C) 18

(D) 36

Spiral Review

3. Find the difference. (Lesson 2.6)

$$1,692$$
$$-\ 1,168$$

(A) 524

(B) 534

(C) 536

(D) 860

4. What number does the model show? (Lesson 1.4)

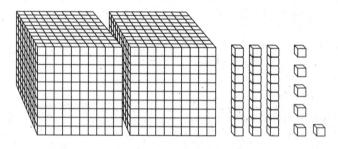

(A) 236

(C) 2,306

(B) 2,036

(D) 2,360

5. Morgan buys a bottle of water for 75¢. She pays with a $5 bill. How much change should she get back? (Lesson 3.9)

(A) $3.00

(B) $3.75

(C) $4.00

(D) $4.25

6. There are 5 pages of photos. Each page has 6 photos. How many photos are there in all? (Lesson 5.6)

(A) 12

(B) 20

(C) 24

(D) 30

Name _____

Distributive Property

Write one way to break apart the array.
Then find the product.

1.

$$(3 \times 7) + (3 \times 7)$$
$$42$$

2.

_____

_____

3.

_____

4.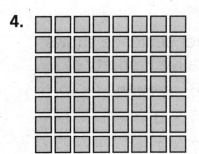

_____

Problem Solving REAL WORLD

5. There are 2 rows of 8 chairs set up in the library for a puppet show. How many chairs are there in all? Use the Distributive Property to solve.

_____

6. A marching band has 4 rows of trumpeters with 10 trumpeters in each row. How many trumpeters are in the marching band? Use the Distributive Property to solve.

_____

Lesson Check

1. Which number sentence shows the Distributive Property?

   Ⓐ $7 \times 6 = 6 \times 7$

   Ⓑ $7 \times (2 \times 3) = (7 \times 2) \times 3$

   Ⓒ $7 \times 6 = (7 \times 3) + (7 \times 3)$

   Ⓓ $7 + 6 = 7 + 3 + 3$

2. What is one way to break apart the array?

   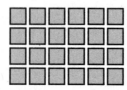

   Ⓐ $(2 \times 6) + (2 \times 6)$

   Ⓑ $(4 \times 2) + (4 \times 2)$

   Ⓒ $(4 \times 4) + (4 \times 4)$

   Ⓓ $(6 \times 3) + (6 \times 3)$

Spiral Review

3. Which number sentence shows the Commutative Property of Multiplication? (Lesson 5.8)

   Ⓐ $3 \times 5 = 5 \times 3$

   Ⓑ $3 + 5 = 7 + 1$

   Ⓒ $3 + 4 = 3 \times 4$

   Ⓓ $3 \times 5 = 3 \times 5$

4. Find the difference. (Lesson 3.10)

   $$\begin{array}{r} \$8.00 \\ -\ \$5.96 \\ \hline \end{array}$$

   Ⓐ $2.04   Ⓒ $3.04

   Ⓑ $2.96   Ⓓ $3.96

5. There are 2,186 fruit snacks in one crate and 1,914 in another crate. How many fruit snacks are there in all? (Lesson 2.3)

   $$\begin{array}{r} 2{,}186 \\ +\ 1{,}914 \\ \hline \end{array}$$

   Ⓐ 3,190

   Ⓑ 4,000

   Ⓒ 4,100

   Ⓓ 4,190

6. Which sport do most students play? (Lesson 4.5)

   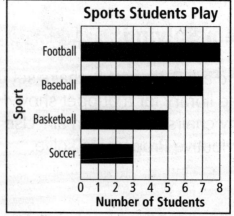

   Ⓐ Football   Ⓒ Basketball

   Ⓑ Baseball   Ⓓ Soccer

Name _____

Multiply with 8

Find the product.

1. $\begin{array}{r} 8 \\ \times\ 2 \\ \hline 16 \end{array}$

2. $\begin{array}{r} 6 \\ \times\ 8 \\ \hline \end{array}$

3. $\begin{array}{r} 8 \\ \times\ 7 \\ \hline \end{array}$

4. $\begin{array}{r} 0 \\ \times\ 8 \\ \hline \end{array}$

5. $\begin{array}{r} 8 \\ \times\ 5 \\ \hline \end{array}$

6. $\begin{array}{r} 8 \\ \times\ 8 \\ \hline \end{array}$

7. $\begin{array}{r} 9 \\ \times\ 8 \\ \hline \end{array}$

8. $\begin{array}{r} 8 \\ \times\ 3 \\ \hline \end{array}$

9. $\begin{array}{r} 8 \\ \times\ 1 \\ \hline \end{array}$

10. $\begin{array}{r} 4 \\ \times\ 8 \\ \hline \end{array}$

11. $8 \times 10 =$ _____

12. $8 \times 8 =$ _____

13. $8 \times 5 =$ _____

14. $3 \times 8 =$ _____

15. _____ $= 4 \times 8$

16. $8 \times$ _____ $= 56$

17. _____ $\times 8 = 48$

18. _____ $= 9 \times 8$

Problem Solving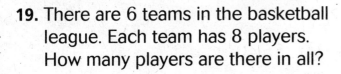

19. There are 6 teams in the basketball league. Each team has 8 players. How many players are there in all?

_____

20. Lynn has 4 stacks of quarters. There are 8 quarters in each stack. How many quarters does Lynn have in all?

_____

21. Tomas is packing 7 baskets for a fair. He is placing 8 apples in each basket. How many apples are there in all the baskets?

_____

22. There are 10 pencils in one box. If Jenna buys 8 boxes, how many pencils will she buy?

_____

Lesson Check

1. Find the product.

$5 \times 8 = $ ■

Ⓐ 30

Ⓑ 32

Ⓒ 42

Ⓓ 40

2. What multiplication fact does this array show?

Ⓐ 2×8 Ⓒ 6×8

Ⓑ 4×8 Ⓓ 8×8

Spiral Review

3. Which number shows eight thousand ninety? (Lesson 1.5)

Ⓐ   890

Ⓑ 8,009

Ⓒ 8,090

Ⓓ 8,900

4. What multiplication sentence shows $3 + 3 + 3 + 3 + 3$? (Lesson 5.2)

Ⓐ 4×3

Ⓑ 5×3

Ⓒ 6×3

Ⓓ 7×3

5. In a class survey, 8 people chose pizza as their favorite lunch. The key for a pictograph is: Each ★ = 2 votes. How many ★ should be next to pizza on the pictograph?

(Lesson 4.4)

Ⓐ 2

Ⓑ 4

Ⓒ 6

Ⓓ 8

6. Annette has two $5 bills, one quarter, and three dimes. How much money does she have in all?

(Lesson 3.6)

Ⓐ $5.40

Ⓑ $5.55

Ⓒ $10.40

Ⓓ $10.55

Name _____

Make a Table · Multiplication

Solve.

1. Henry has a new album for his baseball cards. Some of the pages hold 6 cards and the other pages hold 3 cards. If Henry has 36 cards, how many different ways can he put them in his album?

Pages with 6 Cards	1	2	3	4	5
Pages with 3 Cards	10	8	6	4	2
Total Cards	36	36	36	36	36

Henry can put the cards in his album __5__ ways.

2. Ms. Hernandez has 17 tomato plants that she wants to plant in rows. She will put 2 plants in some rows and 1 plant in the others. How many different ways can she plant the tomato plants? Make a table to solve.

Rows with 2 Plants	
Rows with 1 Plant	
Total Plants	

Ms. Hernandez can plant the tomato plants _____ ways.

3. Bianca has a total of 25¢. She has some nickels and pennies. How many different combinations of nickels and pennies could Bianca have? Make a table to solve.

Number of Nickels	
Number of Pennies	
Total Value	

Bianca could have _____ combinations of 25¢.

Lesson Check

1. The table at the right shows different ways that Cameron can display his 12 model cars on shelves. How many shelves will display 2 cars if 8 of the shelves display 1 car on each?

Shelves with 1 Car	2	4	6	8	10
Shelves with 2 Cars	5	4	3	■	■
Total cars	12	12	12	12	12

Ⓐ 1   Ⓒ 3

Ⓑ 2   Ⓓ 4

Spiral Review

2. Find the sum. (Lesson 2.3)

$$8,257$$
$$+ \ 1,494$$

Ⓐ 9,641

Ⓑ 9,651

Ⓒ 9,741

Ⓓ 9,751

3. At which time are most third graders eating lunch? (Lesson 3.3)

Ⓐ 9:00 A.M.

Ⓑ noon

Ⓒ 10:00 P.M.

Ⓓ midnight

4. Tyler is making a pictograph with this key: Each ⬤ = 1. If a tally table shows ⅧⅡ votes for green, how many ⬤s should Tyler make next to green in the pictograph? (Lesson 4.4)

Ⓐ 5   Ⓒ 7

Ⓑ 6   Ⓓ 8

5. There are 8 dogs in the the parade. There are 0 poodles in the parade. Find how many poodles in all. (Lesson 5.9)

Ⓐ 0   Ⓒ 8

Ⓑ 1   Ⓓ 10

Name _____

Multiply with 9

Find the product.

1. $\begin{array}{r} 9 \\ \times\ 4 \\ \hline 36 \end{array}$

2. $\begin{array}{r} 5 \\ \times\ 9 \\ \hline \end{array}$

3. $\begin{array}{r} 9 \\ \times\ 7 \\ \hline \end{array}$

4. $\begin{array}{r} 2 \\ \times\ 9 \\ \hline \end{array}$

5. $\begin{array}{r} 9 \\ \times\ 9 \\ \hline \end{array}$

6. $\begin{array}{r} 10 \\ \times\ 9 \\ \hline \end{array}$

7. $\begin{array}{r} 3 \\ \times\ 9 \\ \hline \end{array}$

8. $\begin{array}{r} 9 \\ \times\ 8 \\ \hline \end{array}$

9. $\begin{array}{r} 6 \\ \times\ 9 \\ \hline \end{array}$

10. $\begin{array}{r} 9 \\ \times\ 1 \\ \hline \end{array}$

Compare. Write <, >, or =.

11. $9 + 9 \bigcirc 3 \times 9$

12. $9 \times 9 \bigcirc 80$

13. $0 \times 9 \bigcirc 0$

14. $3 \times 9 \bigcirc 9 + 9 + 9$

15. $9 \times 8 \bigcirc 70$

16. $45 \bigcirc 9 \times 6$

Problem Solving REAL WORLD

17. There are 9 positions on the softball team. Three people are trying out for each position. How many people in all are trying out?

_____

18. Carlos bought a book for $9. Now he would like to buy 4 other books for the same price. How much will he have to pay in all for the other 4 books?

_____

Lesson Check

1. Find the product.

7×9

Ⓐ 63

Ⓑ 56

Ⓒ 45

Ⓓ 36

2. Clare is buying 5 tickets for the high school musical. Each ticket costs $9. How much do the tickets cost in all?

Ⓐ $36   Ⓒ $45

Ⓑ $40   Ⓓ $52

Spiral Review

3. The tally table shows the hair color of girls in Kim's class. How many girls have brown hair? **(Lesson 4.1)**

Kim's Class	
Hair Color	Number of Girls
Brown	卌	
Black	|||
Blonde	||||
Red		

Ⓐ 1   Ⓒ 4

Ⓑ 3   Ⓓ 6

4. Which list shows the numbers in order from least to greatest? **(Lesson 1.6)**

Ⓐ 1,143; 2,450; 1,393; 2,484

Ⓑ 1,393; 1,143; 2,450; 2,484

Ⓒ 1,143; 1,393; 2,450; 2,484

Ⓓ 2,484; 2,450; 1,393; 1,143

5. In a pictograph, each picture of a baseball is equal to one game won by a team. The row for the Nationals has 7 baseballs. How many games have the Nationals won? **(Lesson 4.3)**

Ⓐ 7   Ⓒ 21

Ⓑ 14   Ⓓ 28

6. An array has 7 rows with 4 circles in each row. How many circles are in the array? **(Lesson 5.7)**

Ⓐ 11   Ⓒ 28

Ⓑ 14   Ⓓ 30

Name _____

Multiply with 7

Find the product.

1.	2.	3.	4.	5.
$\begin{array}{r} 7 \\ \times\ 5 \\ \hline 35 \end{array}$	$\begin{array}{r} 7 \\ \times\ 1 \\ \hline \end{array}$	$\begin{array}{r} 6 \\ \times\ 7 \\ \hline \end{array}$	$\begin{array}{r} 7 \\ \times\ 4 \\ \hline \end{array}$	$\begin{array}{r} 2 \\ \times\ 7 \\ \hline \end{array}$

6.	7.	8.	9.	10.
$\begin{array}{r} 10 \\ \times\ 7 \\ \hline \end{array}$	$\begin{array}{r} 3 \\ \times\ 7 \\ \hline \end{array}$	$\begin{array}{r} 7 \\ \times\ 9 \\ \hline \end{array}$	$\begin{array}{r} 8 \\ \times\ 7 \\ \hline \end{array}$	$\begin{array}{r} 7 \\ \times\ 0 \\ \hline \end{array}$

Complete.

11. $9 \times 7 = $ _____

12. $7 \times 6 = $ _____

13. $7 + 7 = $ _____ $\times 7$

14. $3 \times 7 = 7 + 7 + $ _____

15. _____ $= 7 \times 7$

16. $7 \times$ _____ $= 35$

Problem Solving REAL WORLD

17. Julie buys a pair of earrings for $7. Now she would like to buy the same kind of earrrings for 2 of her friends. How much will she spend for all 3 pairs of earrings?

_____

18. There are 7 days in 1 week. How many days are in 8 weeks?

_____

Lesson Check

1. Find the product.

$$\begin{array}{r} 7 \\ \times\ 8 \\ \hline \end{array}$$

- Ⓐ 54
- Ⓑ 56
- Ⓒ 64
- Ⓓ 66

2. What product does the array show?

- Ⓐ 14
- Ⓑ 17
- Ⓒ 21
- Ⓓ 24

Spiral Review

3. Find the next number in the pattern. **(Lesson 1.1)**

6, 12, 18, 24, 30, ▪

- Ⓐ 32
- Ⓑ 33
- Ⓒ 36
- Ⓓ 48

4. Round to the nearest ten. **(Lesson 1.7)**

94

- Ⓐ 90
- Ⓑ 94
- Ⓒ 95
- Ⓓ 100

5. How many more people chose retrievers than poodles? **(Lesson 4.1)**

Favorite Breed of Dog	
Dog	Number
Shepherd	58
Retriever	65
Poodle	26

- Ⓐ 31
- Ⓒ 41
- Ⓑ 39
- Ⓓ 49

6. Jack has 5 craft sticks. He needs 4 times as many for a project. How many craft sticks does Jack need altogether? **(Lesson 5.4)**

- Ⓐ 9
- Ⓑ 16
- Ⓒ 20
- Ⓓ 24

Find a Rule

Write a rule for the table. Then complete the table.

1.

Pans	1	2	3	4	5
Muffins	6	12	18	24	30

Multiply the number of pans by 6.

2.

Wagons	2	3	4	5	6
Wheels	8	12	16		

_____

_____

3.

Vases	Flowers
1	7
2	14
3	
4	28
5	
6	

_____

_____

4.

Spiders	Legs
1	8
2	
3	24
4	
5	
6	48

_____

_____

Problem Solving REAL WORLD

5. Caleb buys 5 cartons of yogurt. Each carton has 8 yogurt cups. How many yogurt cups does Caleb buy?

_____

6. Libby bought 4 pencils. Each pencil costs 6¢. How much money did Libby spend on pencils?

_____

Lesson Check

1. Find a rule.

Tables	1	2	3	4	5
Chairs	5	10	15	20	■

Ⓐ Multiply by 3. Ⓒ Add 1.

Ⓑ Multiply by 5. Ⓓ Add 4.

2. Which number completes the table?

Butterflies	3	4	5	6	7
Wings	6	8	10	■	14

Ⓐ 9 Ⓒ 12

Ⓑ 11 Ⓓ 13

Spiral Review

3. The Nile River is 4,132 miles long. The Missouri River is 2,540 miles long. How many miles longer is the Nile River? (Lesson 2.6)

Ⓐ 6,672 miles

Ⓑ 3,878 miles

Ⓒ 2,592 miles

Ⓓ 1,592 miles

4. Ken saves 9¢ every day for 1 week. How much money will Ken have on Day 4? (Lesson 4.2)

Day	1	2	3	4	5	6	7
Amount	9¢	18¢	■	■	■	■	■

Ⓐ 36¢ Ⓒ 24¢

Ⓑ 27¢ Ⓓ 13¢

5. What time does the clock show?

(Lesson 3.1)

Ⓐ 2:15 Ⓒ 3:45

Ⓑ 2:45 Ⓓ 9:15

6. Dane placed 4 pancakes on each of 5 plates. How many pancakes in all are on the plates? (Lesson 5.1)

Ⓐ 9 Ⓒ 20

Ⓑ 16 Ⓓ 24

Name _____

Missing Factors

Find the missing factor.

1. $n \times 3 = 12$

Think: How many groups of 3 equal 12?

$n = \underline{\quad 4 \quad}$

2. $s \times 8 = 64$

$s = \underline{\quad\quad}$

3. $7 \times n = 21$

$n = \underline{\quad\quad}$

4. $y \times 2 = 18$

$y = \underline{\quad\quad}$

5. $5 \times p = 0$

$p = \underline{\quad\quad}$

6. $8 \times t = 56$

$t = \underline{\quad\quad}$

7. $m \times 4 = 28$

$m = \underline{\quad\quad}$

8. $z \times 1 = 9$

$z = \underline{\quad\quad}$

9. $6 \times r = 18$

$r = \underline{\quad\quad}$

10. $u \times 5 = 30$

$u = \underline{\quad\quad}$

11. $4 \times \blacksquare = 24$

$\blacksquare = \underline{\quad\quad}$

12. $w \times 7 = 35$

$w = \underline{\quad\quad}$

13. $b \times 6 = 54$

$b = \underline{\quad\quad}$

14. $5 \times \blacktriangle = 40$

$\blacktriangle = \underline{\quad\quad}$

15. $d \times 3 = 30$

$d = \underline{\quad\quad}$

16. $7 \times k = 42$

$k = \underline{\quad\quad}$

Problem Solving REAL WORLD

17. Carol spent $42 for 6 hats. How much did each hat cost?

_____

18. Mark has a baking tray with 24 cupcakes. There are 4 rows of cupcakes. How many cupcakes are in each row?

_____

Lesson Check

1. Find the missing factor.

$b \times 7 = 56$

Ⓐ $b = 6$

Ⓑ $b = 7$

Ⓒ $b = 8$

Ⓓ $b = 9$

2. What is the missing factor for this array?

$3 \times \blacksquare = 24$

Ⓐ 3   Ⓒ 8

Ⓑ 6   Ⓓ 9

Spiral Review

3. How many tiles are in a 6 × 8 array? (Lesson 5.7)

Ⓐ 40

Ⓑ 48

Ⓒ 56

Ⓓ 64

4. What is another way to write 1,432? (Lesson 1.3)

Ⓐ 1,000 + 40 + 30 + 2

Ⓑ 1,000 + 403 + 2

Ⓒ 1,000 + 402

Ⓓ 1,000 + 400 + 30 + 2

5. Marilyn buys a soda for $1.07. She gives the cashier $1.50. How much change should she get back?

(Lesson 3.9)

Ⓐ 43¢

Ⓑ 45¢

Ⓒ 50¢

Ⓓ 55¢

6. In a group of 10 boys, each boy had 1 hat. How many hats did they have in all? (Lesson 5.9)

Ⓐ 0

Ⓑ 5

Ⓒ 10

Ⓓ 20

Name _____

Chapter 6 Extra Practice

Lesson 6.1 – 6.2

Find the product.

1. $4 \times 3 =$ _____ | **2.** _____ $= 3 \times 0$ | **3.** $10 \times 3 =$ _____ | **4.** _____ $= 5 \times 3$

5. $1 \times 6 =$ _____ | **6.** _____ $= 5 \times 6$ | **7.** $6 \times 4 =$ _____ | **8.** _____ $= 6 \times 7$

9. A room has 3 rows of chairs with 6 chairs in each row. How many chairs are there in all?

10. Jim is buying 6 tickets for a play. If each ticket costs $10, how much will Jim spend?

_____   _____

Lesson 6.3

Write another way to group the factors. Then find the product.

1. $(3 \times 2) \times 4$ | **2.** $2 \times (5 \times 3)$ | **3.** $(1 \times 4) \times 2$

_____ | _____ | _____

_____ | _____ | _____

Lesson 6.4 – 6.5

Write one way to break apart the array. Then find the product.

1.    _____

_____

Find the product.

2. $4 \times 8 =$ _____ | **3.** _____ $= 8 \times 3$ | **4.** $8 \times 5 =$ _____ | **5.** _____ $= 8 \times 10$

Lesson 6.6

Solve.

1. Hailey is handing out 14 stickers. Some students will get 1 sticker, and the others will get 2. How many different ways can she hand them out? Make a table to solve the problem.

Students with 1 Sticker	2
Students with 2 Stickers	6
Total Number of Stickers	14

So, there are _____ different ways to hand them out.

Lesson 6.7 – 6.8

Find the product.

1. $2 \times 9 = $ ____

2. $7 \times 5 = $ ____

3. ____ $= 7 \times 9$

4. ____ $= 7 \times 8$

5. ____ $= 9 \times 6$

6. ____ $= 7 \times 1$

7. $9 \times 8 = $ ____

8. $7 \times 4 = $ ____

9. ____ $= 4 \times 9$

10. ____ $= 7 \times 2$

11. $9 \times 5 = $ ____

12. $9 \times 9 = $ ____

Lesson 6.9 – 6.10

Write a rule for the table. Then complete the table.

1.

Team	2	3	4	5	6
Players	12	18	24		

2.

Tables	4	5	6	7	8
Chairs	16	20		28	

_____

_____

Find the product.

3. $4 \times n = 12$

   $n = $ ____

4. $s \times 9 = 18$

   $s = $ ____

5. $3 \times b = 21$

   $b = $ ____

6. $6 \times d = 54$

   $d = $ ____

© Houghton Mifflin Harcourt Publishing Company

School-Home Letter

Vocabulary

dividend The number that is to be divided in a division problem

dividend, divisor, quotient The parts of a division problem. There are two ways to record division.

$$10 \div 2 = 5$$
↑ dividend   ↑ divisor   ↑ quotient

$$5 \leftarrow \text{quotient}$$
divisor → $2\overline{)10}$
↑ dividend

Dear Family,

During the next few weeks, our math class will be learning about division. We will learn how division is related to subtraction, and how multiplication and division are inverse operations.

You can expect to see homework that provides practice with division.

Here is a sample of how your child will be taught to use repeated subtraction to solve division problems.

🔑 MODEL Use Repeated Subtraction to Divide

This is how we will be using repeated subtraction to divide.

STEP 1

Start with the dividend and subtract the divisor until you reach 0.

$15 \div 5 = $ _____

$$\begin{array}{ccc} 15 & 10 & 5 \\ -5 & -5 & -5 \\ \hline 10 & 5 & 0 \end{array}$$

STEP 2

Count the number of times you subtract 5.

$$\begin{array}{ccc} 15 & 10 & 5 \\ -5 & -5 & -5 \\ \hline 10 & 5 & 0 \end{array}$$ (3 times)

There are 3 groups of 5 in 15.

STEP 3

Record the quotient.

$15 \div 5 = 3$, or

$$5\overline{)15}^{\,3}$$

Fifteen divided by 5 equals 3.

Tips

Counting Back on a Number Line

Counting back on a number line is another way to find a quotient. On a 0–15 number line, for example, start at 15 and count back by 5s to 0. Then count the number of times 5 is subtracted (3 times) to find that $15 \div 5 = 3$.

Activity

Display a number of objects that are divisible by 5. Have your child use repeated subtraction to solve division problems. For example: "Here are 20 crayons. I want to subtract 5 crayons at a time until there are no crayons left. How many times can I subtract?" Check answers by arranging the objects.

Capítulo 7

Carta para la casa

Estimada familia,

Durante las próximas semanas, nuestra clase de matemáticas aprenderá sobre la división. Aprenderemos sobre cómo la división se relaciona con la resta, y cómo la multiplicación y la división son operaciones inversas.

Pueden esperar ver tareas que sirven para practicar la división.

Esta es una muestra de cómo su hijo o hija aprenderá a usar la resta repetida para resolver problemas de división.

Vocabulario

dividendo El número que se divide en un problema de división.

dividendo, divisor, cociente Las partes de un problema de división. Hay dos maneras de anotar la división.

$$10 \quad \div \quad 2 \quad = \quad 5$$

↑   ↑   ↑

dividendo   divisor   cociente

$$\text{divisor} \rightarrow 2\overline{)10} \quad \leftarrow \text{cociente}$$

↑

dividendo

🔒 MODELO   Usar la **resta repetida** para dividir

Así es como usaremos la resta repetida para dividir.

PASO 1

Comience con el dividendo y réstele el divisor hasta llegar a 0.

$15 \div 5 = $ ___

$$\begin{array}{ccc} 15 & 10 & 5 \\ -5 & -5 & -5 \\ \hline 10 & 5 & 0 \end{array}$$

PASO 2

Cuente la cantidad de veces que restó 5.

$$\begin{array}{ccc} 15 & 10 & 5 \\ -5 & -5 & -5 \quad \text{(3 veces)} \\ \hline 10 & 5 & 0 \end{array}$$

Hay 3 grupos de 5 en 15.

PASO 3

Anote el cociente.

$15 \div 5 = 3$, o

$$5\overline{)15}^{\,3}$$

Quince dividido entre 5 es igual a 3.

Pistas

Contar hacia atrás en una recta numérica

Contar hacia atrás en una recta numérica es otra manera de hallar un cociente. En una recta numérica de 0–15, por ejemplo, comience en 15 y cuente hacia atrás de 5 en 5 hasta 0. Después cuente la cantidad de veces que restó 5 (3 veces) para hallar que $15 \div 5 = 3$.

Actividad

Muestre una cantidad de objetos que sea divisible entre 5. Pida a su hijo o hija que use la resta repetida para resolver problemas de división. Por ejemplo: "Aquí hay 20 crayolas. Quiero restar 5 crayolas a la vez hasta que no queden crayolas. ¿Cuántas veces puedo restar?" Compruebe las respuestas ordenando los objetos.

P126

© Houghton Mifflin Harcourt Publishing Company

Name _____

Lesson 7.1

Size of Equal Groups

Use counters or draw a quick picture. Make equal groups. Complete the table.

	Counters	Number of Equal Groups	Number in Each Group
1.	15	3	5
2.	21	7	
3.	28	7	
4.	27	3	
5.	9	3	
6.	18	3	
7.	20	5	
8.	16	8	
9.	28	4	
10.	24	3	

Problem Solving REAL WORLD

11. Alicia has 12 eggs that she will use to make 4 different cookie recipes. If each recipe calls for the same number of eggs, how many eggs will she use in each recipe?

_____

12. Brett picked 27 flowers from the garden. He plans to give an equal number of flowers to each of 3 people. How many flowers will each person get?

_____

© Houghton Mifflin Harcourt Publishing Company

Chapter 7   P127

Lesson Check

1. Ryan has 32 pencils. He wants to put the same number of pencils in each of 4 pencil holders. How many pencils will he put in each pencil holder?

   Ⓐ 3
   Ⓑ 4
   Ⓒ 6
   Ⓓ 8

2. Corinne is setting out 24 plates on 8 tables for a dinner. She sets the same number of plates on each table. How many plates does Corinne set on each table?

   Ⓐ 3
   Ⓑ 4
   Ⓒ 5
   Ⓓ 6

Spiral Review

3. Which shows the number in standard form? **(Lesson 1.4)**

   $3,000 + 400 + 50 + 9$

   Ⓐ 3,000
   Ⓑ 3,400
   Ⓒ 3,059
   Ⓓ 3,459

4. Add. **(Lesson 2.3)**

   $$\begin{array}{r} 2,568 \\ +\ 1,460 \\ \hline \end{array}$$

   Ⓐ 1,108   Ⓒ 3,928
   Ⓑ 3,028   Ⓓ 4,028

5. Which multiplication sentence shows the addition? **(Lesson 5.2)**

   $2 + 2 + 2 + 2 = 8$

   Ⓐ $2 \times 2 = 4$
   Ⓑ $3 \times 2 = 6$
   Ⓒ $4 \times 2 = 8$
   Ⓓ $2 \times 8 = 16$

6. Use the table below.

Number of packs	1	2	3	4	5
Number of yo-yos	3	6	9	12	?

   How many yo-yos would be in 5 packs? **(Lesson 6.9)**

   Ⓐ 10
   Ⓑ 15
   Ⓒ 18
   Ⓓ 20

Name _____

Number of Equal Groups

Draw counters. Then circle equal groups.
Complete the table.

	Counters	Number of Equal Groups	Number in Each Group
1.	24	**3**	8
2.	35		7
3.	30		5
4.	16		4
5.	12		6
6.	32		8
7.	18		3
8.	15		5
9.	28		4
10.	27		3

Problem Solving REAL WORLD

11. In his bookstore, Toby places 21 books on shelves, with 7 books on each shelf. How many shelves does Toby place books on?

_____

12. Mr. Holden has 32 quarters in stacks of 4 on his desk. How many stacks of quarters are on his desk?

_____

Lesson Check

1. Ramon works at a clothing store. He puts 24 pairs of jeans into stacks of 8. How many stacks does Ramon make?

   (A) 5

   (B) 4

   (C) 3

   (D) 2

2. There are 36 people waiting in line for a hay ride. Only 6 people can ride on each wagon. How many wagons are needed for all 36 people?

   (A) 5

   (B) 6

   (C) 7

   (D) 8

Spiral Review

3. Which multiplication sentence does the array show? (Lesson 5.7)

   ○○○○○○○
   ○○○○○○○
   ○○○○○○○
   ○○○○○○○

   (A) 4 × 5 = 20   (C) 4 × 7 = 28

   (B) 4 × 6 = 24   (D) 4 × 8 = 32

4. Estimate the sum. (Lesson 2.1)

   $$229 + 518$$

   (A) 300   (C) 800

   (B) 700   (D) 900

5. What number continues the pattern? (Lesson 1.1)

   3, 6, 9, 12, 15, 18, 21, __

   (A) 23

   (B) 24

   (C) 25

   (D) 26

6. What time does the clock show? (Lesson 3.2)

   (A) 1:40   (C) 8:05

   (B) 8:01   (D) 9:05

Name _____

Divide by 2

Find the quotient. You may want to draw a quick picture to help.

1. $12 \div 2 =$ __6__ | **2.** $18 \div 2 =$ _38_ | **3.** ____ $= 8 \div 2$ | **4.** $10 \div 2 =$ ____

5. ____ $= 14 \div 2$ | **6.** _3_ $= 4 \div 2$ | **7.** $16 \div 2 =$ ____ | **8.** $6 \div 2 =$ ____

9. $2\overline{)18}$ | **10.** $2\overline{)12}$ | **11.** $2\overline{)14}$ | **12.** $2\overline{)2}$

Problem Solving REAL WORLD

13. Mr. Reynolds, the gym teacher, divided a class of 16 students into 2 equal teams. How many students were on each team?

_____

14. Sandra has 10 books. She divides them into groups of 2 each. How many groups did she make?

_____

Lesson Check

1. Divide.

$2\overline{)4}$

Ⓐ 2

Ⓑ 4

Ⓒ 6

Ⓓ 8

2. There are 8 students singing a song in the school musical. Ms. Lang put the students in 2 equal rows. How many students are in each row?

Ⓐ 2

Ⓑ 4

Ⓒ 6

Ⓓ 10

Spiral Review

3. Find the product. (Lesson 5.3)

2×6

Ⓐ 4

Ⓑ 8

Ⓒ 12

Ⓓ 18

4. Find the difference. (Lesson 2.6)

$$5,568$$
$$- 1,280$$

Ⓐ 4,288   Ⓒ 4,388

Ⓑ 4,328   Ⓓ 6,848

5. Barton started his homework at 3:30 P.M. and finished 1 hour 30 minutes later. At what time did Barton finish his homework?

(Lesson 3.4)

Ⓐ 2:00 P.M.

Ⓑ 4:00 P.M.

Ⓒ 5:00 P.M.

Ⓓ 6:30 P.M.

6. A tricycle has 3 wheels. How many wheels are there on 4 tricycles?

(Lesson 6.1)

Ⓐ 7

Ⓑ 9

Ⓒ 12

Ⓓ 15

Name _____

Divide by 5

Find the quotient. You may want to draw a quick picture to help.

1. $15 \div 5 =$ __3__ | **2.** $6 \div 2 =$ _____ | **3.** _____ $= 35 \div 5$ | **4.** $25 \div 5 =$ _____

5. $45 \div 5 =$ _____ | **6.** _____ $= 30 \div 5$ | **7.** $14 \div 2 =$ _____ | **8.** _____ $= 10 \div 2$

9. $5\overline{)40}$ | **10.** $2\overline{)16}$ | **11.** $5\overline{)20}$ | **12.** $5\overline{)10}$

Problem Solving REAL WORLD

13. Joey has 25 pennies. He puts them into groups of 5 to exchange for nickels. How many groups does he make?

_____

14. Forty people signed up to bowl. There will be 5 equal teams. How many people will be on each team?

_____

Lesson Check

1. Divide.

$5\overline{)45}$

- (A) 6
- (B) 7
- (C) 8
- (D) 9

2. Five customers at a plant store bought 15 daisy plants. Each customer bought an equal number. How many daisy plants did each customer buy?

- (A) 2
- (B) 3
- (C) 4
- (D) 5

Spiral Review

3. Erica made a pictograph of the number of movies her friends saw during the summer. Each ☆ equals 5 movies. Rosemarie has 3 stars next to her name. How many movies did she see?

(Lesson 4.4)

- (A) 5
- (C) 15
- (B) 10
- (D) 20

4. What number would you put in a frequency table to show a tally of
$\cancel{|||} \; ||||$? (Lesson 4.2)

- (A) 5
- (B) 8
- (C) 9
- (D) 14

5. A nickel is worth 5¢. How much are 4 nickels worth? (Lesson 5.5)

- (A) 9¢
- (B) 10¢
- (C) 15¢
- (D) 20¢

6. Claire has 3 shells. Ben has 6 times as many shells as Claire. How many shells does Ben have? (Lesson 6.2)

- (A) 3
- (B) 9
- (C) 12
- (D) 18

Name _____

Relate Division and Subtraction

Write a division sentence.

1.

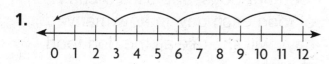

$$12 \div 3 = 4$$

2.

$$
\begin{array}{c c c c}
16 & 12 & 8 & 4 \\
-\ 4 & -\ 4 & -\ 4 & -\ 4 \\
\hline
12 & 8 & 4 & 0
\end{array}
$$

_____

3.

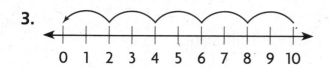

_____

4.

$$
\begin{array}{c c c c}
20 & 15 & 10 & 5 \\
-\ 5 & -\ 5 & -\ 5 & -\ 5 \\
\hline
15 & 10 & 5 & 0
\end{array}
$$

_____

Use a number line or repeated subtraction to solve.

5. $28 \div 7 =$ _____

6. $18 \div 6 =$ _____

Problem Solving REAL WORLD

7. Ms. Costa has 18 pencils. She gives 9 pencils to each of her children. How many children does Ms. Costa have?

_____

8. Randy decides to plant lettuce in his garden. He has 24 lettuce plants. He places 6 plants in each row. How many rows of lettuce are in his garden?

_____

Lesson Check

1. Which division sentence is shown?

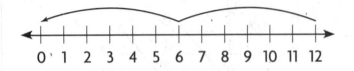

  (A) $3 \times 4 = 12$ (C) $12 \div 3 = 4$

  (B) $12 \div 6 = 2$ (D) $12 \div 4 = 3$

2. Ivana has 35 cups of dog food to feed her dogs. She uses 5 cups of food each day. In how many days will she use all the dog food she has?

  (A) 6 days   (C) 8 days

  (B) 7 days   (D) 9 days

Spiral Review

3. Multiply. (Lesson 6.2)

  6×4

  (A) 10   (C) 24

  (B) 12   (D) 30

4. Find the difference. (Lesson 2.6)

$$\begin{array}{r} 2{,}000 \\ -\ \ \ 985 \\ \hline \end{array}$$

  (A) 1,015   (C) 1,115

  (B) 1,025   (D) 1,125

Use the graph for 5–6.

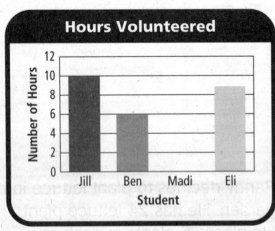

5. How many hours did Eli volunteer? (Lesson 4.6)

  (A) 4 hours   (C) 9 hours

  (B) 8 hours   (D) 10 hours

6. Madi volunteered twice as many hours as Ben. At what number should the bar for Madi stop? (Lesson 4.6)

  (A) 3   (C) 10

  (B) 6   (D) 12

Model with Arrays

Make an array. Solve.

1. How many rows of 4 are in 12?

2. How many rows of 3 are in 21?

3

_____

_____

3. How many rows of 6 are in 30?

4. How many rows of 9 are in 18?

_____

_____

Make an array. Then write a division sentence.

5. 20 tiles in 5 rows

6. 28 tiles in 7 rows

_____

_____

Problem Solving REAL WORLD

7. A dressmaker has 24 buttons. He needs 3 buttons to make one dress. How many dresses can he make with 24 buttons?

8. Liana buys 32 party favors for her 8 guests. She gives an equal number of favors to each guest. How many party favors does each guest get?

_____

_____

Lesson Check

1. How many rows of 6 are in 24?

   (A) 2

   (B) 3

   (C) 4

   (D) 5

2. Which division sentence is shown by the array?

   (A) $12 \div 6 = 2$ (C) $12 \div 2 = 6$

   (B) $12 \div 3 = 4$ (D) $12 \div 1 = 12$

Spiral Review

3. Find the product. (Lesson 6.3)

   $(4 \times 2) \times 3$

   (A) 8

   (B) 9

   (C) 12

   (D) 24

4. Which number is greater than 2,364? (Lesson 1.6)

   (A) 1,958

   (B) 2,401

   (C) 2,187

   (D) 2,356

5. Sam has 7 stacks with 4 quarters each. How many quarters does Sam have? (Lesson 5.4)

   (A) 11

   (B) 12

   (C) 24

   (D) 28

6. What time is 2 hours 30 minutes after 2:15 P.M.? (Lesson 3.4)

   (A) 11:45 A.M.

   (B) 3:45 P.M.

   (C) 4:45 P.M.

   (D) 5:30 P.M.

Name _____

Act It Out · Division

Solve each problem.

1. Six customers at a toy store bought 18 jump ropes. Each customer bought the same number of jump ropes. How many jump ropes did each customer buy?

   3 jump ropes

2. Hiro has 36 pictures of his summer trip. He wants to put them in an album. Each page of the album holds 4 pictures. How many pages will Hiro need for his pictures?

   _____

3. Katia has 42 crayons in a box. She buys a storage bin that has 6 sections. She puts the same number of crayons in each section. How many crayons does Katia put in each section of the storage bin?

   _____

4. Ms. Taylor's students give cards to each of the 3 class parent helpers. There are 24 cards. How many cards will each helper get if they give an equal number of cards to each one?

   _____

5. Jamie divides 20 baseball stickers equally among 5 of his friends. How many stickers does each friend get?

   _____

Lesson Check

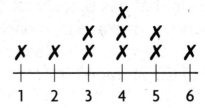

1. Maria buys 15 apples at the store and places them into bags. She puts 5 apples into each bag. How many bags does Maria use for all the apples?

   Ⓐ 2

   Ⓑ 3

   Ⓒ 4

   Ⓓ 10

2. Tom's neighbor is fixing a section of his walkway. He has 32 bricks that he is placing in 8 equal rows. How many bricks will Tom's neighbor place in each row?

   Ⓐ 3

   Ⓑ 4

   Ⓒ 5

   Ⓓ 6

Spiral Review

3. Mason scored 3,485 points in a video game. Libby scored 2,950 points. How many more points did Mason score than Libby? **(Lesson 2.6)**

   Ⓐ 535

   Ⓑ 630

   Ⓒ 1,535

   Ⓓ 6,435

4. How many students practiced the piano more than 3 hours a week?

   (Lesson 4.7)

   Piano Practice Hours

   Ⓐ 2   Ⓒ 8

   Ⓑ 6   Ⓓ 10

5. Which multiplication sentence shows the addition? **(Lesson 5.2)**

   4 + 4 + 4 = 12

   Ⓐ 2 × 4 = 8

   Ⓑ 2 × 6 = 12

   Ⓒ 3 × 4 = 12

   Ⓓ 4 × 4 = 16

6. Find the product. **(Lesson 6.3)**

   (3 × 2) × 5

   Ⓐ 6

   Ⓑ 11

   Ⓒ 25

   Ⓓ 30

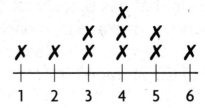

Name _____

Relate Multiplication and Division

Complete the number sentences.

1. $4 \times \underline{}\mathbf{7} = 28$

$28 \div 4 = \underline{}\mathbf{7}$

2. $6 \times \underline{} = 36$

$36 \div 6 = \underline{}$

3. $5 \times \underline{} = 20$

$20 \div 5 = \underline{}$

4. $7 \times \underline{} = 21$

$21 \div 7 = \underline{}$

5. $9 \times \underline{} = 27$

$27 \div 9 = \underline{}$

6. $2 \times \underline{} = 16$

$16 \div 2 = \underline{}$

7. $4 \times \underline{} = 36$

$36 \div 4 = \underline{}$

8. $8 \times \underline{} = 40$

$40 \div 8 = \underline{}$

9. $3 \times \underline{} = 18$

$18 \div 3 = \underline{}$

10. $2 \times \underline{} = 14$

$14 \div 2 = \underline{}$

11. $5 \times \underline{} = 45$

$45 \div 5 = \underline{}$

12. $9 \times \underline{} = 36$

$36 \div 9 = \underline{}$

Problem Solving REAL WORLD

13. Mr. Martin buys 36 muffins for a class breakfast. He places them on plates for his students. If he places 9 muffins on each plate, how many plates does Mr. Martin use?

_____

14. Ralph is the running back on a football team. He ran 32 yards in one game. He ran the same number of yards in each of the 4 quarters of the game. How many yards did Ralph run in each quarter of the game?

_____

Lesson Check

1. Which number will complete the number sentences?

   $6 \times \blacksquare = 24$

   $24 \div 6 = \blacksquare$

   (A) 3

   (B) 4

   (C) 5

   (D) 6

2. Shelly has 14 seashells. She divides them equally between her 2 sisters. How many seashells does each sister get?

   (A) 7

   (B) 8

   (C) 12

   (D) 16

Spiral Review

3. Which shows the Associative Property of Multiplication with $3 \times (3 \times 2)$? (Lesson 6.3)

   (A) $(3 \times 3) \times 2$

   (B) $3 \times (3) \times 2$

   (C) $(3 \times 3 \times 2)$

   (D) $3 \times 3 \times (2)$

4. Eric bought a book for $3.85. He paid with a $5 bill. How much change should Eric get? (Lesson 3.10)

   (A) $0.15

   (B) $1.15

   (C) $2.25

   (D) $8.85

5. The key for a pictograph showing the number of books students read is: Each ▱ = 2 books. How many books did Sharon read, if she has ▱ ▱ ▱ by her name? (Lesson 4.3)

   (A) 2

   (B) 4

   (C) 5

   (D) 6

6. Jun surveyed her friends to find their favorite season. She recorded IﾘI III for summer. How many people chose summer as their favorite season? (Lesson 4.1)

   (A) 5

   (B) 8

   (C) 9

   (D) 12

Fact Families

Write the fact family for the array.

1.

$$2 \times 6 = 12$$
$$6 \times 2 = 12$$
$$12 \div 2 = 6$$
$$12 \div 6 = 2$$

2. ⬜⬜⬜⬜⬜⬜⬜⬜⬜⬜⬜⬜⬜⬜⬜

_____
_____
_____
_____

3. ⬜⬜⬜⬜⬜⬜⬜⬜

_____
_____
_____
_____

Complete the fact family.

4. $4 \times 9 = $ _____

$9 \times$ _____ $= 36$

$36 \div$ _____ $= 4$

_____ $\div 4 = 9$

5. _____ $\times 7 = 35$

_____ $\times 5 = 35$

_____ $\div 7 = 5$

$35 \div 5 = $ _____

6. $6 \times$ _____ $= 18$

$3 \times 6 = $ _____

$18 \div$ _____ $= 3$

_____ $\div 3 = 6$

Write the fact family for the set of numbers.

7. 3, 7, 21

_____
_____
_____
_____

8. 2, 9, 18

_____
_____
_____
_____

9. 4, 8, 32

_____
_____
_____
_____

Problem Solving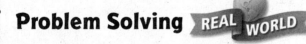

10. CDs are on sale for $5 each. Jennifer has $45 and wants to buy as many as she can. How many CDs can Jennifer buy?

_____

11. Mr. Santana has 21 feet of wrapping paper. He cuts it into sections that are each 3 feet long. How many pieces does Mr. Santana have?

_____

Lesson Check

1. Which number completes the fact family?

   $5 \times \blacksquare = 40$ $40 \div \blacksquare = 5$

   $\blacksquare \times 5 = 40$ $40 \div 5 = \blacksquare$

   (A) 6
   (B) 7
   (C) 8
   (D) 9

2. Which shows the set of numbers for this fact family?

   $4 \times 7 = 28$ $28 \div 4 = 7$

   $7 \times 4 = 28$ $28 \div 7 = 4$

   (A) 3, 6, 18
   (B) 3, 7, 21
   (C) 4, 7, 28
   (D) 4, 8, 32

Spiral Review

3. Which shows $5,000 + 800 + 6$ written in standard form? **(Lesson 1.5)**

   (A) 5,860
   (B) 5,806
   (C) 5,086
   (D) 5,006

4. Find the product. **(Lesson 5.9)**

   5×0

   (A) 0
   (B) 1
   (C) 5
   (D) 10

5. Leslie spends 45 minutes doing her homework. She finishes at 4:15 P.M. At what time did Leslie start her homework? **(Lesson 5.4)**

   (A) 2:30 P.M.
   (B) 3:15 P.M.
   (C) 3:30 P.M.
   (D) 5:00 P.M.

6. Al buys 8 packages of batteries. Each package has 4 batteries. How many batteries did Al buy in all? **(Lesson 6.5)**

   (A) 12
   (B) 16
   (C) 24
   (D) 32

Name _____

Divide by 10

Complete the number sentences.

1. 10 × __**2**__ = 20   20 ÷ 10 = __**2**__ | **2.** 10 × ____ = 70   70 ÷ 10 = ____

3. 10 × ____ = 80   80 ÷ 10 = ____ | **4.** 10 × ____ = 30   30 ÷ 10 = ____

Find the quotient.

5. 60 ÷ 10 = ___ | **6.** 25 ÷ 5 = ____ | **7.** 20 ÷ 2 = ____ | **8.** 50 ÷ 10 = ___

9. 90 ÷ 10 = ___ | **10.** 12 ÷ 2 = ____ | **11.** 30 ÷ 5 = ____ | **12.** 10 ÷ 2 = ____

13. 10)‾40‾ | **14.** 10)‾70‾ | **15.** 5)‾40‾ | **16.** 10)‾20‾

Problem Solving  REAL WORLD

17. Pencils cost 10¢ each. How many pencils can Brent buy with 90¢?

_____

18. Mrs. Marks wants to buy 80 pens. If the pens come in packs of 10, how many packs does she need to buy?

_____

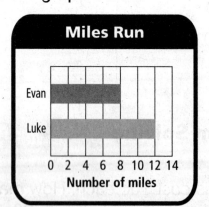

Lesson Check

1. Divide.

$60 \div 10$

Ⓐ 6   Ⓒ 50

Ⓑ 10   Ⓓ 70

2. A florist arranges 10 flowers in each vase. How many vases does the florist need to arrange 40 flowers?

Ⓐ 3   Ⓒ 30

Ⓑ 4   Ⓓ 50

Spiral Review

3. Glenn buys a notebook for $2.79. How much change does he get from a $5 bill? (Lesson 3.9)

Ⓐ $0.21

Ⓑ $2.21

Ⓒ $3.31

Ⓓ $7.79

4. Find the product. (Lesson 6.1)

3×8

Ⓐ 11

Ⓑ 16

Ⓒ 24

Ⓓ 27

5. Mr. Samuels buys a sheet of stamps. There are 4 rows with 7 stamps in each row. How many stamps does Mr. Samuels buy?

(Lesson 5.4)

Ⓐ 11

Ⓑ 14

Ⓒ 21

Ⓓ 28

6. Use the graph below.

How many more miles did Luke run than Evan? (Lesson 4.5)

Ⓐ 2 miles   Ⓒ 8 miles

Ⓑ 4 miles   Ⓓ 20 miles

Name _____

Chapter 7 Extra Practice

Lessons 7.1 - 7.2

Use counters or draw a quick picture. Complete the table.

	Counters	Number of Equal Groups	Number in Each Group
1.	16	4	
2.	21	7	
3.	18		3
4.	4		2

Lessons 7.3 - 7.4

Find the quotient. You may want to draw a quick picture to help.

1. $8 \div 2 =$ _____ | **2.** _____ $= 14 \div 2$ | **3.** $18 \div 2 =$ _____ | **4.** _____ $= 12 \div 2$

5. $15 \div 5 =$ _____ | **6.** _____ $= 45 \div 5$ | **7.** _____ $= 10 \div 5$ | **8.** $40 \div 5 =$ _____

9. There are 12 balloons arranged in 2 equal groups. How many balloons are in each group?

_____

Lesson 7.5

Use a number line or repeated subtraction to solve.

1. $48 \div 8 =$ _____ | **2.** _____ $= 42 \div 6$ | **3.** _____ $= 35 \div 5$ | **4.** _____ $= 54 \div 9$

5. Carter buys 16 bottles of water. He wants to put 8 bottles in each cooler. How many coolers does Carter need?

_____

Lessons 7.6 - 7.7

Use square tiles to make an array. Solve.

1. How many rows of 4 are in 24?

   _____

2. How many rows of 9 are in 36?

   _____

3. How many rows of 4 are in 20?

   _____

4. How many rows of 3 are in 9?

   _____

5. Mr. Cho has 28 shells to display in a case. He wants to put 7 shells in each row. How many rows of shells will there be?

   _____

6. Madison stores her collection of 15 rocks in boxes. If she stores 5 rocks in each box, how many boxes does she use?

   _____

Lesson 7.8

Complete the number sentences.

1. $9 \times$ _____ $= 36$ $36 \div 9 =$ _____   2. $9 \times$ _____ $= 45$ $45 \div 9 =$ _____

Lesson 7.9

Write the fact family for the set of numbers.

1. 3, 5, 15   2. 6, 8, 48   3. 4, 5, 20

   _____   _____   _____

   _____   _____   _____

   _____   _____   _____

   _____   _____   _____

Lesson 7.10

Find the quotient.

1. $70 \div 10 =$ _____ | 2. $50 \div 10 =$ _____ | 3. $40 \div 10 =$ _____ | 4. $90 \div 10 =$ _____

© Houghton Mifflin Harcourt Publishing Company

School-Home Letter

© Houghton Mifflin Harcourt Publishing Company

Vocabulary

array An arrangement of objects in rows and columns

equation A number sentence that uses the equal sign to show that two amounts are equal

expression Part of an equation that combines numbers and operation signs but does not have an equal sign

variable A symbol or a letter that stands for an unknown number

Dear Family,

During the next few weeks, our math class will be learning about division facts and strategies. We will learn strategies to use to divide by 3, 4, 6, 7, 8, and 9. We will also learn the division rules for 1 and 0.

You can expect to see homework that provides practice with dividing by these divisors.

Here is a sample of how your child will be taught to divide.

MODEL Use an Array

This is how we can use arrays to divide.

STEP 1

$20 \div 4 = \blacksquare$

Draw rows of 4 tiles until you have drawn all 20 tiles.

☐ ☐ ☐ ☐
☐ ☐ ☐ ☐
☐ ☐ ☐ ☐
☐ ☐ ☐ ☐
☐ ☐ ☐ ☐

STEP 2

Count the number of rows to find the quotient.

There are 5 rows of 4 tiles.

So, $20 \div 4 = 5$.

Tips

Use a Related Multiplication Fact

Since division is the opposite of multiplication, using a multiplication fact is another way to find a quotient. To divide 20 by 4, for example, think of a related multiplication fact: $4 \times \blacksquare = 20$.
$4 \times 5 = 20$.
So, $20 \div 4 = 5$.

Activity

Provide 12 pennies. Have your child make as many arrays as possible using all 12 pennies. Have your child write a division sentence for each array.

Capítulo 8

Carta
para la casa

Querida familia,

Durante las próximas semanas, en la clase de matemáticas aprenderemos sobre las operaciones de división y sus estrategias. Aprenderemos estrategias para dividir entre 3, 4, 6, 7, 8, y 9 y las reglas de la división para 1 y 0.

Llevaré a la casa tareas que sirven para practicar la división entre estos divisores.

Este es un ejemplo de la manera como aprenderemos a dividir.

Vocabulario

ecuación Una oración numérica que usa el signo de igual para mostrar que dos cantidades son iguales

expresión Parte de una ecuación que combina números y signos de operación, pero no incluye un signo de igual

matriz Una forma de ordenar objetos en filas y columnas

variable Una letra o un símbolo que representa un número desconocido

---

🔑 MODELO Usar una matriz.

Esta es la manera como podemos usar matrices para dividir.

PASO 1

$20 \div 4 = \blacksquare$

Traza filas de 4 fichas cuadradas hasta tener todas las 20 fichas.

☐ ☐ ☐ ☐
☐ ☐ ☐ ☐
☐ ☐ ☐ ☐
☐ ☐ ☐ ☐
☐ ☐ ☐ ☐

PASO 2

Cuenta la cantidad de filas para encontrar el cociente.

Hay 5 filas de 4 fichas.

Por lo tanto,
$20 \div 4 = 5$.

Pistas

Usar una operación de multiplicación relacionada

Dado que la división es opuesta a la multiplicación, usar una operación de multiplicación es otra manera de hallar un cociente. Para dividir 20 entre 4, por ejemplo, piensa en una operación de multiplicación relacionada: $4 \times \blacksquare = 20$. $4 \times 5 = 20$. Por lo tanto, $20 \div 4 = 5$.

Actividad

Dé a su hijo 12 monedas de 1¢. Pídale que haga la mayor cantidad posible de matrices usando las 12 monedas de 1¢. Luego, pídale que escriba un enunciado de división para cada matriz.

© Houghton Mifflin Harcourt Publishing Company

Name _____

Divide by 3

Find the quotient.

1. $18 \div 3 = \underline{6}$

2. $24 \div 3 = \underline{}$

3. $\underline{} = 6 \div 3$

4. $40 \div 5 = \underline{}$

5. $\underline{} = 15 \div 3$

6. $\underline{} = 21 \div 3$

7. $16 \div 2 = \underline{}$

8. $27 \div 3 = \underline{}$

9. $3\overline{)12}$

10. $5\overline{)25}$

11. $3\overline{)24}$

12. $3\overline{)9}$

Problem Solving  REAL WORLD

13. The principal at Miller Street School has 12 packs of new pencils. She will give 3 packs to each third grade class. How many third grade classes are there?

_____

14. Mike has $21 to spend at the mall. He spends all of his money on bracelets for his sisters. They cost $3 each. How many bracelets does he buy?

_____

Lesson Check

1. There are 18 counters divided equally among 3 groups. How many counters are in each group?

Ⓐ 5

Ⓑ 6

Ⓒ 7

Ⓓ 8

2. Find the quotient.

$$3\overline{)27}$$

Ⓐ 6

Ⓑ 7

Ⓒ 8

Ⓓ 9

Spiral Review

3. Which number is less than 5,079? **(Lesson 1.6)**

Ⓐ   579

Ⓑ 5,079

Ⓒ 5,709

Ⓓ 5,790

4. How many students watch less than 3 hours of TV a day? **(Lesson 4.7)**

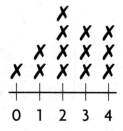

Hours Watching TV

Ⓐ 3   Ⓒ 8

Ⓑ 7   Ⓓ 13

5. Which is an example of the Distributive Property? **(Lesson 6.4)**

Ⓐ $3 \times 6 = 18$

Ⓑ $6 \times 3 = 15 + 3$

Ⓒ $3 \times 6 = 6 \times 3$

Ⓓ $3 \times 6 = (3 \times 2) + (3 \times 4)$

6. Which number completes the number sentences? **(Lesson 7.8)**

$3 \times \blacksquare = 21$ $21 \div 3 = \blacksquare$

Ⓐ 3

Ⓑ 6

Ⓒ 7

Ⓓ 18

Name _____

Divide by 4

Find the quotient.

1. __4__ = 16 ÷ 4 | 2. 20 ÷ 4 = _____ | 3. 12 ÷ 4 = _____ | 4. 10 ÷ 2 = _____

5. 24 ÷ 3 = _____ | 6. _____ = 8 ÷ 2 | 7. 32 ÷ 4 = _____ | 8. _____ = 28 ÷ 4

9. 4)‾36‾ | 10. 4)‾8‾ | 11. 4)‾24‾ | 12. 5)‾30‾

Problem Solving

13. Ms. Higgins has 28 students in her gym class. She puts them in 4 equal groups. How many students are in each group?

_____

14. Andy has 36 CDs. He buys a case that holds 4 CDs in each section. How many sections can he fill?

_____

Lesson Check

1. Find the quotient.

$16 \div 4$

- (A) 3
- (B) 4
- (C) 5
- (D) 6

2. Tori has a bag of 32 markers to share equally among 3 friends and herself. How many markers will Tori and each of her friends get?

- (A) 6
- (B) 7
- (C) 8
- (D) 9

Spiral Review

3. Find the product. (Lesson 6.1)

3×7

- (A) 18
- (B) 21
- (C) 24
- (D) 28

4. Find the difference. (Lesson 2.3)

$$3,985$$
$$- \ 2,349$$

- (A) 636
- (B) 1,636
- (C) 1,644
- (D) 6,334

5. Which is an example of the Commutative Property of Multiplication? (Lesson 5.8)

- (A) $3 \times 6 = 2 \times 9$
- (B) $2 \times 4 = 5 + 3$
- (C) $4 \times 5 = 5 \times 4$
- (D) $2 \times 5 = 5 + 5$

6. Emily has 18 marbles. She puts the same number of marbles in each of 3 bags. How many marbles does she put in each bag? (Lesson 7.1)

- (A) 6
- (B) 7
- (C) 15
- (D) 21

Name _____

Division Rules for 1 and 0

Find the quotient.

1. $3 \div 1 = \underline{3}$

2. $8 \div 8 = \underline{\hspace{1cm}}$

3. $\underline{\hspace{1cm}} = 0 \div 6$

4. $2 \div 2 = \underline{\hspace{1cm}}$

5. $\underline{\hspace{1cm}} = 9 \div 1$

6. $0 \div 2 = \underline{\hspace{1cm}}$

7. $21 \div 3 = \underline{\hspace{1cm}}$

8. $\underline{\hspace{1cm}} = 0 \div 4$

9. $7\overline{)7}$

10. $2\overline{)12}$

11. $9\overline{)0}$

12. $1\overline{)5}$

Problem Solving  REAL WORLD

13. Jamie has a cheese pizza and a veggie pizza at her party. Everyone ate all but 2 pieces of the cheese pizza. How many of each kind of pizza can Jamie and her dad each eat as leftovers later?

_____

_____

14. Jon has 6 kites. He and his friends will each fly 1 kite. How many people in all will fly a kite?

_____

Lesson Check

1. Find the quotient.

$5 \div 5$

Ⓐ 0   Ⓒ 5

Ⓑ 1   Ⓓ 10

2. Find the quotient.

$0 \div 1$

Ⓐ 0   Ⓒ 2

Ⓑ 1   Ⓓ 3

Spiral Review

3. Find the quotient. (Lesson 7.2)

$16 \div 2$

Ⓐ 7

Ⓑ 8

Ⓒ 14

Ⓓ 18

4. Which shows a way to break apart the array to find the product? (Lesson 6.4)

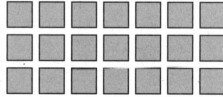

Ⓐ $(3 \times 5) + (3 \times 2)$

Ⓑ $(2 \times 8) + (1 \times 8)$

Ⓒ $(4 \times 7) + (1 \times 7)$

Ⓓ $(3 \times 6) + (3 \times 3)$

5. Lisa has two $1 bills, 1 quarter, 2 dimes, and 1 nickel. How much money does she have in all? (Lesson 3.6)

Ⓐ $1.50

Ⓑ $2.35

Ⓒ $2.50

Ⓓ $3.25

6. Use the graph.

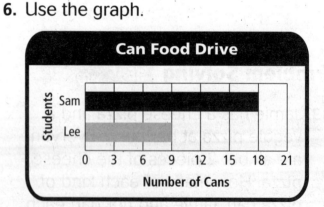

How many more cans did Sam bring in than Lee? (Lesson 4.5)

Ⓐ 4   Ⓒ 7

Ⓑ 5   Ⓓ 9

Name _____

Divide by 6

Find the missing factor and quotient.

1. $6 \times \underline{\ 7\ } = 42 \quad 42 \div 6 = \underline{\ 7\ }$ | **2.** $6 \times \underline{\ \ \ } = 18 \quad 18 \div 6 = \underline{\ \ \ }$

3. $4 \times \underline{\ \ \ } = 24 \quad 24 \div 4 = \underline{\ \ \ }$ | **4.** $6 \times \underline{\ \ \ } = 54 \quad 54 \div 6 = \underline{\ \ \ }$

Find the quotient.

5. $\underline{\ \ \ } = 24 \div 6$ | **6.** $48 \div 6 = \underline{\ \ \ }$ | **7.** $\underline{\ \ \ } = 6 \div 6$ | **8.** $12 \div 6 = \underline{\ \ \ }$

9. $6)\overline{36}$ | **10.** $6)\overline{0}$ | **11.** $6)\overline{30}$ | **12.** $1)\overline{6}$

Problem Solving  REAL WORLD

13. Lucas has 36 pages of a book left to read. If he reads 6 pages a day, how many days will it take Lucas to finish the book?

14. Juan has $24 to spend at the bookstore. If books cost $6 each, how many books can he buy?

_____   _____

Lesson Check

1. Find the quotient.

   $54 \div 6$

   Ⓐ 6
   Ⓑ 7
   Ⓒ 8
   Ⓓ 9

2. Which is the missing factor and quotient?

   $6 \times \blacksquare = 42 \qquad 42 \div 6 = \blacksquare$

   Ⓐ 6
   Ⓑ 7
   Ⓒ 8
   Ⓓ 9

Spiral Review

3. The key for a pictograph is: Each 📖 = 10 books. There are 4 📖 next to Carol's name. How many books has she read? **(Lesson 4.3)**

   Ⓐ 4
   Ⓑ 14
   Ⓒ 40
   Ⓓ 44

4. Mrs. Simms buys 4 toy trucks. How many batteries does she need for the 4 toy trucks? **(Lesson 6.6)**

Trucks	1	2	3	4
Batteries	4	8	12	■

   Ⓐ 8   Ⓒ 16
   Ⓑ 15   Ⓓ 20

5. Which multiplication sentence shows the addition? **(Lesson 5.2)**

   $3 + 3 + 3 + 3 = 12$

   Ⓐ $2 \times 6 = 12$
   Ⓑ $3 \times 3 = 9$
   Ⓒ $2 \times 4 = 8$
   Ⓓ $4 \times 3 = 12$

6. Find the product. **(Lesson 6.7)**

   3×9

   Ⓐ 36
   Ⓑ 27
   Ⓒ 18
   Ⓓ 12

Name _____

Divide by 7

Find the missing factor and quotient.

1. $7 \times \underline{\textbf{6}} = 42 \quad 42 \div 7 = \underline{\textbf{6}}$

2. $7 \times \underline{\hphantom{00}} = 35 \quad 35 \div 7 = \underline{\hphantom{00}}$

3. $7 \times \underline{\hphantom{00}} = 7 \quad 7 \div 7 = \underline{\hphantom{00}}$

4. $5 \times \underline{\hphantom{00}} = 20 \quad 20 \div 5 = \underline{\hphantom{00}}$

Find the quotient.

5. $56 \div 7 = e$

$e = \underline{\hphantom{00000}}$

6. $k = 32 \div 4$

$k = \underline{\hphantom{00000}}$

7. $g = 49 \div 7$

$g = \underline{\hphantom{00000}}$

8. $28 \div 7 = s$

$s = \underline{\hphantom{00000}}$

9. $7\overline{)21}$

10. $7\overline{)14}$

11. $6\overline{)48}$

12. $7\overline{)63}$

Problem Solving REAL WORLD

13. Twenty-eight players sign up for basketball. The coach puts 7 players on each team. How many teams are there?

_____

14. Roberto read 42 books over 7 months. He read the same number of books each month. How many books did Roberto read each month?

_____

Lesson Check

1. Find the quotient.

$49 \div 7$

Ⓐ 6

Ⓑ 7

Ⓒ 8

Ⓓ 9

2. Which is the missing factor and quotient?

$7 \times \blacksquare = 63$

$63 \div 7 = \blacksquare$

Ⓐ 6   Ⓒ 8

Ⓑ 7   Ⓓ 9

Spiral Review

3. Maria has 3 pencils. Her brother has 6 times as many pencils. How many pencils does Maria's brother have? (Lesson 6.2)

Ⓐ 9

Ⓑ 12

Ⓒ 18

Ⓓ 24

4. Kaitlyn makes 4 bracelets. She uses 8 beads for each bracelet. How many beads does she use in all? (Lesson 6.5)

Ⓐ 12

Ⓑ 16

Ⓒ 32

Ⓓ 40

5. There are 7 days in 1 week. How many days are there in 5 weeks? (Lesson 6.8)

Ⓐ 42 days

Ⓑ 35 days

Ⓒ 28 days

Ⓓ 12 days

6. Which division sentence is represented by the following? (Lesson 7.5)

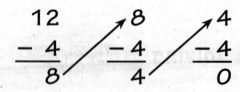

Ⓐ $12 \div 4 = 3$

Ⓑ $8 \div 2 = 4$

Ⓒ $12 \div 2 = 6$

Ⓓ $10 \div 5 = 2$

Name _____

Divide by 8

Find the missing factor and quotient.

1. $8 \times \underline{\textbf{4}} = 32$ $32 \div 8 = \underline{\textbf{4}}$

2. $3 \times \underline{\quad} = 27$ $27 \div 3 = \underline{\quad}$

3. $8 \times \underline{\quad} = 8$ $8 \div 8 = \underline{\quad}$

4. $8 \times \underline{\quad} = 72$ $72 \div 8 = \underline{\quad}$

Find the quotient.

5. $\underline{\quad} = 24 \div 8$

6. $40 \div 8 = \underline{\quad}$

7. $\underline{\quad} = 56 \div 8$

8. $14 \div 2 = \underline{\quad}$

9. $8\overline{)64}$

10. $7\overline{)28}$

11. $8\overline{)16}$

12. $8\overline{)48}$

Problem Solving  REAL WORLD

13. Sixty-four students are going on a field trip. There is 1 adult for every 8 students. How many adults are there?

_____

14. Mr. Chen spends $32 for tickets to a play. If the tickets cost $8 each, how many tickets does Mr. Chen buy?

_____

Lesson Check

1. Find the quotient.

$72 \div 8$

(A) 6

(B) 7

(C) 8

(D) 9

2. Find the missing factor and quotient.

$8 \times \blacksquare = 40$

$40 \div 8 = \blacksquare$

(A) 4

(B) 5

(C) 6

(D) 7

Spiral Review

3. Find the product. (Lesson 6.3)

$(3 \times 2) \times 5$

(A) 6

(B) 10

(C) 20

(D) 30

4. Which has the same product as 4×9? (Lesson 5.8)

(A) 3×8

(B) 9×4

(C) 5×6

(D) 7×2

5. Kyle has 15 counters. He puts them into 3 equal groups. How many counters are in each group? (Lesson 7.1)

(A) 4

(B) 5

(C) 6

(D) 12

6. Which division sentence is shown by the array? (Lesson 7.6)

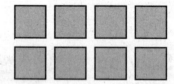

(A) $16 \div 8 = 2$

(B) $8 \div 1 = 8$

(C) $8 \div 2 = 4$

(D) $16 \div 4 = 4$

Name _____

Divide by 9

Find the quotient.

1. __4__ = 36 ÷ 9 | **2.** 30 ÷ 6 = _____ | **3.** _____ = 81 ÷ 9 | **4.** 27 ÷ 9 = _____

5. 48 ÷ 8 = g | **6.** s = 72 ÷ 9 | **7.** m = 0 ÷ 9 | **8.** 54 ÷ 9 = n

g = _____ | s = _____ | m = _____ | n = _____

9. 9)‾6‾3‾ | **10.** 9)‾1‾8‾ | **11.** 7)‾4‾9‾ | **12.** 9)‾4‾5‾

Problem Solving

13. A crate of oranges has trays inside which hold 9 oranges each. There are 72 oranges in the crate. If the trays are filled, how many trays are there?

_____

14. Hector has 45 new baseball cards. He puts them in a binder that holds 9 cards on each page. How many pages does he fill?

_____

Lesson Check

1. Find the quotient.

$54 \div 9$

(A) 5

(B) 6

(C) 7

(D) 8

2. Mr. Robinson sets 36 glasses on a table. He puts the same number of glasses in each of 9 rows. How many glasses does he put in each row?

(A) 4   (C) 6

(B) 5   (D) 7

Spiral Review

3. Find the quotient. (Lesson 7.4)

$5\overline{)40}$

(A) 6

(B) 7

(C) 8

(D) 9

4. Find the product. (Lesson 6.5)

$$\begin{array}{r} 8 \\ \times\,7 \\ \hline \end{array}$$

(A) 49

(B) 56

(C) 63

(D) 64

5. Bridget plants 12 tomato plants in 3 equal rows. How many tomato plants does she put in each row? (Lesson 7.7)

(A) 36

(B) 15

(C) 9

(D) 4

6. Carla packs 4 boxes of books. Each box has 9 books. How many books does Carla pack? (Lesson 6.7)

(A) 36

(B) 27

(C) 13

(D) 5

© Houghton Mifflin Harcourt Publishing Company

Name _____

Act It Out · Division

Solve the problem.

1. Jack has 3 boxes of pencils with the same number of pencils in each box. His mother gives him 4 more pencils. Now Jack has 28 pencils. How many pencils are in each box?

   Think: I can start with 28 counters to act out the problem.

   8 pencils

2. The art teacher has 48 paintbrushes. She puts 8 paintbrushes on each table in her classroom. How many tables are in her classroom?

   _____

3. Ricardo has 2 cases of video games with the same number in each. He gives 4 games to his brother. Ricardo has 12 games left. How many video games were in each case?

   _____

4. Patty has $25 to spend on gifts for her friends. If each gift costs $5, how many gifts can she buy?

   _____

5. Joe has a collection of 35 DVD movies. He received 8 of them as gifts. Joe bought the rest of his movies over 3 years. If he bought the same number of movies each year, how many movies did Joe buy last year?

   _____

6. Elizabeth makes 18 cookies for the members of her chess club. If each member gets 2 cookies, how many members are in the chess club?

   _____

Lesson Check

1. Casey has $36. If she wants to buy shirts for $6 each, how many shirts can she buy?

   (A) 5
   (B) 6
   (C) 7
   (D) 8

2. Jacob and Nicole set up chairs for the winter concert at school. There are 72 chairs in 9 equal rows. How many chairs are in each row?

   (A) 6
   (B) 7
   (C) 8
   (D) 9

Spiral Review

3. Estimate the sum. (Lesson 2.1)

   $$\begin{array}{r} 4{,}987 \\ +\ 1{,}009 \\ \hline \end{array}$$

   (A) 4,000
   (B) 5,000
   (C) 6,000
   (D) 7,000

4. Find the sum. (Lesson 2.2)

   $$\begin{array}{r} 345 \\ +\ 126 \\ \hline \end{array}$$

   (A) 119
   (B) 219
   (C) 461
   (D) 471

5. Meredith practices the piano for 3 hours each week. How many hours will she practice in 8 weeks? (Lesson 6.1)

   (A) 18 hours
   (B) 21 hours
   (C) 24 hours
   (D) 27 hours

6. Brad has 12 counters. He puts 4 counters in each group. How many groups of counters does Brad make? (Lesson 7.2)

   (A) 3
   (B) 4
   (C) 6
   (D) 8

Expressions and Equations

Draw a line to match each story with the expression or equation.

1. Janell has 3 shelves with 9 books on each shelf.

2. Mr. Hanson's third-grade class made 50 muffins. They sold 37 muffins at a bake sale.

3. Tim has 36 shells. He gives an equal number of shells to each of 4 friends. How many shells does each friend receive?

4. Lin ran 9 miles last week and 3 miles this week. How many miles did Lin run in all?

- $36 \div 4 = s$

- 3×9

- $9 + 3 = m$

- $50 - 37$

---

5. Write an expression to show how much money is saved on Day 4. Then complete the table.

Day	1	2	3	4
Cents	8	16	24	

_____

Problem Solving REAL WORLD

6. Miss Jackson bought 23 yards of fabric. She used 16 yards to make curtains. How many yards, *y*, does she have left? Write an equation to solve.

_____

_____

7. Write a math story for the expression 3×6.

_____

_____

_____

© Houghton Mifflin Harcourt Publishing Company

Lesson Check

1. Mr. Delgado has 9 paint jars. His art class uses 3 jars. Which equation could be used to find how many jars, *j*, are left?

   Ⓐ $9 + 3 = j$
   Ⓑ $9 - 3 = j$
   Ⓒ $9 \times 3 = j$
   Ⓓ $9 \div 3 = j$

2. Which expression shows how many tickets are in 4 books?

Books	1	2	3	4
Tickets	5	10	15	■

   Ⓐ 1×4
   Ⓑ 4×4
   Ⓒ 4×5
   Ⓓ $30 + 4$

Spiral Review

3. What is the missing factor? (Lesson 6.10)

   $■ \times 9 = 63$

   Ⓐ 9
   Ⓑ 8
   Ⓒ 7
   Ⓓ 6

4. Fifteen people went camping. Eight people were adults. Each adult brought 3 bottles of water. How many bottles is that in all? (Lesson 5.6)

   Ⓐ 8
   Ⓑ 18
   Ⓒ 23
   Ⓓ 24

5. Paco makes 9 puppets. Each puppet needs 4 buttons. How many buttons does Paco need? (Lesson 6.7)

   Ⓐ 5
   Ⓑ 13
   Ⓒ 32
   Ⓓ 36

6. There are 45 people going on a trip. Each van holds 9 people. How many vans are needed for the trip? (Lesson 7.5)

   Ⓐ 5
   Ⓑ 8
   Ⓒ 36
   Ⓓ 54

Name _____

Chapter 8 Extra Practice

Lessons 8.1 - 8.2

Find the quotient.

1. 6 ÷ 3 = _____ | **2.** _____ = 21 ÷ 3 | **3.** _____ = 24 ÷ 3 | **4.** _____ = 18 ÷ 3

5. 28 ÷ 4 = _____ | **6.** _____ = 16 ÷ 4 | **7.** _____ = 20 ÷ 4 | **8.** _____ = 32 ÷ 4

9. Mr. Song spends $27 on sports drinks. Each bottle costs $3. How many bottles does Mr. Song buy? _____

Lesson 8.3

Find the quotient.

1. 4 ÷ 1 = _____ | **2.** _____ = 0 ÷ 5 | **3.** _____ = 0 ÷ 8 | **4.** _____ = 3 ÷ 3

5. 1)$\overline{8}$ | **6.** 9)$\overline{0}$ | **7.** 6)$\overline{6}$ | **8.** 7)$\overline{0}$

Lessons 8.4 - 8.5

Find the missing factor and quotient.

1. 7 × _____ = 35   35 ÷ 7 = _____ | **2.** 6 × _____ = 54   54 ÷ 6 = _____

Find the quotient.

3. 36 ÷ 6 = _____ | **4.** 48 ÷ 6 = _____ | **5.** 7)$\overline{63}$ | **6.** 7)$\overline{56}$

7. An artist places 42 small paintings in 6 equal rows. How many paintings are in each row? _____

Lessons 8.6 – 8.7

Find the quotient.

1. $40 \div 8 =$ _____

2. _____ $= 24 \div 8$

3. $72 \div 9 =$ _____

4. _____ $= 8 \div 1$

5. $9)\overline{45}$

6. $9)\overline{63}$

7. $8)\overline{32}$

8. $9)\overline{0}$

9. $36 \div 9 = m$

$m =$ _____

10. $18 \div 9 = d$

$d =$ _____

11. $48 \div 8 = b$

$b =$ _____

12. $56 \div 8 = p$

$p =$ _____

Lesson 8.8

Solve.

1. At the store, there are 5 vases. Each vase has the same number of flowers. Twelve flowers are sold. Now there are 28 flowers left. How many flowers were in each vase?

2. Lizzy bought 4 bags of apples, with the same number of apples in each bag. Her mom gave her 8 more apples. Now Lizzy has 36 apples. How many apples were in each bag?

Lesson 8.9

Write an expression. Then write an equation to solve.

1. Mr. Sheldon buys 4 bags of hot dog buns, with the same number of buns in each bag. He buys 32 buns in all. How many hot dog buns, b, are in each bag?

2. There are 24 cans of soup in one box. There are 48 cans of soup in another box. How many cans, c, of soup are there in both boxes?

School-Home Letter

© Houghton Mifflin Harcourt Publishing Company

Vocabulary

fraction A number that names part of a whole or part of a group

numerator The part of a fraction above the line that tells how many equal parts are being counted

denominator The part of a fraction below the line that tells how many equal parts are in the whole or in the group

Dear Family,

During the next few weeks, our math class will be learning about fractions. We will learn to identify, read, and write fractions as part of a whole and as part of a group.

You can expect to see homework that provides practice with fractions.

Here is a sample of how your child will be taught to find a fractional part of a group.

🔑 MODEL   Find How Many in a Fractional Part of a Group

This is how we will be finding how many in a fractional part of a group.

Tips

Equal Groups or Parts

Before you name a fraction, be sure there are equal groups or parts.

STEP 1

Find $\frac{2}{3}$ of 9.

Put 9 counters on your MathBoard.

STEP 2

Since the denominator of $\frac{2}{3}$ is 3, place the counters in 3 equal groups.

STEP 3

Since the numerator of $\frac{2}{3}$ is 2, count the number of counters in two of the groups.

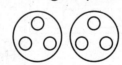

There are 6 counters in 2 groups.

So, $\frac{2}{3}$ of 9 = 6.

Activity

Display a group of 12 objects, such as crayons. Have your child find fractional parts of the group by counting objects in equal groups. Ask your child to find these fractional groups of 12: $\frac{1}{2}$ (6), $\frac{3}{4}$ (9), $\frac{4}{6}$ (8).

Carta para la casa

Vocabulario

fracción Un número que representa una parte de un todo o una parte de un grupo

numerador La parte de una fracción que está encima de la barra y que indica cuántas partes iguales del entero se están tomando en cuenta

denominador La parte de una fracción que está debajo de la barra y que indica cuántas partes iguales hay en el entero o en el grupo

Querida familia,

Durante las próximas semanas, en la clase de matemáticas aprenderemos sobre las fracciones. Aprenderemos a identificar, leer y escribir fracciones como parte de un todo y como parte de un grupo.

Llevaré a la casa tareas que sirven para practicar las fracciones.

Este es un ejemplo de la manera como aprenderemos a hallar una parte fraccionaria de un grupo.

🔑 MODELO Hallar cuántos hay en una parte fraccionaria de un grupo

Así es como hallaremos cuántos hay en una parte fraccionaria de un grupo.

Pistas

Grupos o partes iguales

Antes de que nombres una fracción, asegúrate de que haya grupos o partes iguales.

PASO 1	PASO 2	PASO 3
Halla $\frac{2}{3}$ de 9.	Dado que el denominador de $\frac{2}{3}$ es 3, coloca las fichas en 3 grupos iguales.	Dado que el numerador de $\frac{2}{3}$ es 2, cuenta la cantidad de fichas en dos de los grupos.
Coloca 9 fichas en el *MathBoard*.		

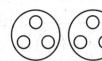

Hay 6 fichas en 2 grupos. Por lo tanto,

$\frac{2}{3}$ de 9 = 6.

Actividad

Muestre un grupo de 12 objetos, como crayolas. Pida a su hijo que halle las partes fraccionarias del grupo contando objetos en grupos iguales. Luego, pídale que halle estos grupos fraccionarios de 12: $\frac{1}{2}$ (6), $\frac{3}{4}$ (9), $\frac{4}{6}$ (8).

Name _____

Equal Parts of a Whole

Write the number of equal parts.
Then write the name for the parts.

1.

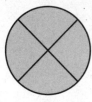

_____ 4 _____ equal parts

_____ fourths _____

2.

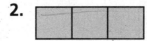

_____ 3 _____ equal parts

_____ thirds _____

3.

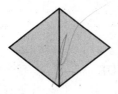

_____ 2 _____ equal parts

_____ half _____

4.

_____ 6 _____ equal parts

_____ one six _____

Write whether each shape is divided into *equal* parts or *unequal* parts.

5.

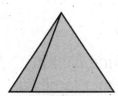

_____ unequal _____ parts

6.

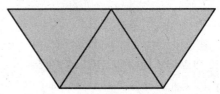

_____ equal _____ parts

Problem Solving REAL WORLD

7. Larry cuts a round pizza into eight equal slices. What is the name for the parts?

_____ c _____

8. Sandra is making a place mat. She divides it into 6 equal parts to color. What is the name for the parts?

_____

Lesson Check

© Houghton Mifflin Harcourt Publishing Company

1. How many equal parts are in the shape?

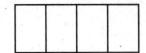

   (A) 3

   (B) 4

   (C) 5

   (D) 6

2. What is the name for the equal parts of the whole?

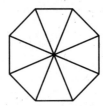

   (A) fourths   (C) eighths

   (B) sixths   (D) tenths

Spiral Review

3. Use a related multiplication fact to find the quotient. (Lesson 8.5)

   49 ÷ 7

   (A) 6   (C) 8

   (B) 7   (D) 9

4. Find the missing factor and quotient. (Lesson 5.5)

   $9 \times \boxed{} = 45$

   $45 \div 9 = \boxed{}$

   (A) 4   (C) 6

   (B) 5   (D) 7

5. Which is a way to model 294?

   (Lesson 1.3)

   (A) 29 tens 14 ones

   (B) 294 hundreds

   (C) 294 tens

   (D) 2 hundreds 94 ones

6. Which number sentence is NOT included in the same fact family as $3 \times 8 = 24$? (Lesson 7.9)

   (A) $8 \times 3 = 24$

   (B) $24 \div 8 = 3$

   (C) $24 \div 3 = 8$

   (D) $24 \div 4 = 6$

Name _____

Equal Shares

Draw lines to show how much each person gets. Write the answer.

1. 6 friends share 3 sandwiches equally.

$\underline{\text{3 sixths or 1 half}}$

2. 8 classmates share 4 pizzas equally.

_____

3. 4 teammates share 5 granola bars equally.

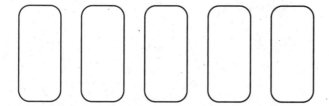

_____

Problem Solving REAL WORLD

4. Two sisters share 5 oranges equally. How much of an orange does each sister get?

_____

5. Six neighbors share 2 pies equally. How much of a pie does each neighbor get?

_____

Lesson Check

1. Three friends share 2 fruit bars equally. How much of a fruit bar does each friend get?

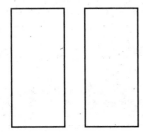

(A) 1 third   (C) 3 thirds

(B) 2 thirds   (D) 3 halves

2. Four brothers share 3 pizzas equally. How much of a pizza does each brother get?

(A) 3 halves

(B) 4 thirds

(C) 3 fourths

(D) 2 fourths

Spiral Review

3. Divide. (Lesson 8.1)

$$3\overline{)27}$$

(A) 6

(B) 7

(C) 8

(D) 9

4. Cayden put 4 cookies in each of 7 bags. How many cookies did he put in bags? (Lesson 5.4)

(A) 11   (C) 32

(B) 28   (D) 40

5. Tom earned $5 per hour raking leaves. He earned $35. For how many hours did he rake leaves?

(Lesson 7.4)

(A) 5 hours

(B) 6 hours

(C) 7 hours

(D) 35 hours

6. James ate lunch at the time shown on the clock. At what time did he eat lunch? (Lesson 3.1)

(A) 12:15   (C) 12:00

(B) 11:30   (D) 11:45

Name _____

Unit Fractions of a Whole

Write the number of equal parts in the whole.
Then write the fraction that names the shaded part.

1.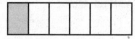

_____6_____ equal parts

_____$\frac{1}{6}$_____

2.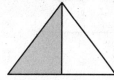

_____ equal parts

_____

3.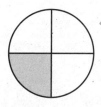

_____ equal parts

_____

4.

_____ equal parts

_____

5.

_____ equal parts

_____

6.

_____ equal parts

_____

Problem Solving

7. Tyler made a pan of cornbread. He cut it into 10 equal pieces and ate 1 piece. What fraction of the cornbread did Tyler eat?

_____

8. Anna cut an apple into 4 equal pieces. She gave 1 piece to her sister. What fraction of the apple did Anna give to her sister?

_____

Lesson Check

1. What fraction names the shaded part?

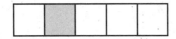

(A) $\frac{1}{3}$

(B) $\frac{1}{4}$

(C) $\frac{1}{5}$

(D) $\frac{1}{6}$

2. Gina cut a fruit bar into 3 equal parts. She ate 1 part. What fraction of the fruit bar did Gina eat?

(A) $\frac{1}{2}$

(B) $\frac{1}{3}$

(C) $\frac{1}{4}$

(D) $\frac{1}{5}$

Spiral Review

3. Alex has 5 lizards. He divides them equally among 5 cages. How many lizards does Alex put in each cage?

(Lesson 7.4)

(A) 0

(B) 1

(C) 5

(D) 10

4. Find the product. (Lesson 5.9)

$8 \times 1 = $ ▢

(A) 0

(B) 1

(C) 8

(D) 9

5. Which number is greater than 6,184? (Lesson 1.6)

(A) 6,148

(B) 6,099

(C) 6,084

(D) 6,186

6. What is the value of the underlined digit? (Lesson 1.4)

3,287

(A) 2 thousands

(B) 2 hundreds

(C) 2 tens

(D) 2 ones

Fractions of a Whole

Write a fraction in numbers and in words
to name the shaded part.

1.

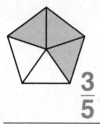

$\dfrac{3}{5}$

_____

_____ three _____ fifths

2.

_____

_____ eighths

3.

_____

_____ thirds

4.

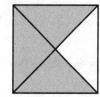

_____

_____ fourths

Write a fraction that names the point.

5.

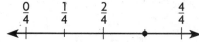

_____

6.

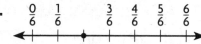

_____

Problem Solving REAL WORLD

7. Emma makes a poster for the
school's spring concert. She divides
the poster into 8 equal sections. She
uses two of the sections for the title.
What fraction of the poster does
Emma use for the title?

_____

8. Lucas makes a flag. It has 10 equal
parts. Four of the parts are red. What
fraction of the flag is red?

_____

Lesson Check

★TEST PREP

1. What fraction names the shaded part?

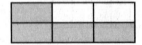

- Ⓐ $\frac{4}{6}$
- Ⓑ $\frac{2}{4}$
- Ⓒ $\frac{4}{8}$
- Ⓓ $\frac{2}{6}$

2. What fraction, in words, names the shaded part?

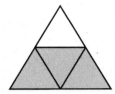

- Ⓐ one fourth
- Ⓑ one third
- Ⓒ three fourths
- Ⓓ four thirds

Spiral Review

3. Subtract. (Lesson 2.6)

$$\begin{array}{r} 3,409 \\ - \ 1,508 \\ \hline \end{array}$$

- Ⓐ 1,901
- Ⓒ 2,901
- Ⓑ 2,101
- Ⓓ 4,917

4. Add. (Lesson 2.3)

$$\begin{array}{r} 4,751 \\ + \ 5,163 \\ \hline \end{array}$$

- Ⓐ 9,914
- Ⓒ 8,914
- Ⓑ 9,314
- Ⓓ 1,934

5. Alex has the money shown. How much money does he have in all?

(Lesson 3.6)

- Ⓐ 39¢
- Ⓒ 59¢
- Ⓑ 46¢
- Ⓓ 69¢

6. How many students chose swimming? (Lesson 4.3)

Favorite Activity	
Skating	☺ ☺
Swimming	☺ ☺ ☺ ☺ ☺
Biking	☺ ☺ ☺ ☺
Key: Each ☺ = 5 votes.	

- Ⓐ 5
- Ⓒ 20
- Ⓑ 10
- Ⓓ 25

Name _____

Fractions Greater Than 1

Each shape is 1 whole. Write a fraction greater
than 1 for the parts that are shaded.

1.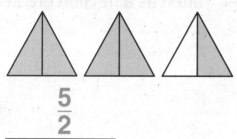

$\dfrac{5}{2}$

_____

2.

_____

3.

_____

4.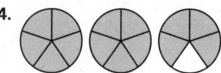

_____

Use the number line for 5–7.
Write the fraction greater than 1 as a mixed number.

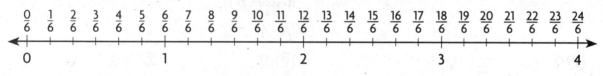

5. $\dfrac{7}{6}$

6. $\dfrac{14}{6}$

7. $\dfrac{19}{6}$

_____   _____   _____

Problem Solving REAL WORLD

8. Rachel gave $\dfrac{1}{4}$ of a pie to each of
5 friends. How many pies did she
give to her friends in all? Write the
mixed number.

_____

9. Ms. Fuller has $2\dfrac{2}{3}$ pies left over from
her party. Write the number of pies
left over as a fraction greater than 1.

_____

Lesson Check

1. Each shape is 1 whole. What mixed number is modeled by the shaded parts?

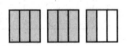

(A) $1\frac{1}{3}$

(B) $2\frac{1}{3}$

(C) $2\frac{1}{2}$

(D) $2\frac{2}{3}$

2. Alex's family ate $1\frac{7}{8}$ pizzas for dinner. Which shows this mixed number written as a fraction greater than 1?

(A) $\frac{9}{8}$

(B) $\frac{15}{8}$

(C) $\frac{16}{8}$

(D) $\frac{17}{8}$

Spiral Review

3. Add. (Lesson 2.3)

$$\begin{array}{r} 1,598 \\ + \ 1,431 \\ \hline \end{array}$$

(A) 2,029

(B) 2,929

(C) 3,019

(D) 3,029

4. Dylan has read 6 books. Kylie has read twice as many books as Dylan. How many books has Kylie read?

(Lesson 5.3)

(A) 4

(C) 10

(B) 8

(D) 12

5. Lindsay has $1.00 in dimes. How many dimes does she have?

(Lesson 7.10)

(A) 11

(B) 10

(C) 2

(D) 1

6. Matt bought a yo-yo for $2.59. How much change did he get from $3.00? (Lesson 3.9)

(A) $1.51

(B) $1.41

(C) $0.51

(D) $0.41

Name _____

Fractions of a Group

Write a fraction to name the shaded part of the group.

1.

2.

_____   _____

Write a mixed number and a fraction greater than 1 to name the part filled.

3.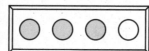

4.

_____   _____

Draw a quick picture. Then, write a fraction to name the shaded part of the group.

5. Draw 4 circles.
   Shade 2 circles.

6. Draw 6 circles.
   Make 3 groups.
   Shade 2 groups.

_____   _____

Problem Solving

7. Brian has 3 basketball cards and 7 baseball cards. What fraction of Brian's cards are baseball cards?

8. Sophia has 2 purple flowers, 6 pink flowers, and 4 yellow flowers. What fraction of Sophia's flowers are NOT yellow?

_____   _____

Lesson Check

1. What fraction of the group is shaded?

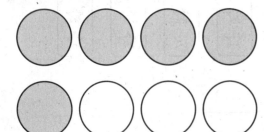

- Ⓐ $\frac{5}{3}$
- Ⓑ $\frac{5}{8}$
- Ⓒ $\frac{3}{5}$
- Ⓓ $\frac{3}{8}$

2. What fraction of the group is shaded?

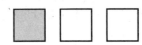

- Ⓐ $\frac{1}{3}$
- Ⓑ $\frac{1}{2}$
- Ⓒ $\frac{2}{3}$
- Ⓓ $\frac{2}{1}$

Spiral Review

3. Which number sentence does the array show? (Lesson 6.8)

- Ⓐ $4 \times 7 = 28$
- Ⓑ $3 \times 8 = 24$
- Ⓒ $3 \times 7 = 21$
- Ⓓ $3 \times 6 = 18$

4. Juan has 136 baseball cards and 89 football cards. How many more baseball cards than football cards does Juan have? (Lesson 2.5)

- Ⓐ 17
- Ⓑ 29
- Ⓒ 36
- Ⓓ 47

5. Jasmine went to the store after breakfast but before noon. What time did she go to the store? (Lesson 3.3)

- Ⓐ 2:00 A.M.
- Ⓒ 2:00 P.M.
- Ⓑ 10:45 P.M.
- Ⓓ 10:45 A.M.

6. Add. (Lesson 3.10)

$$\$2.76 + 1.19$$

- Ⓐ $1.19
- Ⓒ $3.95
- Ⓑ $2.76
- Ⓓ $4.95

Find Part of a Group

Circle equal groups to solve.

1. $\frac{3}{4}$ of 12 = __9__

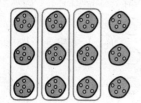

2. $\frac{7}{8}$ of 16 = _____

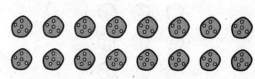

3. $\frac{6}{10}$ of 10 = _____

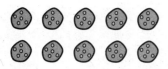

4. $\frac{2}{3}$ of 9 = _____

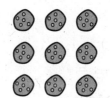

5. $\frac{1}{6}$ of 18 = _____

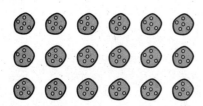

6. $\frac{4}{5}$ of 10 = _____

Problem Solving REAL WORLD

7. Marco drew 20 pictures. He drew $\frac{3}{4}$ of them in art class. How many pictures did Marco draw in art class?

_____

8. Caroline has 10 marbles. One half of them are blue. How many of Caroline's marbles are blue?

_____

Name _____

Draw a Diagram · Fractions

Solve. Show your work.

1. Katrina has 8 ribbons for her hair. Three fourths of the ribbons are blue. How many of Katrina's ribbons are blue?

   6 ribbons

2. Ms. Perez has 20 math workbooks for her third grade class. She gives $\frac{1}{10}$ of them to another third grade teacher. How many workbooks does she give away?

3. Brianna has 16 pieces of play jewelry. Five eighths of the pieces are bracelets. How many bracelets does Brianna have?

4. Ramal has 12 pages in a stamp album filled. Two thirds of the pages are filled with stamps of famous people. How many pages in Ramal's album are filled with stamps of famous people?

5. Justin helped repair 15 bicycles over the weekend at his dad's bicycle shop. One fifth of the bicycles were mountain bikes. How many mountain bikes did Justin help repair?

6. Layla collects interesting pencils. She has a total of 18 pencils. She received $\frac{4}{6}$ of the pencils as gifts. How many of Layla's pencils were gifts?

Lesson Check

1. Devon's little brother has 12 blocks. One fourth of them are red. How many of the blocks are red?

   (A) 3   (C) 6

   (B) 4   (D) 8

2. There were 20 juice boxes sold in the cafeteria at lunch. Three fifths of them were apple juice. How many boxes of apple juice were sold?

   (A) 3   (C) 12

   (B) 5   (D) 15

Spiral Review

3. Tiffany read that 2,431 people went to the county fair last week. Which is the best estimate of the number of people who went to the fair last week? (Lesson 1.7)

   (A) 1,000   (C) 3,000

   (B) 2,000   (D) 4,000

4. Subtract. (Lesson 2.6)

   $$3,458$$
   $$- \ 1,267$$

   (A) 2,291   (C) 2,191

   (B) 2,211   (D) 2,181

5. Ken has 54 marbles. He and 5 friends share them equally. How many marbles does each person get? (Lesson 8.7)

   (A) 5

   (B) 6

   (C) 9

   (D) 11

6. Morgan got out of school at the time shown on the clock. At what time did Morgan get out of school?

   (Lesson 3.2)

   (A) 3:00

   (B) 2:55

   (C) 2:50

   (D) 2:11

Name _____

Chapter 9 Extra Practice

Lesson 9.1

Write the number of equal parts. Then write the name for the parts.

1.

____ equal parts

_____

2.

____ equal parts

_____

3.

____ equal parts

_____

Lesson 9.2

Draw lines to show how much each person gets. Write the answer.

1. 4 friends share 3 oranges equally.

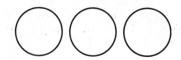

_____

2. 3 sisters share 5 sandwiches equally.

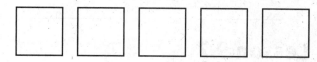

_____

Lessons 9.3 - 9.4

Write a fraction in numbers and in words to name the shaded part.

1.

_____ fifths

2.

_____ eighths

3.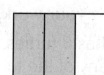

_____ thirds

Lesson 9.5

Each shape is 1 whole. Write a fraction greater than 1 for the parts that are shaded.

1.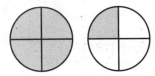

2.

_____   _____

Lesson 9.6

Write a mixed number and a fraction greater than 1 to name the part filled.

1.

2.

_____ _____   _____ _____

Lesson 9.7

Circle equal groups to solve.

1. $\frac{1}{3}$ of 6 = _____

○ ○ ○
○ ○ ○

2. $\frac{2}{5}$ of 10 = _____

○ ○ ○ ○ ○
○ ○ ○ ○ ○

3. $\frac{5}{5}$ of 5 = _____

○ ○ ○ ○ ○

Lesson 9.8

Solve. Show your work.

1. Beatriz has 8 turtles. Two fourths of them are box turtles. How many of the turtles are box turtles?

_____

2. Josh has a job walking dogs. He walks a total of 18 dogs each week. Today, he is walking $\frac{1}{3}$ of the dogs. How many dogs is Josh walking today?

_____

School-Home Letter

© Houghton Mifflin Harcourt Publishing Company

Dear Family,

During the next few weeks, our math class will be learning more about fractions. We will learn how to compare fractions, order fractions, and find equivalent fractions.

You can expect to see homework that provides practice with fractions.

Here is a sample of how your child will be taught to compare fractions that have the same numerator.

Vocabulary

equivalent fractions Two or more fractions that name the same amount

greater than (>) A symbol used to compare two numbers, with the greater number given first

less than (<) A symbol used to compare two numbers, with the lesser number given first

🔑 MODEL Compare Fractions with the Same Numerator

This is one way we will be comparing fractions that have the same numerator.

STEP 1

Compare $\frac{4}{10}$ and $\frac{4}{6}$.

Look at the numerators.

Each numerator is 4.

The numerators are the same.

STEP 2

Since the numerators are the same, look at the denominators, 10 and 6.

The more pieces a whole is divided into, the smaller the pieces are. Tenths are smaller pieces than sixths.

So, $\frac{4}{10}$ is a smaller fraction of the whole than $\frac{4}{6}$.

$\frac{4}{10}$ is less than $\frac{4}{6}$. $\frac{4}{10} < \frac{4}{6}$

Tips

Identifying Fewer Pieces

The fewer pieces a whole is divided into, the larger the pieces are. For example, when a whole is divided into 6 equal pieces, the pieces are larger than when the same size whole is divided into 10 equal pieces. So, $\frac{4}{6}$ is greater than (>) $\frac{4}{10}$.

Activity

Play a card game to help your child practice comparing fractions. On several cards, write a pair of fractions with the same numerator and draw a circle between the fractions. Players take turns drawing a card and telling whether *greater than* (>) or *less than* (<) belongs in the circle.

Carta para la casa

Vocabulario

fracciones equivalentes Dos o más fracciones que representan la misma cantidad

mayor que Símbolo que se usa para comparar dos números. El número mayor se escribe primero ($>$)

menor que Símbolo que se usa para comparar dos números. El número menor se escribe primero ($<$)

Querida familia,

Durante las próximas semanas, en la clase de matemáticas aprenderemos más sobre las fracciones. Aprenderemos a comparar y ordenar fracciones, y a hallar fracciones equivalentes.

Llevaré a la casa tareas para practicar las fracciones.

Este es un ejemplo de la manera como aprenderemos a comparar fracciones que tienen el mismo numerador.

MODELO Comparar fracciones que tienen el mismo denominador

Esta es una manera como compararemos fracciones que tienen el mismo numerador.

Paso 1

Compara $\frac{4}{10}$ y $\frac{4}{6}$.

Mira los numeradores.

Cada numerador es 4.

Los numeradores son iguales.

Paso 2

Dado que los numeradores son iguales, Mira los denominadores 10 y 6.

Entre más piezas se divida un entero, las piezas serán más pequeñas. Los décimos son piezas más pequeñas que los sextos.

Por lo tanto, $\frac{4}{10}$ es una fracción menor del entero que $\frac{4}{6}$.

$\frac{4}{10}$ es menor que $\frac{4}{6}$. $\frac{4}{10} < \frac{4}{6}$

Pistas

Identificar menos piezas

Entre menos piezas se divida un entero, las piezas serán más grandes. Por ejemplo, si un entero se divide en 6 piezas iguales, las piezas son más grandes que las piezas del mismo entero, si éste se divide en 10 piezas iguales. Por lo tanto, $\frac{4}{6}$ es mayor que ($>$) $\frac{4}{10}$.

Actividad

Ayude a su hijo a comparar fracciones jugando con tarjetas de fracciones. En varias tarjetas, escriba pares de fracciones con el mismo numerador y dibuje un círculo entre las fracciones. Túrnense para dibujar cada tarjeta y decir qué debe ir en el círculo: "mayor que" o "menor que."

Name _____

Act It Out · Compare Fractions

Solve.

1. Luis skates $\frac{2}{5}$ mile from his home to school. Isabella skates $\frac{3}{4}$ mile to get to school. Who skates farther?

   Think: Use fraction strips to act it out.

   _____ Isabella _____

2. Sandra makes a pizza. She puts mushrooms on $\frac{2}{6}$ of the pizza. She adds green peppers to $\frac{5}{8}$ of the pizza. Which topping covers more of the pizza?

   _____

3. The jars of paint in the art room have different amounts of paint. The green paint jar is $\frac{2}{8}$ full. The purple paint jar is $\frac{4}{6}$ full. Which paint jar is less full?

   _____

4. Jan has a recipe for bread. She uses $\frac{6}{8}$ cup of flour and $\frac{1}{3}$ cup of chopped onion. Which ingredient does she use more of, flour or onion?

   _____

5. Edward walked $\frac{3}{4}$ mile from his home to the park. Then he walked $\frac{2}{4}$ mile from the park to the library. Which distance is shorter?

   _____

Lesson Check

1. Ali and Jonah collect seashells in identical buckets. When they are finished, Ali's bucket is $\frac{2}{3}$ full and Jonah's bucket is $\frac{3}{5}$ full. Which statement correctly compares the fractions?

   (A) $\frac{2}{3} = \frac{3}{5}$ (C) $\frac{3}{5} < \frac{2}{3}$

   (B) $\frac{2}{3} < \frac{3}{5}$ (D) $\frac{3}{5} > \frac{2}{3}$

2. Rosa paints a wall in her bedroom. She puts green paint on $\frac{5}{8}$ of the wall and blue paint on $\frac{3}{8}$ of the wall. Which statement correctly compares the fractions?

   (A) $\frac{5}{8} > \frac{3}{8}$ (C) $\frac{3}{8} > \frac{5}{8}$

   (B) $\frac{5}{8} < \frac{3}{8}$ (D) $\frac{3}{8} = \frac{5}{8}$

Spiral Review

3. Dan divides a pie into eighths. How many equal parts are there? (Lesson 9.1)

   (A) 3
   (B) 6
   (C) 8
   (D) 10

4. Which shows equal parts? (Lesson 9.1)

   (A) 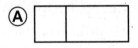   (C)

   (B)   (D)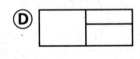

5. Charles places 30 pictures on his bulletin board in 6 equal rows. How many pictures are in each row?

   (Lesson 7.8)

   (A) 3
   (B) 4
   (C) 5
   (D) 6

6. Which is a rule for the table? (Lesson 6.9)

Tables	1	2	3	4	5
Chairs	5	10	15	20	25

   (A) Add 1.
   (B) Add 4.
   (C) Multiply by 2.
   (D) Multiply by 5.

Name

Compare Fractions Using Benchmarks

Use the benchmarks on the number line to help you compare. Write < or >.

1. Compare $\frac{2}{8}$ and $\frac{3}{4}$.

$\frac{2}{8}$ $<$ $\frac{3}{4}$

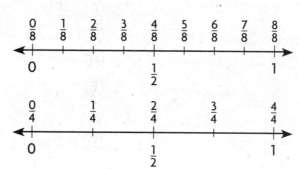

Compare. Write < or >.

2. $\frac{1}{8}$ $\bigcirc$ $\frac{6}{10}$

3. $\frac{4}{12}$ $\bigcirc$ $\frac{4}{6}$

4. $\frac{2}{8}$ $\bigcirc$ $\frac{1}{2}$

5. $\frac{3}{5}$ $\bigcirc$ $\frac{3}{3}$

6. $\frac{4}{3}$ $\bigcirc$ $\frac{5}{10}$

7. $\frac{9}{12}$ $\bigcirc$ $\frac{1}{3}$

8. $\frac{4}{6}$ $\bigcirc$ $\frac{7}{5}$

9. $\frac{2}{4}$ $\bigcirc$ $\frac{6}{9}$

10. $\frac{11}{10}$ $\bigcirc$ $\frac{1}{4}$

Problem Solving REAL WORLD

11. Erika ran $\frac{3}{8}$ mile. Maria ran $\frac{3}{4}$ mile. Which distance is greater?

12. Carlos finished $\frac{1}{3}$ of his art project on Monday. Tyler finished $\frac{1}{2}$ of his art project on Monday. Who finished more of his art project on Monday?

Lesson Check

TEST PREP

1. Which symbol makes the statement true?

$\frac{4}{6} \bullet \frac{3}{8}$

(A) >
(B) <
(C) =
(D) none

2. Which symbol makes the statement true?

$\frac{3}{5} \bullet \frac{3}{2}$

(A) >
(B) <
(C) =
(D) none

Spiral Review

3. At Linda's party, 3 pizzas were eaten. There were 8 guests at the party. If each guest ate an equal amount of pizza, how much pizza did each guest eat? (Lesson 9.2)

(A) 8 halves
(B) 8 thirds
(C) 3 fifths
(D) 3 eighths

4. Ronald has 6 bags of trail mix he wants to share equally among 4 friends. How much of the bags of trail mix will each friend get? (Lesson 9.2)

(A) 2 sixths
(B) 1 half
(C) 4 sixths
(D) 6 fourths

5. Find the quotient. (Lesson 8.1)

$18 \div 3 = \blacksquare$

(A) 7
(B) 6
(C) 5
(D) 4

6. Pilar arranges 40 tiles in an array. She places 5 tiles in each row. How many rows of 5 does Pilar make? (Lesson 7.6)

(A) 10
(B) 9
(C) 8
(D) 7

© Houghton Mifflin Harcourt Publishing Company

P196

Name _____

Compare Fractions with the Same Numerator

Compare. Write < or >.

1. $\frac{1}{8}$ $\bigcirc$< $\frac{1}{2}$

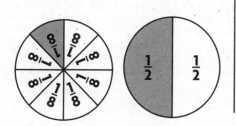

2. $\frac{3}{8}$ $\bigcirc$ $\frac{3}{6}$

3. $\frac{2}{3}$ $\bigcirc$ $\frac{2}{4}$

4. $\frac{2}{10}$ $\bigcirc$ $\frac{2}{8}$

5. $\frac{3}{12}$ $\bigcirc$ $\frac{3}{10}$

6. $\frac{1}{5}$ $\bigcirc$ $\frac{1}{6}$

7. $\frac{5}{6}$ $\bigcirc$ $\frac{5}{10}$

8. $\frac{4}{5}$ $\bigcirc$ $\frac{4}{10}$

9. $\frac{6}{12}$ $\bigcirc$ $\frac{6}{9}$

Problem Solving REAL WORLD

10. Javier is buying food in the lunch line. The tray of salad plates is $\frac{3}{9}$ full. The tray of fruit plates is $\frac{3}{5}$ full. Which tray is more full?

    _____

11. Rachel bought some buttons. Of the buttons, $\frac{3}{5}$ are yellow and $\frac{3}{10}$ are red. Rachel bought more of which color buttons?

    _____

Lesson Check

1. Which symbol makes the statement true?

$\frac{3}{4}$ ● $\frac{3}{12}$

(A) >
(B) <
(C) =
(D) none

2. Which symbol makes the statement true?

$\frac{2}{5}$ ● $\frac{2}{3}$

(A) >
(B) <
(C) =
(D) none

Spiral Review

3. Anita divided a circle into 6 equal parts and shaded 1 of the parts. Which fraction names the part she shaded? (Lesson 9.3)

(A) $\frac{1}{6}$ (C) $\frac{5}{6}$

(B) $\frac{1}{5}$ (D) $\frac{1}{1}$

4. Which fraction names the shaded part of the rectangle? (Lesson 9.4)

(A) $\frac{1}{8}$ (C) $\frac{6}{8}$

(B) $\frac{2}{8}$ (D) $\frac{8}{8}$

5. Chip worked at the animal shelter for 6 hours each week for several weeks. He worked for a total of 42 hours. Which of the following shows how to find the number of weeks Chip worked at the animal shelter? (Lesson 8.4)

(A) $6 + w = 42$

(B) $42 - w = 6$

(C) $42 \div 6 = w$

(D) $w \times 2 = 6$

6. Mr. Jackson has 20 quarters. If he gives 4 quarters to each of his children, how many children does Mr. Jackson have? (Lesson 7.7)

(A) 3
(B) 4
(C) 5
(D) 6

Name _____

Compare Fractions

Compare. Write < or >. Write the strategy you used.

1. $2\frac{3}{8}$ ⬡< $2\frac{3}{4}$

   Think: The whole numbers are the same. Compare the fractions. Is $\frac{3}{8}$ greater than or less than $\frac{1}{2}$? Is $\frac{3}{4}$ greater than or less than $\frac{1}{2}$?

   <u>same whole number;</u>

   <u>benchmarks</u>

2. $1\frac{2}{3}$ ◯ $1\frac{7}{8}$

   _____

   _____

3. $2\frac{1}{4}$ ◯ $1\frac{3}{8}$

   _____

   _____

4. $\frac{3}{5}$ ◯ $\frac{2}{5}$

   _____

   _____

5. $3\frac{4}{6}$ ◯ $3\frac{1}{8}$

   _____

   _____

6. $\frac{5}{6}$ ◯ $\frac{9}{10}$

   _____

   _____

Problem Solving 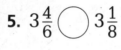 REAL WORLD

7. At the third-grade party, two groups each had their own pizzas. The blue group ate $1\frac{7}{8}$ pizzas. The green group ate $1\frac{2}{8}$ pizzas. Which group ate more of their pizzas?

   _____

8. Ben and Antonio both take the same bus to school. Ben's ride is $2\frac{3}{8}$ miles. Antonio's ride is $2\frac{3}{4}$ miles. Who has a longer bus ride?

   _____

Lesson Check

1. Which symbol makes the statement true?

   $1\frac{4}{5}$ ● $1\frac{11}{12}$

   (A) >

   (B) <

   (C) =

   (D) none

2. Which symbol makes the statement true?

   $2\frac{7}{10}$ ● $2\frac{2}{6}$

   (A) >

   (B) <

   (C) =

   (D) none

Spiral Review

3. Hari gave $\frac{1}{3}$ of a granola bar to each of 5 friends. How many granola bars did Hari give to his friends in all? (Lesson 9.5)

   (A) $\frac{3}{5}$

   (B) $1\frac{1}{3}$

   (C) $1\frac{2}{3}$

   (D) 2

4. Each shape is 1 whole. Which mixed number is represented by the shaded part of the model? (Lesson 9.5)

   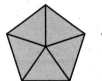

   (A) $\frac{3}{5}$ (C) $1\frac{3}{5}$

   (B) $1\frac{2}{5}$ (D) $2\frac{2}{3}$

5. Which related multiplication fact can you use to find $16 \div \blacksquare = 8$? (Lesson 8.6)

   (A) $4 \times 4 = 16$

   (B) $8 \times 2 = 16$

   (C) $8 \times 1 = 8$

   (D) $4 \times 2 = 8$

6. What is the missing factor? (Lesson 6.10)

   $9 \times \blacksquare = 36$

   (A) 7

   (B) 6

   (C) 4

   (D) 3

Order Fractions

Write the numbers in order from greatest to least.

1. $\frac{1}{3}, \frac{5}{8}, \frac{1}{4}$

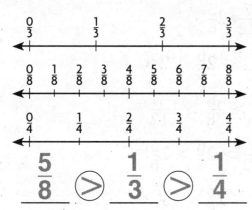

$$\frac{5}{8} \; \bigcirc{>} \; \frac{1}{3} \; \bigcirc{>} \; \frac{1}{4}$$

2. $1\frac{2}{5}, 1\frac{2}{8}, 1\frac{6}{10}$

_____ $\bigcirc$ _____ $\bigcirc$ _____

Write the numbers in order from least to greatest.

3. $\frac{4}{6}, \frac{1}{3}, \frac{3}{8}$

4. $\frac{1}{2}, \frac{1}{8}, \frac{1}{5}$

5. $2\frac{7}{8}, 1\frac{7}{12}, 2\frac{3}{4}$

6. $1\frac{2}{3}, 1\frac{4}{9}, 1\frac{3}{6}$

Problem Solving REAL WORLD

7. Mr. Ruiz is making a bar graph for a bulletin board. He has one strip of paper that is $\frac{2}{4}$ foot long. A second strip is $\frac{11}{12}$ foot, and a third strip is $\frac{4}{6}$ foot. What is the order of the lengths of paper from least to greatest?

_____

8. Danny, Joe, and Nicole are making chalk drawings during recess. The length of Danny's drawing is $2\frac{1}{4}$ feet. Joe's drawing is $2\frac{7}{8}$ feet. Nicole's drawing is $2\frac{1}{8}$ feet. What is the order of the lengths of the drawings from greatest to least?

_____

Lesson Check

1. Which list orders the fractions from least to greatest?

   $\frac{1}{3}, \frac{1}{8}, \frac{1}{5}$

   (A) $\frac{1}{8} < \frac{1}{3} < \frac{1}{5}$

   (B) $\frac{1}{3} > \frac{1}{5} > \frac{1}{8}$

   (C) $\frac{1}{8} < \frac{1}{5} < \frac{1}{3}$

   (D) $\frac{1}{5} > \frac{1}{8} > \frac{1}{3}$

2. Which list orders the mixed numbers from greatest to least?

   $2\frac{6}{8}, 1\frac{7}{12}, 2\frac{5}{6}$

   (A) $1\frac{7}{12} < 2\frac{6}{8} < 2\frac{5}{6}$

   (B) $2\frac{5}{6} > 2\frac{6}{8} > 1\frac{7}{12}$

   (C) $1\frac{7}{12} > 2\frac{6}{8} > 2\frac{5}{6}$

   (D) $2\frac{6}{8} < 2\frac{5}{6} < 1\frac{7}{12}$

Spiral Review

3. What fraction of the group of cars is shaded? (Lesson 9.6)

   (A) $\frac{3}{8}$ (C) $\frac{5}{8}$

   (B) $\frac{1}{2}$ (D) $\frac{3}{5}$

4. Wendy has 6 pieces of fruit. Of these, 2 pieces are bananas. What fraction of Wendy's fruit is bananas?

   (Lesson 9.6)

   (A) $\frac{2}{6}$ (C) $\frac{4}{6}$

   (B) $\frac{2}{4}$ (D) $\frac{2}{2}$

5. Each member of the art club is given 1 award. If 9 awards are given, how many members does the art club have? (Lesson 8.3)

   (A) 10
   (B) 9
   (C) 8
   (D) 1

6. The number sentence is an example of which multiplication property? (Lesson 6.4)

   $6 \times 7 = (6 \times 5) + (6 \times 2)$

   (A) Associative
   (B) Commutative
   (C) Distributive
   (D) Identity

Name _____

Model Equivalent Fractions

Shade the model. Then divide the pieces to find the equivalent fraction.

1.

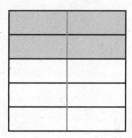

$$\frac{2}{5} = \frac{4}{10}$$

2.

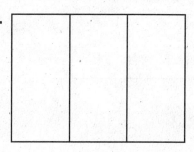

$$\frac{1}{3} = \frac{\square}{6}$$

3.

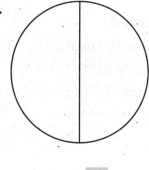

$$\frac{1}{2} = \frac{\square}{4}$$

4.

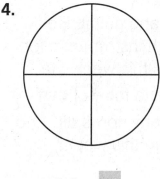

$$\frac{3}{4} = \frac{\square}{8}$$

Problem Solving REAL WORLD

5. Mike says that $\frac{2}{3}$ of his fraction model is shaded blue. Ryan says that $\frac{4}{6}$ of the same model is shaded blue. Are the two fractions equivalent? If so, what is another equivalent fraction?

6. Brett shaded $\frac{4}{16}$ of his piece of notebook paper. Aisha says he shaded $\frac{1}{4}$ of the paper. Are the two fractions equivalent? If so, what is another equivalent fraction?

_____   _____

Lesson Check

1. Find the fraction equivalent to $\frac{2}{3}$.

Ⓐ $\frac{3}{2}$　　　Ⓒ $\frac{3}{6}$

Ⓑ $\frac{4}{6}$　　　Ⓓ $\frac{1}{3}$

2. Find the fraction equivalent to $\frac{1}{4}$.

Ⓐ $\frac{1}{2}$　　　Ⓒ $\frac{2}{8}$

Ⓑ $\frac{2}{4}$　　　Ⓓ $\frac{6}{8}$

Spiral Review

3. Eric plays piano and guitar. He practiced on both instruments for a total of 8 hours this week. He practiced the piano for $\frac{3}{4}$ of that time. For how many hours did Eric practice the piano this week?

(Lesson 9.7)

Ⓐ 3 hours　　　Ⓒ 5 hours

Ⓑ 4 hours　　　Ⓓ 6 hours

4. Kylee bought a pack of 12 cookies. Two-thirds of the cookies are peanut butter. How many of the cookies in the pack are peanut butter? (Lesson 9.7)

Ⓐ 6　　　Ⓒ 8

Ⓑ 7　　　Ⓓ 9

5. There are 56 students going to the game. The coach puts 7 students in each van. Which number sentence can be used to find how many vans are needed to get the students to the game? (Lesson 8.5)

Ⓐ $56 + 7 = $ ■

Ⓑ ■ $+ 7 = 56$

Ⓒ ■ $\times 7 = 56$

Ⓓ $56 - 7 = $ ■

6. Which number sentence can be used to describe the picture?

(Lesson 7.3)

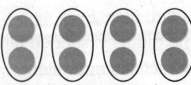

Ⓐ $2 + 4 = 6$

Ⓑ $4 - 2 = 2$

Ⓒ $4 \times 1 = 4$

Ⓓ $8 \div 2 = 4$

Equivalent Fractions

Each shape is 1 whole. Shade the model to find
the equivalent fraction.

1.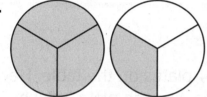

$$\frac{2}{3} = \frac{4}{6}$$

2.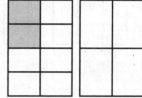

$$\frac{2}{8} = \frac{\boxed{}}{4}$$

3.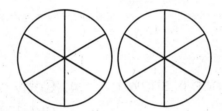

$$\frac{4}{3} = \frac{\boxed{}}{6}$$

Use the number lines to find the equivalent fraction.

4. $\frac{1}{2} = \frac{\boxed{}}{6}$

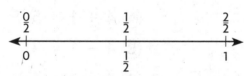

5. $\frac{6}{6} = \frac{2}{\boxed{}}$

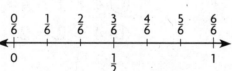

Problem Solving REAL WORLD

6. Mr. Sudo has an attendance chart.
He says that $\frac{3}{4}$ of the students have
never missed a day of school. What
is an equivalent fraction for $\frac{3}{4}$?

$$\frac{3}{4} = \frac{\boxed{}}{8}$$

7. Brenda's class has an outdoor
vegetable garden. Carrots make
up $\frac{4}{10}$ of the garden. What is an
equivalent fraction for $\frac{4}{10}$?

$$\frac{4}{10} = \frac{\boxed{}}{5}$$

Lesson Check

1. Which fraction is equivalent to $\frac{8}{10}$?

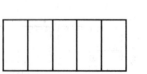

- Ⓐ $\frac{4}{20}$
- Ⓒ $\frac{3}{4}$
- Ⓑ $\frac{3}{5}$
- Ⓓ $\frac{4}{5}$

2. Which fraction is equivalent to $\frac{1}{3}$?

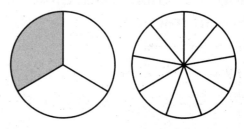

- Ⓐ $\frac{1}{9}$
- Ⓒ $\frac{3}{9}$
- Ⓑ $\frac{3}{12}$
- Ⓓ $\frac{2}{3}$

Spiral Review

3. Which number sentence is shown by the array? **(Lesson 7.8)**

- Ⓐ $8 - 2 = 6$
- Ⓑ $8 \times 1 = 8$
- Ⓒ $2 + 8 = 10$
- Ⓓ $16 \div 2 = 8$

4. Cody put 4 plates on the table. He put 1 apple on each plate. Which number sentence can be used to find the total number of apples on the table? **(Lesson 5.9)**

- Ⓐ $4 + 1 = 5$
- Ⓑ $4 - 1 = 3$
- Ⓒ $4 \times 1 = 4$
- Ⓓ $4 \div 2 = 2$

5. Which number sentence is in the same fact family as $7 \times 3 = 21$?

(Lesson 7.9)

- Ⓐ $7 + 3 = 10$
- Ⓑ $7 - 3 = 4$
- Ⓒ $7 \times 2 = 14$
- Ⓓ $21 \div 3 = 7$

6. Find the quotient. **(Lesson 8.2)**

$4\overline{)36}$

- Ⓐ 9
- Ⓑ 8
- Ⓒ 7
- Ⓓ 6

Name _____

Chapter 10 Extra Practice

Lesson 10.1

Solve. Show your work.

1. Nina finished $\frac{4}{8}$ of her homework before dinner. Ed finished $\frac{7}{8}$ of his homework before dinner. Who finished the greater part of homework?

 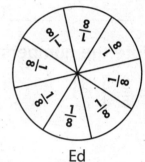

Nina   Ed

_____

2. Rafael walked $\frac{2}{3}$ mile and then rode his scooter $\frac{5}{6}$ mile. Which distance is farther?

$\frac{1}{3}$	$\frac{1}{3}$	$\frac{1}{3}$

$\frac{1}{6}$	$\frac{1}{6}$	$\frac{1}{6}$	$\frac{1}{6}$	$\frac{1}{6}$	$\frac{1}{6}$

_____ mile is farther.

Lessons 10.2 - 10.3

Compare. Write < or >.

1. $\frac{2}{6} \bigcirc \frac{3}{4}$

2. $\frac{6}{8} \bigcirc \frac{1}{4}$

3. $\frac{3}{2} \bigcirc \frac{2}{4}$

4. $\frac{1}{6} \bigcirc \frac{1}{8}$

5. $\frac{2}{3} \bigcirc \frac{2}{6}$

6. $\frac{3}{10} \bigcirc \frac{3}{12}$

Lesson 10.4

Compare. Write < or >. Write the strategy you used.

1. $1\frac{4}{5} \bigcirc 2\frac{1}{2}$

2. $4\frac{5}{6} \bigcirc 4\frac{1}{6}$

3. $\frac{7}{8} \bigcirc \frac{4}{5}$

_____ _____ _____

_____ _____ _____

Lesson 10.5

Write the numbers in order from greatest to least.

1. $\frac{1}{2}, \frac{1}{4}, \frac{5}{8}$

2. $\frac{2}{3}, \frac{1}{6}, \frac{9}{10}$

Write the numbers in order from least to greatest.

3. $\frac{3}{5}, \frac{5}{4}, \frac{3}{8}$

4. $2\frac{1}{3}, 2\frac{6}{10}, 3\frac{1}{2}$

Lessons 10.6 - 10.7

Each shape is 1 whole. Shade the model to find the equivalent fraction.

1.

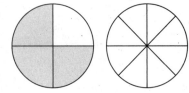

$\frac{3}{4} = \frac{\blacksquare}{8}$

2.

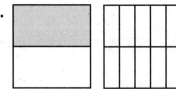

$\frac{1}{2} = \frac{\blacksquare}{10}$

Use the number lines to find the equivalent fraction.

3. $\frac{1}{3} = \frac{\blacksquare}{12}$

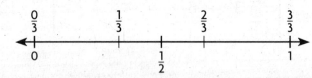

4. $\frac{12}{12} = \frac{3}{\blacksquare}$

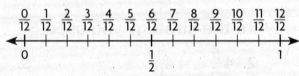

5. Traci has 4 whole sandwiches. Each sandwich is cut in half. What fraction names all the sandwich halves?

_____

6. Alex is reading a book. He has $\frac{4}{6}$ of the chapters left to read. Write an equivalent fraction for $\frac{4}{6}$.

_____

© Houghton Mifflin Harcourt Publishing Company

School-Home Letter

Vocabulary

congruent Shapes that have the same size and the same shape

Dear Family,

During the next few weeks, our math class will be learning more about plane shapes. We will learn how to combine, separate, and transform plane shapes.

You can expect to see homework that provides practice with shapes.

Here is a sample of how your child will be taught to identify congruent shapes.

🔑 MODEL Identify Congruent Shapes

This is how we will be identifying congruent shapes.

Which shape appears to be congruent to shape A?

STEP 1

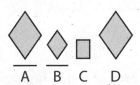

A   B   C   D

Look at shape A and shape B to see if they are the same shape and the same size.

They are the same shape. They are not the same size.

Shape B is not congruent to shape A.

STEP 2

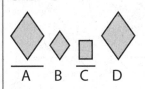

A   B   C   D

Look at shape A and shape C to see if they are the same shape and the same size.

They are not the same shape. They are not the same size.

Shape C is not congruent to shape A.

STEP 3

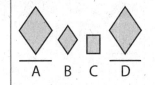

A   B   C   D

Look at shape A and shape D to see if they are the same shape and the same size.

They are the same shape. They are the same size.

Shape D is congruent to shape A.

Tips

Checking to See If Shapes Are Congruent

Some pairs of shapes, such as paper cutouts and pattern blocks, can be placed on top of one another to see if they are the same shape and size.

Activity

Point out pairs of objects around the house that have congruent and noncongruent shapes, such as plates, books, and photos. Have your child identify and explain which shapes are congruent and which are not.

Carta para la casa

Vocabulario

figuras congruentes Las figuras que tienen el mismo tamaño y la misma forma

Querida familia,

Durante las próximas semanas, en la clase de matemáticas estudiaremos más acerca de las figuras planas. Aprenderemos a combinar, separar y transformar figuras planas.

Llevaré a la casa tareas con actividades con figuras.

Este es un ejemplo de la manera como aprenderemos a identificar figuras congruentes.

🔑 MODELO Identificar figuras congruentes

Así es como identificaremos figuras congruentes.
¿Qué figura parece ser congruente con la figura A?

PASO 1

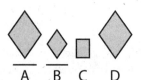

A   B   C   D

Observa la figura A y la figura B para ver si tienen la misma forma y el mismo tamaño.

Tienen la misma forma. No tienen el mismo tamaño.

La figura B no es congruente con la figura A.

PASO 2

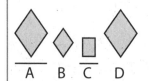

A   B   C   D

Observa la figura A y la figura C para ver si tienen la misma forma y el mismo tamaño.

No tienen la misma forma. No tienen el mismo tamaño.

La figura C no es congruente con la figura A.

PASO 3

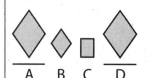

A   B   C   D

Observa la figura A y la figura D para ver si tienen la misma forma y el mismo tamaño.

Tienen la misma forma. Tienen el mismo tamaño.

La figura D es congruente con la figura A.

Pistas

Comprobar si dos figuras son congruentes

Algunos pares de figuras, como los recortes de papel y los bloques de figuras geométricas, pueden ponerse uno encima del otro para ver si tienen la misma forma y el mismo tamaño.

Actividad

Por pares, elija objetos que haya en la casa y que tengan o no tengan figuras congruentes, como platos, libros y fotos. Pida a su hijo que identifique y explique qué figuras son congruentes y cuáles no lo son.

Describe Plane Shapes

Write whether each is a *point, line, line segment,* or *ray*.

1.

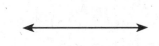

point
_____

2.

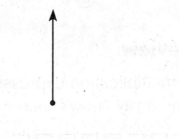

_____

3.

_____

4.

_____

5.

_____

6.

_____

Problem Solving REAL WORLD

7. Carl wants to show a closed shape in his drawing. Show and explain how to make the drawing a closed shape.

_____
_____

8. The shape of a fish pond at a park is shown below. Is the shape open or closed?

_____
_____

Lesson Check

1. How many line segments does this shape have?

Ⓐ 2   Ⓒ 4

Ⓑ 3   Ⓓ 5

2. Which of these is part of a line, has one endpoint, and continues in one direction?

Ⓐ ray

Ⓑ line

Ⓒ line segment

Ⓓ point

Spiral Review

3. Which multiplication expression does the array show? **(Lesson 5.7)**

Ⓐ 3 × 8   Ⓒ 8 × 5

Ⓑ 4 × 8   Ⓓ 4 × 9

4. Find the missing factor and quotient. **(Lesson 7.9)**

$9 \times \boxed{} = 27$

$27 \div 9 = \boxed{}$

Ⓐ 3

Ⓑ 4

Ⓒ 5

Ⓓ 6

5. Which fraction is equivalent to $\frac{4}{8}$? **(Lesson 10.6)**

Ⓐ $\frac{3}{4}$ Ⓒ $\frac{1}{4}$

Ⓑ $\frac{1}{2}$ Ⓓ $\frac{1}{8}$

6. There were 5 people on the bus. When the bus got to the last stop, there were 30 people on it. Which expression could be used to find how many more people got on the bus? **(Lesson 8.9)**

Ⓐ 30 + 5   Ⓒ 30 × 5

Ⓑ 30 − 5   Ⓓ 30 ÷ 5

Name _____

Classify Angles

Use the corner of a sheet of paper to tell whether the
angle is *right, acute,* or *obtuse.*

1.

_____acute_____

2.

_____

3.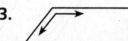

_____

Write how many of each type of angle the shape has.

4.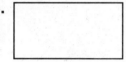

_____ right

_____ acute

_____ obtuse

5.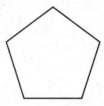

_____ right

_____ acute

_____ obtuse

6.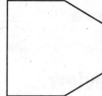

_____ right

_____ acute

_____ obtuse

Problem Solving REAL WORLD

7. Jeff has a square piece of art paper.
   He cuts across it from one corner
   to the opposite corner to make
   two pieces. What is the total number
   of sides and angles in both of the
   new shapes?

8. Kaylee tells Aimee that the shape
   of a stop sign has at least one right
   angle. Aimee says that there are no
   right angles. Who is correct? **Explain.**

_____

_____

_____

_____

Lesson Check

1. What is a name for this angle?

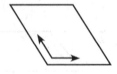

   Ⓐ right
   Ⓑ acute
   Ⓒ obtuse
   Ⓓ scalene

2. How many right angles does this shape appear to have?

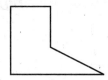

   Ⓐ 1
   Ⓑ 2
   Ⓒ 3
   Ⓓ 4

Spiral Review

3. Subtract. (Lesson 2.6)

$$5,458 - 2,225$$

   Ⓐ 3,233
   Ⓑ 3,283
   Ⓒ 7,683
   Ⓓ 8,683

4. Which symbol makes the statement true? (Lesson 10.4)

$$1\frac{6}{12} \bigcirc 1\frac{1}{2}$$

   Ⓐ >
   Ⓑ <
   Ⓒ =
   Ⓓ ÷

5. What is the eighth number in the pattern? (Lesson 6.9)

   4, 8, 12, 16, 20

   Ⓐ 32
   Ⓑ 40
   Ⓒ 44
   Ⓓ 50

6. Find the quotient. (Lesson 8.7)

   $45 \div 9 =$ ▨

   Ⓐ 3
   Ⓑ 4
   Ⓒ 5
   Ⓓ 6

Name _____

Identify Polygons

Is the shape a polygon? Write *yes* or *no*.

1.
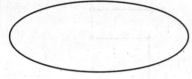

_no_

2.

_____

3.
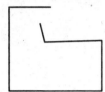

_____

4.
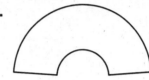

_____

Write the number of sides and the number of vertices.
Then name the polygon.

5.
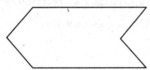

_____ sides

_____ vertices

_____

6.
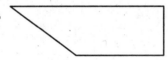

_____ sides

_____ vertices

_____

Problem Solving REAL WORLD

7. Mr. Murphy has an old coin that has ten sides. If its shape is a polygon, how many vertices does the old coin have?

_____

8. Lin says that an octagon has six sides. Chris says that it has eight sides. Whose statement is correct?

_____

Lesson Check

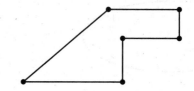

1. Which is a name for this polygon?

- Ⓐ hexagon
- Ⓑ octagon
- Ⓒ quadrilateral
- Ⓓ pentagon

2. How many sides does this polygon have?

- Ⓐ 4
- Ⓑ 5
- Ⓒ 6
- Ⓓ 7

Spiral Review

3. Compare. (Lesson 1.6)

12,450 ◯ 1,245

- Ⓐ >
- Ⓑ <
- Ⓒ =
- Ⓓ +

4. Erica has 9 necklaces. One third of the necklaces are blue. How many necklaces are blue? (Lesson 9.8)

- Ⓐ 2
- Ⓑ 3
- Ⓒ 6
- Ⓓ 9

5. There are 30 desks in a classroom set up in 6 equal rows. How many desks are in each row? (Lesson 8.8)

- Ⓐ 5
- Ⓑ 6
- Ⓒ 30
- Ⓓ 36

6. April has 18 pens. She wants to put the same number of pens in each of 3 bags. How many pens should she put in each bag? (Lesson 7.1)

- Ⓐ 3
- Ⓑ 6
- Ⓒ 9
- Ⓓ 18

Name _____

Describe Lines

Look at the dashed sides of the polygon. Tell if they appear to be *intersecting, perpendicular,* or *parallel.* Write all the words that describe the sides.

1.

_____parallel_____

2.

_____

3.

_____

4.

_____

5.

_____

6.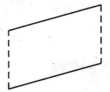

_____

7.

_____

8.

_____

9.

_____

Problem Solving REAL WORLD

10. Tamara is thinking of a shape. It has 2 pairs of parallel sides and 4 right angles. All the sides are the same length. Draw Tamara's shape.

11. Niko is thinking of a shape with three straight sides. Each side is a different length. Draw Niko's shape.

Lesson Check

1. How many pairs of parallel sides does the quadrilateral appear to have?

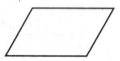

Ⓐ 1   Ⓒ 3

Ⓑ 2   Ⓓ 4

2. Which sides appear to be parallel?

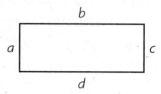

Ⓐ *a* and *c* only

Ⓑ *b* and *d* only

Ⓒ *a* and *b, c* and *d*

Ⓓ *a* and *c, b* and *d*

Spiral Review

3. Compare. (Lesson 10.1)

$\frac{1}{3} \bigcirc \frac{3}{4}$

Ⓐ >

Ⓑ <

Ⓒ =

Ⓓ ×

4. There were 20 students in a class. The students were separated into 4 equal groups. Which expression tells the number of students in each group? (Lesson 8.9)

Ⓐ 20 + 4

Ⓑ 20 − 4

Ⓒ 20 × 4

Ⓓ 20 ÷ 4

5. Joe earns $5 a day for 3 days. Which number sentence shows how much money he earned?

(Lesson 7.2)

Ⓐ 5 + 5 + 5 = 15

Ⓑ 5 − 3 = 2

Ⓒ 3 + 3 + 3 = 9

Ⓓ 5 + 3 = 8

6. Which fraction names the shaded part? (Lesson 9.3)

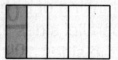

Ⓐ $\frac{1}{3}$ Ⓒ $\frac{1}{5}$

Ⓑ $\frac{1}{4}$ Ⓓ $\frac{4}{5}$

Name _____

Classify Quadrilaterals

Circle all the words that describe the quadrilateral.

1.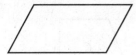

(parallelogram)

rectangle

rhombus

trapezoid

2.

parallelogram

rectangle

rhombus

trapezoid

3.

square

rectangle

rhombus

trapezoid

Use the quadrilaterals below for 4–6.

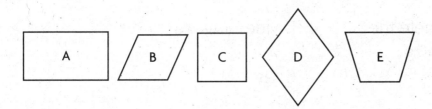

4. Which quadrilateral(s) appear to have only 1 pair of parallel sides?

_____

5. Which quadrilateral(s) appear to have 4 right angles?

_____

6. Which quadrilateral(s) appear to have 4 equal sides?

_____

Problem Solving REAL WORLD

7. A picture on the wall in Jeremy's class has 4 right angles, 4 equal sides, and 2 pairs of parallel sides. What word best describes the picture?

_____

8. Sofia has a plate that has 4 equal sides, 2 pairs of parallel sides, and no right angles. What word best describes the plate?

_____

Lesson Check

1. Which name describes the quadrilateral?

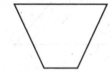

   (A) square

   (B) trapezoid

   (C) rhombus

   (D) rectangle

2. Which quadrilaterals appear to have 2 pairs of parallel sides?

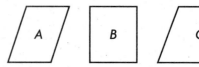

   (A) A and B

   (B) A, B, and C

   (C) A

   (D) B

Spiral Review

3. Which number will complete the number sentences? (Lesson 7.8)

   $5 \times \blacksquare = 35$

   $35 \div 5 = \blacksquare$

   (A) 5   (C) 7

   (B) 6   (D) 8

4. Divide. (Lesson 8.4)

   $6\overline{)48}$

   (A) 8

   (B) 9

   (C) 10

   (D) 11

5. Jen says that $\frac{4}{5}$ of students in her class are wearing the color blue. Which fraction describes the number of students wearing blue? (Lesson 10.7)

   (A) $\frac{4}{10}$ (C) $\frac{8}{10}$

   (B) $\frac{5}{10}$ (D) $\frac{10}{10}$

6. How many right angles does the shape appear to have? (Lesson 11.2)

   (A) 1   (C) 3

   (B) 2   (D) 4

© Houghton Mifflin Harcourt Publishing Company

Name _____

Classify Triangles

Write *right*, *obtuse*, or *acute* to describe the triangle.

1.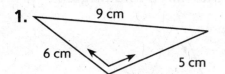

_____obtuse_____

2.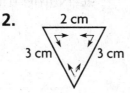

_____

3.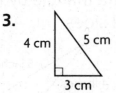

_____

A triangle has sides with these lengths. Write *equilateral*, *isosceles*, or *scalene* to describe the triangle.

4. 6 inches, 8 inches, 10 inches

_____

5. 11 inches, 10 inches, 11 inches

_____

6. 7 inches, 7 inches, 7 inches

_____

7. 105 inches, 105 inches, 105 inches

_____

8. 9 inches, 12 inches, 15 inches

_____

9. 10 inches, 10 inches, 15 inches

_____

Problem Solving REAL WORLD

10. Chris is making a painting with only triangles. He wants each side of the triangles to be the same length. What kind of triangle will he paint? Draw an example of the triangle.

_____

11. Jaime says that a right triangle can be an equilateral triangle. Is she correct? Use a drawing to explain your answer.

_____

_____

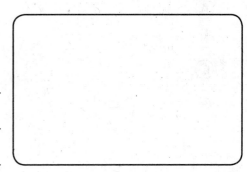

Lesson Check

1. Name the triangle by the number of equal sides.

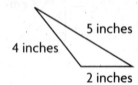

4 inches 5 inches 2 inches

   Ⓐ scalene
   Ⓑ isosceles
   Ⓒ equilateral
   Ⓓ acute

2. Name the triangle by its angles.

   Ⓐ scalene
   Ⓑ obtuse
   Ⓒ right
   Ⓓ acute

Spiral Review

3. Compare. (Lesson 3.7)

   2 quarters, 3 dimes, 1 nickel

   ◯ 3 quarters, 1 dime, 2 nickels

   Ⓐ <   Ⓒ =
   Ⓑ >   Ⓓ +

4. Which fraction of the rectangles has been shaded? (Lesson 9.6)

   Ⓐ $\frac{1}{3}$ Ⓒ $\frac{1}{2}$
   Ⓑ $\frac{2}{3}$ Ⓓ $\frac{3}{3}$

5. Which symbol makes the statement true? (Lesson 10.3)

   $\frac{4}{5}$ ◯ $\frac{4}{8}$

   Ⓐ >
   Ⓑ <
   Ⓒ =
   Ⓓ ÷

6. Find the quotient. (Lesson 7.10)

   $60 \div 10 =$ ▢

   Ⓐ 6
   Ⓑ 10
   Ⓒ 50
   Ⓓ 70

Name _____

Combine and Separate Shapes

Name a new shape that can be made by combining
two of the pattern block shapes shown.

1.

2.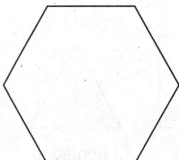

parallelogram _____   _____

Draw a diagonal and write the names of
the new shapes.

3.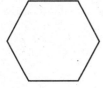

4.

5.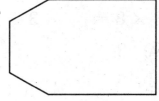

_____   _____   _____

_____   _____   _____

Problem Solving

6. Ray traced some pattern blocks to
make the shape at the right. Name
the blocks he could have combined.

_____

_____

_____

Lesson Check

1. Which shape can be made by combining the pattern blocks shown?

 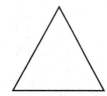

Ⓐ rhombus   Ⓒ pentagon

Ⓑ trapezoid   Ⓓ hexagon

2. Samuel cut this shape on a diagonal. What shapes did he make?

Ⓐ 2 triangles   Ⓒ 2 rhombuses

Ⓑ 2 rectangles   Ⓓ 2 trapezoids

Spiral Review

3. What is the missing factor? (Lesson 6.10)

$3 \times 8 = \boxed{} \times 3$

Ⓐ 3

Ⓑ 5

Ⓒ 8

Ⓓ 24

4. Find the quotient. (Lesson 8.1)

$3\overline{)30}$

Ⓐ 3

Ⓑ 9

Ⓒ 10

Ⓓ 30

5. How many equal parts are in the whole? (Lesson 9.1)

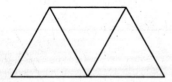

Ⓐ 2

Ⓑ 3

Ⓒ 6

Ⓓ 8

6. Which fraction is equivalent to $\frac{4}{10}$? (Lesson 10.6)

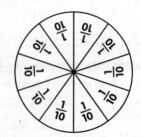

Ⓐ $\frac{1}{10}$ Ⓒ $\frac{2}{5}$

Ⓑ $\frac{1}{4}$ Ⓓ $\frac{10}{10}$

Identify Congruent Shapes

Look at the first shape. Tell if it appears to be congruent to the second shape. Write *yes* or *no*.

1.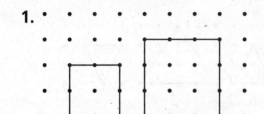

____no____

2.
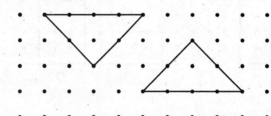

_____

3.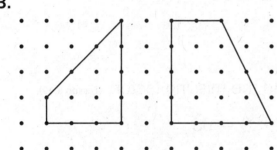

_____

4.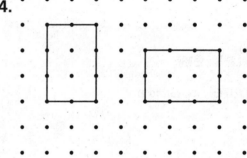

_____

Problem Solving  REAL WORLD

5. Juanita drew one square with sides of 3 inches and another square with sides of 5 inches. Are the squares congruent? **Explain**.

_____

_____

_____

_____

6. Paul has four quarters. He stacks the quarters one on top of the other. Are they all congruent? **Explain**.

_____

_____

_____

_____

Lesson Check

1. Which two shapes appear to be congruent?

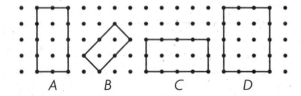

Ⓐ A and B

Ⓑ B and C

Ⓒ A and C

Ⓓ C and D

2. Which two shapes appear to be congruent?

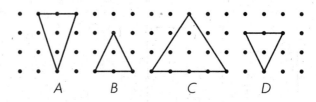

Ⓐ C and B

Ⓑ B and D

Ⓒ A and C

Ⓓ C and D

Spiral Review

3. Compare. (Lesson 10.2)

$$\frac{3}{4} \bigcirc \frac{7}{8}$$

Ⓐ >   Ⓒ =

Ⓑ <   Ⓓ ÷

4. Find the missing factor. (Lesson 6.10)

$\blacksquare \times 9 = 63$

Ⓐ 6   Ⓒ 8

Ⓑ 7   Ⓓ 9

5. What is the value of 1 quarter, 4 dimes, and 3 nickels? (Lesson 3.6)

Ⓐ $0.75

Ⓑ $0.80

Ⓒ $0.85

Ⓓ $0.90

6. Name the triangle by the number of equal sides. (Lesson 11.6)

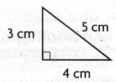

Ⓐ scalene

Ⓑ isosceles

Ⓒ equilateral

Ⓓ acute

Name _____

Identify Symmetry

Does the dashed line appear to be a line of symmetry? Write *yes* or *no*.

1.

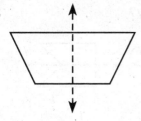

_____yes_____

2.

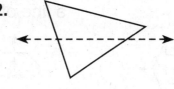

_____

3.

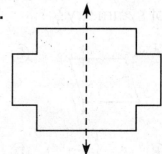

_____

4.

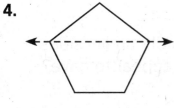

_____

5.

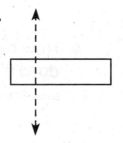

_____

6.

_____

Problem Solving REAL WORLD

7. Finish this drawing so it has a line of symmetry. Draw the line segments and line of symmetry.

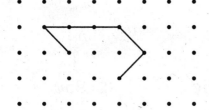

8. Finish this drawing so it has a line of symmetry. Draw the line segments and the line of symmetry.

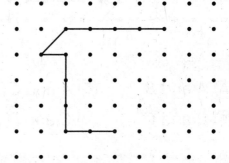

Lesson Check

1. For which shape does the dashed line appear to be a line of symmetry?

   Ⓐ 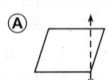   Ⓒ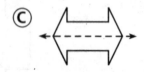

   Ⓑ 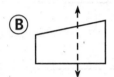   Ⓓ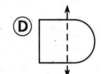

2. For which shape does the dashed line appear to NOT be a line of symmetry?

   Ⓐ   Ⓒ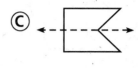

   Ⓑ 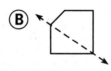   Ⓓ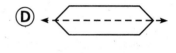

Spiral Review

3. Order the fractions from least to greatest. **(Lesson 10.5)**

   $\frac{3}{4}, \frac{3}{6}, \frac{1}{3}$

   Ⓐ $\frac{1}{3}, \frac{3}{6}, \frac{3}{4}$ Ⓒ $\frac{3}{4}, \frac{1}{3}, \frac{3}{6}$

   Ⓑ $\frac{1}{3}, \frac{3}{4}, \frac{3}{6}$ Ⓓ $\frac{3}{4}, \frac{3}{6}, \frac{1}{3}$

4. How many pairs of parallel sides does the shape appear to have?

   (Lesson 11.4)

   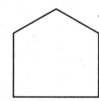

   Ⓐ 1   Ⓒ 4

   Ⓑ 2   Ⓓ 5

5. Which two shapes appear to be congruent? **(Lesson 11.8)**

   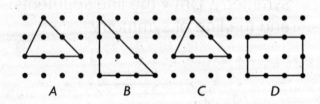

   Ⓐ A and B   Ⓒ A and C

   Ⓑ B and C   Ⓓ C and D

6. What is the total value of the coins?

   (Lesson 3.6)

   Ⓐ 85¢   Ⓒ 95¢

   Ⓑ 90¢   Ⓓ $1.00

Name _____

Draw Lines of Symmetry

Draw the line or lines of symmetry. Then write the number of lines of symmetry the shape has.

1.

5 lines

_____

2.

_____

3.

_____

4.

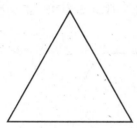

_____

5.

_____

6.

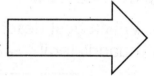

_____

Problem Solving REAL WORLD

7. Manny draws the rhombus shown below. He says there are two lines of symmetry. Is he correct? **Explain**.

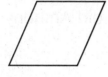

_____

_____

_____

_____

8. Kayla draws a large letter B on a piece of paper. How many lines of symmetry are there? Draw the line or lines of symmetry.

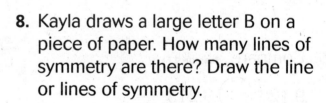

Lesson Check

1. How many lines of symmetry does the shape below have?

Ⓐ 0   Ⓒ 2

Ⓑ 1   Ⓓ 4

2. How many lines of symmetry does the shape below have?

Ⓐ 0   Ⓒ 2

Ⓑ 1   Ⓓ 4

Spiral Review

3. Which best describes the quadrilateral? **(Lesson 11.5)**

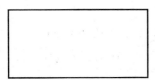

Ⓐ square

Ⓑ rhombus

Ⓒ rectangle

Ⓓ trapezoid

4. How many sides does this shape have? **(Lesson 11.3)**

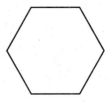

Ⓐ 4   Ⓒ 6

Ⓑ 5   Ⓓ 7

5. Compare. **(Lesson 1.6)**

9,123 ◯ 9,213

Ⓐ <

Ⓑ >

Ⓒ =

Ⓓ ÷

6. Anthony cuts a pizza into 8 equal slices. He ate 1 slice. What fraction of the pizza did Anthony eat?

(Lesson 9.3)

Ⓐ $\frac{1}{2}$ Ⓒ $\frac{1}{4}$

Ⓑ $\frac{4}{8}$ Ⓓ $\frac{1}{8}$

Name _____

Draw a Diagram · Plane Shapes

Solve each problem. Then draw the blocks.

1. Carly traced pattern blocks to make the design at the right. What block or blocks can she add so the design will have at least 1 line of symmentry?

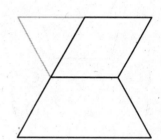

   ___1 triangle___

2. Brad traced pattern blocks to make the design at the right. What block or blocks can he add so the design will NOT have a line of symmentry?

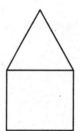

   _____

3. Paula traced pattern blocks to make the design at the right. What block or blocks can she add so the design will have at least 2 lines of symmentry?

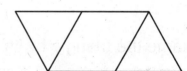

   _____

4. Jeff traced pattern blocks to make the design at the right. What block can he add so the design will NOT have a line of symmetry?

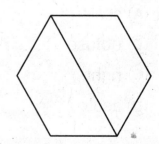

   _____

Lesson Check

1. How many lines of symmetry does the shape appear to have?

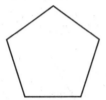

- (A) 1
- (B) 3
- (C) 5
- (D) 7

2. Which shape has exactly 4 lines of symmetry?

- (A) triangle
- (B) pentagon
- (C) square
- (D) trapezoid

Spiral Review

3. Compare. **(Lesson 10.3)**

$$\frac{3}{4} \bigcirc \frac{3}{6}$$

- (A) <
- (B) >
- (C) =
- (D) ÷

4. Divide. **(Lesson 7.10)**

$$80 \div 10 = \blacksquare$$

- (A) 8
- (B) 9
- (C) 10
- (D) 70

5. Name the triangle by its angles.

(Lesson 11.6)

- (A) scalene
- (B) obtuse
- (C) right
- (D) acute

6. What is the total value of the coins shown? **(Lesson 3.6)**

- (A) 35¢
- (B) 45¢
- (C) 50¢
- (D) 55¢

Name _____

Slides, Flips, and Turns

Tell how the shape was moved. Write *slide, flip,* or *turn*.

1.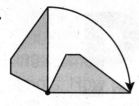

_____

2.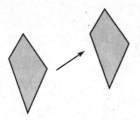

_____

3.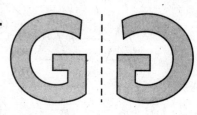

_____

4.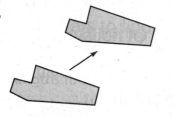

_____

5.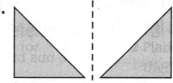

_____

6.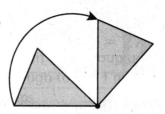

_____

7.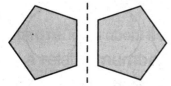

_____

8.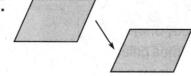

_____

9.

_____

Problem Solving REAL WORLD

10. If the shape below is flipped, what would it look like? Draw how the shape will look after it is flipped over the dashed line.

11. As time passed, did the hands of the clock move by a slide, a flip, or a turn?

_____

Lesson Check

1. Which shows a turn?

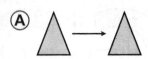 

Ⓐ Ⓒ

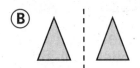 

Ⓑ Ⓓ

2. What describes how the letter P moved?

Ⓐ not congruent   Ⓒ slide

Ⓑ turn   Ⓓ flip

Spiral Review

3. What multiplication sentence is modeled by the picture? (Lesson 5.4)

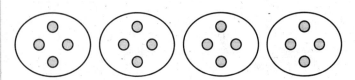

Ⓐ $4 \times 4 = 16$ Ⓒ $1 \times 4 = 4$

Ⓑ $3 \times 4 = 12$ Ⓓ $0 \times 4 = 0$

4. Find the difference. (Lesson 2.6)

$$3,000$$
$$-985$$

Ⓐ 2,015   Ⓒ 2,115

Ⓑ 2,025   Ⓓ 2,125

5. What is the missing factor and quotient? (Lesson 8.6)

$8 \times \boxed{} = 72$

$72 \div 8 = \boxed{}$

Ⓐ 6   Ⓒ 8

Ⓑ 7   Ⓓ 9

6. Use the array to find 6×6. (Lesson 6.2)

Ⓐ 24   Ⓒ 36

Ⓑ 30   Ⓓ 42

© Houghton Mifflin Harcourt Publishing Company

Name _____

Chapter 11 Extra Practice

Lesson 11.1 - 11.3

Write the name of the polygon.

1.

2.

3.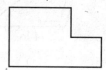

_____   _____   _____

4.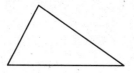

5.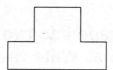

6.

_____   _____   _____

Lesson 11.4

Look at the dashed sides in the polygon. Tell if they appear to be *intersecting*, *perpendicular*, or *parallel*. Write all the words that describe the sides.

1.

2.

3.

_____   _____   _____

Lesson 11.5

Circle all the words that describe the quadrilateral.

1.

parallelogram

trapezoid

rectangle

2.

square

rhombus

trapezoid

3.

trapezoid

rectangle

parallelogram

Lesson 11.6

Name the triangle. Write *equilateral, isosceles,* or *scalene.* Write *right, obtuse,* or *acute.*

1.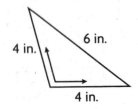

2.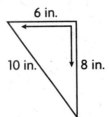

3.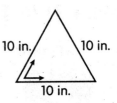

_____   _____   _____

Lesson 11.7–11.8

Draw a line that separates the shape into two congruent shapes. Tell if that line is a diagonal. Write *yes* or *no.*

1.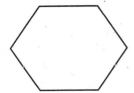

2.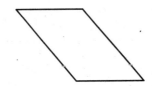

3.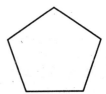

_____   _____   _____

Lesson 11.9–11.11

Draw the line or lines of symmetry. Then write the number of lines of symmetry that the figure has.

1.

2.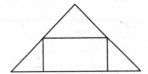

3.

_____   _____   _____

Lesson 11.12

Tell how the shape was moved. Write slide, *flip,* or *turn.*

1.

2.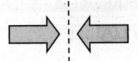

3.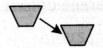

_____   _____   _____

Vocabulary

three-dimensional shape A solid shape that has length, width, and height

net A two-dimensional pattern that can be folded to make a three-dimensional shape

pattern unit The part of a pattern that repeats

Dear Family,

During the next few weeks, our math class will be learning about three-dimensional shapes and geometric patterns.

You can expect to see homework that asks students to identify and combine solid shapes and identify and make patterns with shapes.

Here is a sample of how your child will be taught to use pattern blocks to make a repeating pattern.

🔑 MODEL Make a Repeating Pattern

This is how we will be making a repeating pattern of shapes.

STEP 1 Choose three different pattern blocks. Make a pattern unit.

 The pattern unit is square, triangle, trapezoid.

STEP 2 Repeat the pattern unit at least three times.

 Tips

Extending the Pattern

Students can use a pattern unit to extend a pattern. To find the eleventh shape in the pattern shown, students can look at three repetitions of the pattern unit, then count two more shapes to find that the eleventh shape is a triangle.

Activity

Have your child trace three different shapes to make a pattern unit. Have your child repeat the pattern unit at least three times to make a repeating pattern.

Carta para la casa

Vocabulario

figura tridimensional Un cuerpo geométrico que tiene longitud, ancho y altura

plantilla Un patrón bidimensional que puede doblarse para hacer una figura tridimensional

unidad de patrón La parte de patrón que se repite

Querida familia,

Durante las próximas semanas, en la clase de matemáticas aprenderemos sobre figuras tridimensionales y patrones geométricos.

Llevaré a casa tareas con actividades para identificar y combinar figuras geométricas, y para identificar y hacer patrones con figuras.

Este es un ejemplo de la manera como aprenderemos a usar figuras de bloques de patrón para hacer un patrón que se repite.

MODELO Hacer un patrón que se repite

Así es como haremos un patrón de figuras que se repite.

PASO 1 Elige tres bloques de patrón diferentes. Haz una unidad de patrón.

La unidad de patrón es cuadrado, triángulo, trapecio.

PASO 2 Repite la unidad de patrón al menos tres veces.

Pistas

Extender el patrón

Los estudiantes pueden usar una unidad de patrón para extender el patrón. Para hallar la onceava figura de este patrón, los estudiantes pueden ver las tres repeticiones de la unidad de patrón, y luego contar dos figuras más para hallar que la onceava figura es un triángulo.

Actividad

Pida a su hijo(a) que trace tres figuras diferentes para hacer una unidad de patrón. Pídale que repita la unidad al menos tres veces, para hacer un patrón que se repite.

Name _____

Identify Solid Shapes

Name the solid shape that the object is shaped like.

1.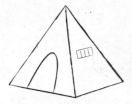

square
pyramid

2.

_____

3.

_____

4.

_____

Name the solid shape. Then write the number of faces, edges, and vertices.

5.

_____

_____ faces

_____ edges

_____ vertices

6.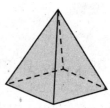

_____

_____ faces

_____ edges

_____ vertices

Problem Solving REAL WORLD

7. Lou found a block shaped like a rectangular prism. How many faces does the block have?

_____

8. Nadine traces a solid shape that has 4 triangles and 1 square as faces. What shape does Nadine trace?

_____

Lesson Check

1. Which solid shape does the object look like?

Ⓐ cone   Ⓒ cylinder

Ⓑ cube   Ⓓ sphere

2. How many vertices does this solid shape have?

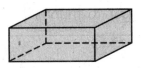

Ⓐ 4   Ⓒ 8

Ⓑ 6   Ⓓ 12

Spiral Review

3. Gwen has 12 flowers and 4 vases. She puts an equal number of flowers in each vase. How many flowers does Gwen put in each vase? **(Lesson 8.2)**

Ⓐ 16

Ⓑ 8

Ⓒ 4

Ⓓ 3

4. Which model shows the greatest fraction shaded? **(Lesson 10.1)**

Ⓐ 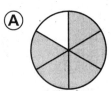   Ⓒ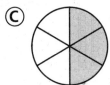

Ⓑ 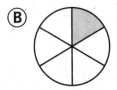   Ⓓ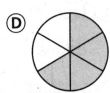

5. Which of the following shapes is a polygon? **(Lesson 11.3)**

Ⓐ   Ⓒ

Ⓑ    Ⓓ

6. Lindsay flew 2,576 miles to Phoenix. Rounded to the nearest thousand, how many miles did she fly? **(Lesson 1.7)**

Ⓐ 2,000 miles

Ⓑ 2,500 miles

Ⓒ 2,600 miles

Ⓓ 3,000 miles

Name _____

Model Solid Shapes

Name a solid shape that can be made from the pattern.

1.

2.
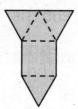

3.
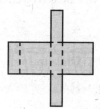

cone
_____

_____

_____

Draw a line to match the pattern with the solid shape.

4.
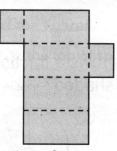

5.
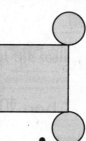

6.
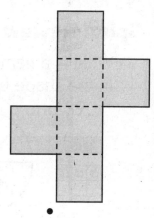

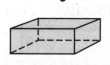

Problem Solving REAL WORLD

7. Kareem makes a cardboard house in art class. He makes a solid shape for the house from the net at the right. What solid shape is like the house?

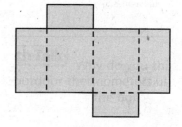

_____

Lesson Check

1. How many rectangles are in a net of a rectangular prism?

- Ⓐ 4
- Ⓑ 6
- Ⓒ 8
- Ⓓ 12

2. Which solid shape can be made from this pattern?

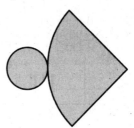

- Ⓐ cone
- Ⓒ rectangular prism
- Ⓑ cube
- Ⓓ square pyramid

Spiral Review

3. What is a name for the equal parts in the shape below? (Lesson 9.1)

- Ⓐ thirds
- Ⓒ sixths
- Ⓑ fourths
- Ⓓ eighths

4. Which model shows a fraction greater than $\frac{1}{2}$ shaded? (Lesson 10.2)

Ⓐ 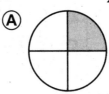   Ⓒ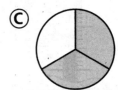

Ⓑ 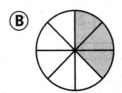   Ⓓ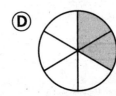

5. Mrs. Mott has 63 tomato plants. She wants to plant 7 rows of tomatoes with an equal number in each row. How many tomato plants should she plant in each row?

(Lesson 8.5)

- Ⓐ 7
- Ⓒ 9
- Ⓑ 8
- Ⓓ 70

6. How many lines of symmetry does the shape below appear to have?

(Lesson 11.10)

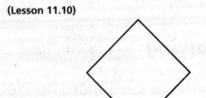

- Ⓐ 0
- Ⓒ 4
- Ⓑ 2
- Ⓓ 8

Name _____

Combine Solid Shapes

Name the solid shapes you could use to model the real world object.

1.

2.

3.

sphere,
rectangular
prism

_____   _____

_____   _____

_____   _____

Name the solid shapes that were combined to make the shape.

4.

5.

6.

_____   _____   _____

_____   _____   _____

Problem Solving REAL WORLD

7. Darren combines a cube and square pyramid. Draw a picture to show the new shape.

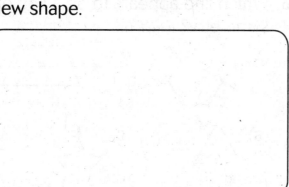

8. Liza cuts a cube in half. What two shapes does she make?

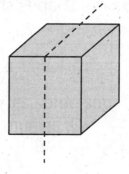

_____

Lesson Check

1. Which new shape was made by combining a cube and a cone?

   Ⓐ

   Ⓒ

   Ⓑ

   Ⓓ

2. Which solid shapes could be used to make a model of the desk?

   Ⓐ square pyramid, spheres

   Ⓑ rectangular prisms, cones

   Ⓒ cube, cylinders

   Ⓓ rectangular prisms, cylinders

Spiral Review

3. Which of the fractions is the greatest? (Lesson 10.3)

   Ⓐ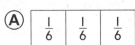

   Ⓑ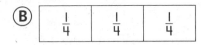

   Ⓒ
$\frac{1}{8}$	$\frac{1}{8}$	$\frac{1}{8}$

   Ⓓ
$\frac{1}{5}$	$\frac{1}{5}$	$\frac{1}{5}$

4. Mika watches a movie. The movie begins at 3:20 P.M. and ends at 5:35 P.M. How long does the movie last? (Lesson 3.4)

   Ⓐ 1 hour 15 minutes

   Ⓑ 2 hours 5 minutes

   Ⓒ 2 hours 15 minutes

   Ⓓ 2 hours 35 minutes

5. Which pair of shapes shows a slide? (Lesson 11.12)

   Ⓐ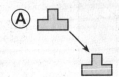

   Ⓒ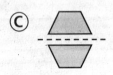

   Ⓑ

   Ⓓ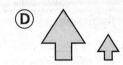

6. Which line appears to be a line of symmetry? (Lesson 11.9)

   Ⓐ

   Ⓒ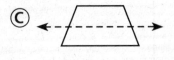

   Ⓑ

   Ⓓ

Identify Relationships

Name a solid shape that has the view shown.

1.

2.

3.

rectangular

prism

_____   _____   _____

Draw two views of the solid shape.

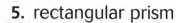

4. square pyramid

5. rectangular prism

6. cube

Problem Solving REAL WORLD

7. Hakim uses a stamp pad and solid shapes to make a border of rectangles and squares around a painting. Name two solid shapes he could use to make the border.

_____

_____

_____

8. Marissa pressed blocks into clay to make a pattern of shapes. She made a *circle, triangle, circle* pattern unit. Name two blocks she could have used to make the pattern.

_____

_____

_____

Lesson Check

1. Which solid shape could have this view?

- Ⓐ sphere
- Ⓒ square pyramid
- Ⓑ cube
- Ⓓ rectangular prism

2. Which could be a view of a cone?

Ⓐ 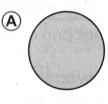 Ⓒ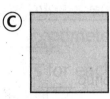

Ⓑ  Ⓓ

Spiral Review

3. Harrison made the line plot below to show how many home runs each player on his team made.

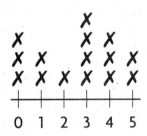

Number of Home Runs

How many players hit 3 home runs? (Lesson 4.7)

- Ⓐ 1
- Ⓒ 3
- Ⓑ 2
- Ⓓ 4

4. Ms. Townsend has 48 markers. She divides them equally among 8 students. How many markers does each student receive? (Lesson 8.6)

- Ⓐ 5
- Ⓑ 6
- Ⓒ 7
- Ⓓ 8

5. Four friends equally share 3 apples. How much of an apple does each person receive? (Lesson 9.2)

- Ⓐ 3 sixths
- Ⓒ 2 halves
- Ⓑ 4 thirds
- Ⓓ 3 fourths

6. Kalisha drew a cube. How many faces does a cube have? (Lesson 12.1)

- Ⓐ 5
- Ⓒ 8
- Ⓑ 6
- Ⓓ 12

Name _____

Patterns with Shapes

Circle the pattern unit. Draw the next two shapes.

1.

2. ○ ▽ ○ ○ ○ ▽ ○ ○ ▽ ○ ○ ___ ___

Write a rule to describe the pattern.

3.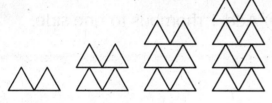

_____

_____

4.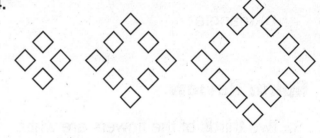

_____

_____

Problem Solving REAL WORLD

5. A growing pattern has 2 triangles, then 4 triangles, then 6 triangles, then 8 triangles. What rule can you use to describe the pattern?

_____

6. Draw a repeating pattern using a square and a triangle.

Lesson Check

1. Find the pattern unit. What is the thirteenth shape?

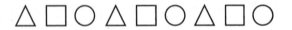

- (A) square
- (B) circle
- (C) rectangle
- (D) triangle

2. Look at the pattern. Which rule describes the pattern?

- (A) Add 1 triangle to one side.
- (B) Add 1 rhombus to each side.
- (C) Add 1 triangle to each side.
- (D) Add 1 rhombus to one side.

Spiral Review

3. Two-thirds of the flowers are white. How many flowers are white? (Lesson 9.7)

- (A) 4
- (C) 2
- (B) 3
- (D) 1

4. Divide. (Lesson 7.4)

$5\overline{)35}$

- (A) 5
- (C) 7
- (B) 6
- (D) 8

5. Which fraction is less than $\frac{1}{2}$?

(Lesson 10.2)

- (A) $\frac{2}{6}$
- (B) $\frac{3}{5}$
- (C) $\frac{5}{8}$
- (D) $\frac{3}{4}$

6. Caitlin completed $\frac{3}{4}$ of the race. Ashley completed $\frac{3}{6}$ of the race. Which comparison is correct?

(Lesson 10.3)

- (A) $\frac{3}{4} > \frac{3}{6}$
- (B) $\frac{3}{6} > \frac{3}{4}$
- (C) $\frac{3}{4} < \frac{3}{6}$
- (D) $\frac{3}{4} = \frac{3}{6}$

Name _____

Make a Pattern

Look at the pattern. Draw the next shape. What is the pattern unit?

1.

_____

2.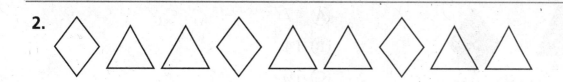

_____

3. **Here are two combined trapezoids. How many sides will five combined trapezoids have?** _____ **Complete the table.**

Trapezoids	Sides
1	
2	
3	
4	
5	

Problem Solving REAL WORLD

4. Fiona makes a pattern of squares by combining toothpicks. The first two squares are shown. How many toothpicks does Fiona need to make a row with 5 squares?

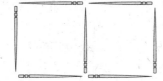

_____

5. Ken makes a pattern by combining two hexagon blocks. The first two shapes are shown. If he continues the pattern, how many sides will 6 hexagons in a row have?

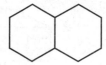

_____

Lesson Check

Use this pattern for 1–2.

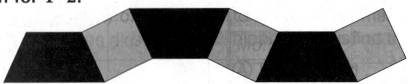

1. If the pattern continues, what shape will the ninth figure be?

   Ⓐ

   Ⓒ

   Ⓑ

   Ⓓ

2. If the pattern continues, how many sides will 7 combined shapes have?

   Ⓐ 7

   Ⓑ 14

   Ⓒ 16

   Ⓓ 28

Spiral Review

3. Tina shares 56 baseball cards equally with 7 friends. How many cards does each friend receive?

   (Lesson 8.5)

   Ⓐ 7   Ⓒ 9

   Ⓑ 8   Ⓓ 10

4. Which fraction names the shaded part? (Lesson 9.4)

   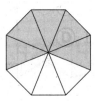

   Ⓐ $\frac{3}{8}$ Ⓑ $\frac{5}{8}$ Ⓒ $\frac{3}{5}$ Ⓓ $\frac{8}{5}$

5. Which solid shape could have a square as one of its views? (Lesson 12.4)

   Ⓐ   Ⓒ

   Ⓑ   Ⓓ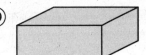

6. What is the next shape in the pattern below? (Lesson 12.5)

   Ⓐ ☆   Ⓒ ⬭

   Ⓑ △   Ⓓ ☐

Name _____

Find a Pattern · Plane Shapes

Solve.

1. Rosalie is making the pattern below. How many tiles will be in the sixth figure?

_____**13 tiles**_____

2. Derek is making a pattern using counters. He has 65 counters. Does he have enough counters to make the next figure in the pattern? How many counters are in the next figure?

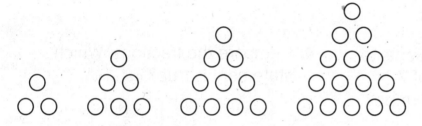

_____

_____

3. Charlie makes this pattern. What shape will the fifteenth figure in the pattern be?

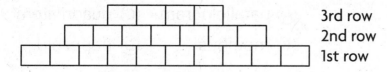

_____

4. Kirby is making a necklace with some square beads, 8 star beads, and 6 triangle beads. She uses twice as many square beads as triangle beads. How many beads does she use in all?

_____

5. Desiree is making the design below on a scarf using stamp blocks. What is a rule for her pattern?

3rd row
2nd row
1st row

_____

Lesson Check

1. Deon is making the pattern below on a belt. What will he make next to continue the pattern?

   (A) 1 sun, 3 stars

   (B) 1 sun, 4 stars

   (C) 2 suns, 3 stars

   (D) 2 suns, 4 stars

2. Latoya is making a pattern with cubes. She uses the rule *subtract 4*. She puts 20 cubes in the first row. How many cubes will Latoya put in the fourth row ?

   (A) 16

   (B) 12

   (C) 8

   (D) 4

Spiral Review

3. Jaycc has 28 books. He wants to put the books in groups of 7. How many groups will there be?

   (Lesson 7.2)

   (A) 4   (C) 21

   (B) 5   (D) 35

4. Compare the fractions. Which statement is true? (Lesson 10.4)

$\frac{1}{3}$				$\frac{1}{3}$	
$\frac{1}{8}$	$\frac{1}{8}$	$\frac{1}{8}$	$\frac{1}{8}$		

   (A) $\frac{1}{8} > \frac{1}{3}$ (C) $\frac{4}{8} < \frac{2}{3}$

   (B) $\frac{4}{8} = \frac{2}{3}$ (D) $\frac{4}{8} > \frac{2}{3}$

5. How many lines of symmetry does this letter appear to have? (Lesson 11.10)

H

   (A) 1

   (B) 2

   (C) 3

   (D) 4

6. Maya used toothpicks to make the shape below. Which is NOT a name for the shape she made? (Lesson 11.5)

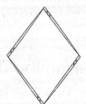

   (A) parallelogram   (C) quadrilateral

   (B) rhombus   (D) trapezoid

Chapter 12 Extra Practice

Lesson 12.1

Name the solid shape that the object is shaped like.

1.

2.

3.

_____

_____

_____

4.

5.

6.

_____

_____

_____

Lesson 12.2

Name a solid shape that can be made from the net.

1.

2.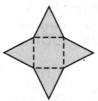

3.

_____

_____

_____

Lesson 12.3

Name the solid shapes that were combined to make the shape.

1.

2.

3.

_____

_____

_____

Lesson 12.4

Name a solid shape that has the view shown.

1.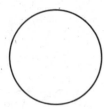

2.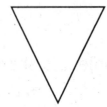

3.

_____   _____   _____

_____   _____   _____

Lesson 12.5 (pp. 499–502)

Circle the pattern unit. Draw the missing shapes.

1. 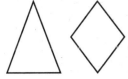  __  ____

Lesson 12.6

1. Here are two combined rhombuses.

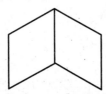

How many sides will 7 combined rhombuses have? _____

Lesson 12.7

1. Jannelle uses square tiles to make a pattern. The first 4 rows are shown. How many tiles in all will she need to complete 6 rows?

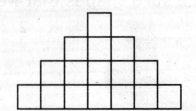

_____

School-Home Letter

© Houghton Mifflin Harcourt Publishing Company

Dear Family,

During the next few weeks, our math class will be learning about measurement. We will learn to measure length, capacity, weight, and mass. We will also learn to find the perimeter and area of shapes.

You can expect to see homework that provides practice with measurement.

Here is a sample of how your child will be taught to find perimeter.

Vocabulary

length The measurement of the distance between two points

foot (ft) A customary unit used to measure length or distance that is equal to 12 inches

yard (yd) A customary unit used to measure length or distance that is equal to 3 feet

meter (m) A metric unit used to measure length or distance that is equal to 100 centimeters

perimeter The distance around a shape

🔒 MODEL Find Perimeter

These are two ways to find perimeter.

Count squares.

Find the perimeter of the shape by counting the sides.

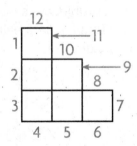

Perimeter is the distance around a shape.

So, the perimeter is 12 units.

Use addition.

Find the perimeter of the rectangle.

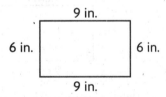

Perimeter = length + width + length + width

Add: 9 + 6 + 9 + 6 = 30 inches

So, the perimeter is 30 inches.

Tips

Using Addition with Rectangles.

Sometimes not all lengths of the sides of a rectangle are given. You can use properties of rectangles to find the missing sides.

Activity

Have your child practice finding the perimeter of items around the house. Find and measure the sides of items that have plane shapes, such as an envelope, a place mat, a square potholder, a pennant, or a rug.

Capítulo 13

Carta para la casa

Querida familia,

Durante las próximas semanas, en la clase de matemáticas aprenderemos acerca de la medición. Aprenderemos a medir la longitud, la capacidad, el peso y la masa. También aprenderemos a hallar el perímetro y el área de las figuras.

Llevaré a la casa tareas que sirven para practicar la medición.

Este es un ejemplo de la manera como aprenderemos a hallar el perímetro.

Vocabulario

longitud La medida de la distancia entre dos puntos

metro Una unidad del sistema métrico que se usa para medir longitud o distancia y que es igual a 100 centímetros.

perímetro La distancia alrededor de una figura

pie (ft) Una unidad del sistema usual que se usa para medir longitud o distancia y que es igual a 12 pulgadas

yarda (yd) Una unidad del sistema usual que se usa para medir longitud o distancia y que es igual a 3 pies

---

🔑 MODELO Hallar el perímetro

Estas son dos maneras de hallar el perímetro.

Contar cuadrados.	Usar la suma.
Halla el perímetro de la figura contando los lados	Halla el perímetro del rectángulo.

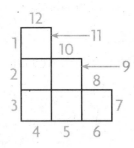

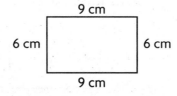

Pistas

Usar suma con rectángulos

A veces no se dan las longitudes de los lados de un rectángulo. Puedes usar propiedades de rectángulos para hallar los lados que faltan.

El perímetro es la distancia alrededor de una figura.

Por tanto, el perímetro es 12 unidades.

Perímetro = largo + ancho + largo + ancho

Sumo: 9 + 6 + 9 + 6 = 30 centímetros

Por tanto, el perímetro es 30 pulgadas.

Actividad

Pida a su hijo que practique hallando el perímetro de algunos objetos de la casa. Hallen y midan los lados de objetos que tengan formas planas, como un sobre, un individual para la mesa, un agarrador de ollas cuadrado, un banderín o un tapete.

Name _____

Customary Units for Length

Choose the unit you would use to measure the length. Write _inch_, _foot_, _yard_, or _mile_.

1.

2.

3.

foot

_____   _____   _____

4. Any length that measures 3 feet can be renamed as 1 yard. Suppose the length of the black line is 9 feet. What is that length renamed as yards?

9 feet = _____ yards

5. Any length that measures 12 inches can be renamed as 1 foot. Suppose the length of the black line is 36 inches. What is that length as feet?

36 inches = _____ feet

Problem Solving

6. Nina measured a bookshelf and said that it was 2 yards wide. Carly measured the same bookshelf and said it was 2 feet wide. The bookshelf is 24 inches wide. Who is correct?

_____

7. Mike is looking at a map of the United States. His family is driving to the next state to visit relatives. Which customary unit of measure will they use to tell how far they will drive?

_____

Lesson Check

1. Which customary unit of measure would be the best to measure the length of a classroom?

   Ⓐ milliliter

   Ⓑ foot

   Ⓒ mile

   Ⓓ liter

2. Which customary unit of measure would be the best to measure the width of a clipboard?

   Ⓐ inch

   Ⓑ yard

   Ⓒ mile

   Ⓓ liter

Spiral Review

3. Which of the following is a pentagon? (Lesson 11.3)

   Ⓐ   Ⓒ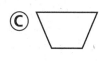

   Ⓑ 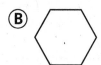   Ⓓ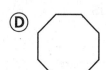

4. The roller coaster has 72 seats. There are 9 seats in each row. How many rows of seats does the roller coaster have? (Lesson 8.7)

   Ⓐ 7

   Ⓑ 8

   Ⓒ 9

   Ⓓ 10

5. What fraction names the shaded part? (Lesson 9.4)

   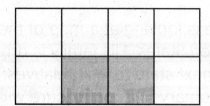

   Ⓐ $\frac{1}{8}$ Ⓒ $\frac{2}{4}$

   Ⓑ $\frac{2}{8}$ Ⓓ $\frac{4}{8}$

6. Which symbol makes the statement true? (Lesson 10.2)

   $$\frac{3}{10} \; \bullet \; \frac{1}{5}$$

   Ⓐ >

   Ⓑ <

   Ⓒ =

   Ⓓ none

Name _____

Measure to the Nearest Half Inch

Measure the length to the nearest half inch.

1.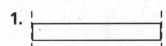

$1\frac{1}{2}$ inches

2.

_____ inches

3.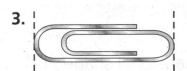

_____ inches

4.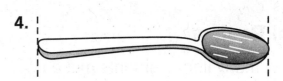

_____ inches

Use a ruler. Draw a line for the length.

5. $3\frac{1}{2}$ inches

Problem Solving REAL WORLD

6. Catherine is measuring the width of one of her books. It is $3\frac{1}{2}$ inches wide. This length is between which two inch marks on the ruler?

_____

_____

7. Eddie measures the length of his pencil sharpener. It is $1\frac{1}{2}$ inches long. This length is between which two inch marks on the ruler?

_____

_____

Lesson Check

1. Measure to the nearest half inch.

- Ⓐ 1 inch
- Ⓒ 2 inches
- Ⓑ $1\frac{1}{2}$ inches
- Ⓓ $2\frac{1}{2}$ inches

2. Measure to the nearest half inch.

- Ⓐ $\frac{1}{2}$ inch
- Ⓒ $1\frac{1}{2}$ inches
- Ⓑ 1 inch
- Ⓓ 2 inches

Spiral Review

3. How many line segments make up this shape? **(Lesson 11.1)**

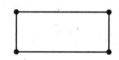

- Ⓐ 4
- Ⓑ 3
- Ⓒ 2
- Ⓓ 1

4. What three-dimensional shape did Vicki draw? **(Lesson 12.1)**

- Ⓐ rectangular prism
- Ⓑ square pyramid
- Ⓒ cube
- Ⓓ cylinder

5. There are 20 students in the third grade chorus. There are an equal number of students in each of 2 rows. How many students are in each row? **(Lesson 7.3)**

- Ⓐ 40
- Ⓑ 20
- Ⓒ 10
- Ⓓ 5

6. Which fraction is equivalent to $\frac{6}{10}$? **(Lesson 10.7)**

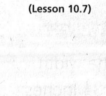

- Ⓐ $\frac{1}{5}$
- Ⓒ $\frac{3}{5}$
- Ⓑ $\frac{2}{5}$
- Ⓓ $\frac{6}{5}$

© Houghton Mifflin Harcourt Publishing Company

Name _____

Measure to the Nearest Fourth Inch

Essential Question How can you measure length to the nearest fourth inch?

Activity You have learned to use a ruler to measure length to the nearest half inch.

You can also measure an object to the nearest fourth inch. What is the length of the crayon to the nearest fourth inch?

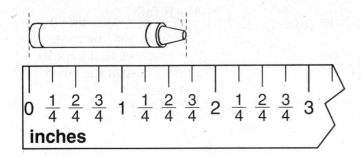

Line up the left end of the crayon with the zero mark on the ruler.

The tip of the crayon is between the

whole-inch marks _____ and _____.

The tip of the crayon is between the

fourth-inch marks _____ and _____.

The tip is closest to the _____ inch mark.

So, to the nearest fourth inch, the crayon

is _____ inches long.

• **What if** you want to have a measurement that is closer to an object's actual length? **Explain** why measuring to the nearest fourth inch is better than measuring to the nearest half inch.

_____

_____

The fourth-inch marks on a ruler divide each whole inch into four equal parts.

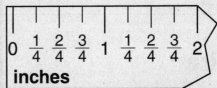

You can think of fraction strips to help.

| $\frac{1}{4}$ | $\frac{1}{4}$ | $\frac{1}{4}$ | $\frac{1}{4}$ |

| $\frac{1}{4}$ | $\frac{1}{4}$ | $\frac{1}{4}$ | $\frac{1}{4}$ |

$\frac{4}{4}$ inch = 1 inch

$\frac{2}{4}$ inch = $\frac{1}{2}$ inch

| $\frac{1}{2}$ | |
| $\frac{1}{4}$ | $\frac{1}{4}$ |

Math Talk Can an object measure 2 inches when it is measured to the nearest fourth inch? **Explain.**

Think About It

1. **Apply** Measure the length of 10 crayons to the nearest fourth inch. Make a line plot. Draw an X for each crayon.

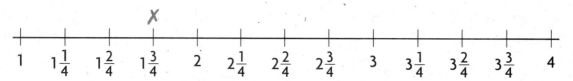

Length of Crayons Measured to the Nearest Fourth Inch

2. **Describe** any patterns you see in your line plot.

_____

_____

> **Math Talk** How do you think your line plot compares to line plots your classmates made? **Explain.**

Practice

Measure the length to the nearest fourth inch.

3.

The end is between the fourth-inch marks _____ and _____.

The length to the nearest fourth inch is _____ inches.

4.

The length to the nearest fourth inch is _____ inches.

5. Draw a line that is $3\frac{3}{4}$ inches when measured to the nearest fourth inch.

6. ⭐ **Test Prep** What is the length of the pasta to the nearest fourth inch?

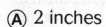

Ⓐ 2 inches   Ⓒ $2\frac{1}{2}$ inches

Ⓑ $2\frac{1}{4}$ inches   Ⓓ $2\frac{3}{4}$ inches

Name _____

Metric Units for Length

**Choose the unit you would use to measure the length.
Write *millimeter*, *centimeter*, *meter*, or *kilometer*.**

1.

millimeter or centimeter

2. Glennville

Wallistown

_____

3.

_____

4. distance from your knee to your foot

_____

5. distance traveled on a field trip

_____

6. height of a door

_____

7. length of a driveway

_____

8. length of a ladybug

_____

9. length of a paintbrush

_____

Problem Solving REAL WORLD

10. Anna takes her brother to the park to play. It takes her 10 minutes to walk to the park. Is the park 1 centimeter, 1 meter, or 1 kilometer from Anna's house?

_____

11. At the doctor's office, Henry will get his height measured. Do you think Henry's height will be 100 centimeters, 100 meters, or 100 kilometers?

_____

Lesson Check

1. Which metric unit of measure would be the best to measure the length of an airplane?

   (A) centimeter

   (B) decimeter

   (C) meter

   (D) mile

2. Which metric unit of measure would be the best to measure the length of a piece of spaghetti?

   (A) centimeter

   (B) decimeter

   (C) meter

   (D) mile

Spiral Review

3. What is the name of this polygon?
   (Lesson 11.3)

   (A) triangle

   (B) hexagon

   (C) quadrilateral

   (D) pentagon

4. Which multiplication sentence does the array show? (Lesson 5.7)

   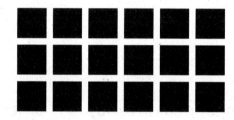

   (A) $2 \times 6 = 12$

   (B) $3 \times 6 = 18$

   (C) $3 \times 7 = 21$

   (D) $4 \times 6 = 24$

5. Melissa had an appointment with Dr. Mundo fifteen minutes after nine. What is another way to write this time? (Lesson 3.1)

   (A) 8:45

   (B) 9:00

   (C) 9:15

   (D) 9:45

6. Which symbol makes the statement true? (Lesson 10.3)

   $$\frac{7}{8} \bigcirc \frac{7}{10}$$

   (A) <

   (B) >

   (C) =

   (D) none

Name _____

Centimeters, Decimeters, and Meters

Measure the length to the nearest centimeter.

1.

   __3__ centimeters

2.

   _____ centimeters

Circle the best estimate.

3. width of eye glasses

   12 cm   12 dm   12 m

4. height of a palm tree

   6 cm   6 dm   6 m

5. width of a CD case

   16 cm   16 dm   16 m

6. length of a shoe box

   3 cm   3 dm   3 m

Use a ruler. Draw a line for the length.

7. 5 centimeters

Problem Solving REAL WORLD

8. Ben says his computer screen is 5 decimeters long. Kim says her computer screen is 52 centimeters long. Whose computer screen is longer? **Explain** how you know.

   _____

   _____

   _____

9. David's poster is 62 centimeters long. Ted's poster is 7 decimeters long. Whose poster is longer? **Explain**.

   _____

   _____

   _____

Lesson Check

1. Which of these is the best estimate for the width of a door?

   Ⓐ 1 centimeter

   Ⓑ 1 decimeter

   Ⓒ 1 meter

   Ⓓ 1 kilometer

2. Which of these is the best estimate for the length of a toothpick?

   Ⓐ 5 centimeters

   Ⓑ 5 decimeters

   Ⓒ 5 meters

   Ⓓ 5 kilometers

Spiral Review

3. Which shape does NOT appear to be congruent to the hexagon? **(Lesson 11.8)**

Ⓐ   Ⓒ

Ⓑ   Ⓓ

4. How many triangles are in a net of a square pyramid? **(Lesson 12.2)**

   Ⓐ 0

   Ⓑ 1

   Ⓒ 4

   Ⓓ 5

5. Which metric unit of measure would be best to measure the length around a playground? **(Lesson 13.3)**

   Ⓐ millimeter

   Ⓑ centimeter

   Ⓒ meter

   Ⓓ kilometer

6. Stephanie has $2.37 saved in her coin bank. Which amount of money is less than Stephanie's amount? **(Lesson 3.7)**

   Ⓐ $3.52

   Ⓑ $2.40

   Ⓒ $2.73

   Ⓓ $2.23

Name _____

Investigate: Model Perimeter

Find the perimeter of the shape. Each unit is 1 centimeter.

1.

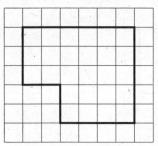

_____ **22** centimeters

2.

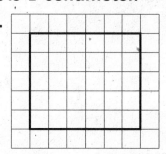

_____ centimeters

3.

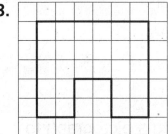

_____ centimeters

4.

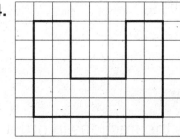

_____ centimeters

Find the perimeter.

5. A shape has two sides that are 4 meters and two sides that are 2 meters.

_____ meters

6. A shape has sides that measure 4 inches, 7 inches, 1 inch, and 3 inches.

_____ inches

Problem Solving REAL WORLD

7. Patrick draws a square that measures 5 centimeters on each side. What is the perimeter?

_____

8. Jillian makes a shape using modeling clay. The sides are 8 inches, 3 inches, 5 inches, and 4 inches. What is the perimeter?

_____

Lesson Check

1. Find the perimeter of the shape. Each unit is 1 centimeter.

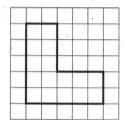

   Ⓐ 14 centimeters

   Ⓑ 16 centimeters

   Ⓒ 18 centimeters

   Ⓓ 20 centimeters

2. Find the perimeter of the shape. Each unit is 1 centimeter.

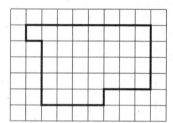

   Ⓐ 19 centimeters

   Ⓑ 26 centimeters

   Ⓒ 33 centimeters

   Ⓓ 55 centimeters

Spiral Review

3. Which shows the fractions in order from least to greatest? **(Lesson 10.5)**

$$\frac{1}{2}, \frac{1}{5}, \frac{7}{10}$$

   Ⓐ $\frac{1}{5} < \frac{7}{10} < \frac{1}{2}$

   Ⓑ $\frac{1}{5} < \frac{1}{2} < \frac{7}{10}$

   Ⓒ $\frac{7}{10} < \frac{1}{5} < \frac{1}{2}$

   Ⓓ $\frac{1}{2} < \frac{7}{10} < \frac{1}{5}$

4. Edward is making a pictograph to show his friends' favorite types of sports. He plans to use a soccer ball for every 2 people. How many soccer balls will he need to show that 6 people chose tennis? **(Lesson 4.3)**

   Ⓐ 2   Ⓒ 6

   Ⓑ 3   Ⓓ 8

5. Which pair of shapes shows a slide? **(Lesson 11.12)**

   Ⓐ S Ƨ   Ⓒ S S

   Ⓑ S s   Ⓓ S ꙅ

6. Which number completes the table? **(Lesson 6.9)**

Number of Tickets	1	2	3	4	5
Cost (in dollars)	3	6	▪	12	15

   Ⓐ 3   Ⓒ 12

   Ⓑ 9   Ⓓ 18

Name _____

Measure Perimeter

Use a centimeter ruler to find the perimeter.

1.

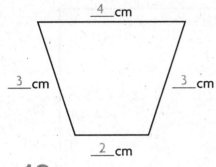

___4___ cm

___3___ cm   ___3___ cm

___2___ cm

___12___ centimeters

2.

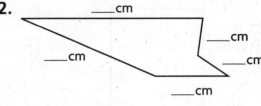

_____ cm

_____ cm

_____ cm

_____ cm

_____ cm

_____ centimeters

Use an inch ruler to find the perimeter.

3.

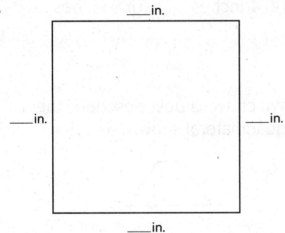

_____ in.

_____ in.   _____ in.

_____ in.

_____ inches

4.

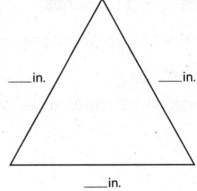

_____ in.   _____ in.

_____ in.

_____ inches

Problem Solving REAL WORLD

5. Evan has a square sticker that measures 3 inches on each side. What is the perimeter of the sticker?

_____

6. Sophie draws a shape that has 6 sides. Each side is 2 centimeters. What is the perimeter of the shape?

_____

Lesson Check

1. Use an inch ruler to find the perimeter.

  (A) 4 inches   (C) 6 inches
  (B) 5 inches   (D) 7 inches

2. Use an inch ruler to find the perimeter.

  (A) 2 inches   (C) 6 inches
  (B) 4 inches   (D) 8 inches

Spiral Review

3. Describe the dashed lines. (Lesson 11.4)

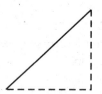

  (A) parallel   (C) perpendicular
  (B) rhombus   (D) equilateral

4. Which word best describes the quadrilateral shown? (Lesson 11.5)

  (A) trapezoid   (C) square
  (B) triangle   (D) parallelogram

5. Jamie's family ate $1\frac{3}{4}$ pies for dessert. Which shows this mixed number as a fraction greater than 1? (Lesson 9.5)

  (A) $\frac{3}{4}$ (C) $\frac{8}{4}$
  (B) $\frac{7}{4}$ (D) $\frac{13}{4}$

6. Which shows the mixed numbers in order from greatest to least? (Lesson 10.5)

  (A) $1\frac{3}{4} > 1\frac{2}{8} > 2\frac{1}{4}$

  (B) $2\frac{1}{4} < 1\frac{3}{4} < 1\frac{2}{8}$

  (C) $1\frac{2}{8} > 1\frac{3}{4} > 2\frac{1}{4}$

  (D) $2\frac{1}{4} > 1\frac{3}{4} > 1\frac{2}{8}$

Change Customary Units for Length

Essential Question How can you change a customary unit for length to a smaller or larger unit?

> **Remember**
> 12 inches = 1 foot
> 3 feet = 1 yard

Real World Evan drew a line 18 inches long. He knew it was longer than 1 foot. How can he rename the length in feet and inches?

One Way Draw a picture.

18 inches
_____

Each ☐ represents 1 inch, so 12 ☐s represent 1 foot.

Count 12 ☐s and draw a line to show 1 foot.

There are _____ ☐s left over.

So, Evan's line is _____ foot _____ inches long.

Another Way Use a number line.

Evan is 53 inches tall. How tall is Evan in feet and inches?

You can use a number line to mark length in feet and inches.

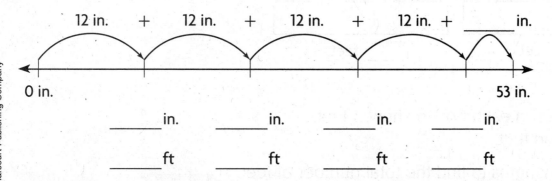

Count by 12s to show each foot on the number line.
Count the number of feet. Then count the left over inches.

So, Evan is _____ feet _____ inches tall.

Activity

Materials ■ inch ruler ■ measuring tape

STEP 1 Write your height in inches. _____ inches

STEP 2 Use the number line to rename your height using feet and inches.

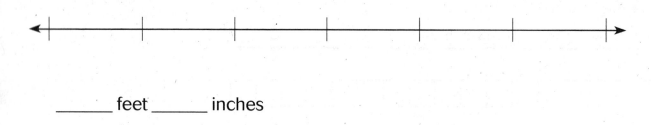

_____ feet _____ inches

Try This! Change to smaller units.

You have learned to change smaller units to larger units. You can also change larger units to smaller units.

The form on the right is used to order wood at Harry's Hardware Store. Jared needs to order boards that are 2 yards long. Rename the 2 yards as feet to fill out the order form.

STEP 1 Each box shows a board that is 1 yard long. Label each length in yards.

```
┌─────────────────────────┐
│ Harry's                 │
│ Hardware Store          │
│                         │
│        Order Form       │
│                         │
│  Name Jared _____ │
│                         │
│  Length of wood ____feet│
└─────────────────────────┘
```

___ yard   ___ yard

┌──────────────┐ ┌──────────────┐
│   │ │   │
└──────────────┘ └──────────────┘

___ feet   ___ feet

STEP 2 Draw lines in each box to show 3 feet. Label the length in feet.

STEP 3 Add the lengths to find the total number of feet.

_____ feet + _____ feet = _____ feet

Write the length in the order form.

> **Math Talk** How is changing to smaller units different from changing to larger units?

Name _____

Think About It

1. **Explain** how you can use a number line to change yards to feet.

_____

_____

2. **Explain** how you can rename a measurement in yards and feet as feet.

_____

_____

Practice

3. Rename 25 inches using feet and inches.

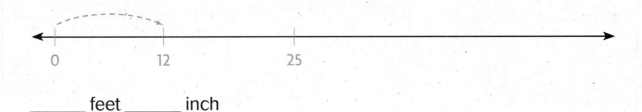

_____ feet _____ inch

4. Rename 8 feet using yards and feet.

_____ yards _____ feet

5. Rename 3 yards as feet.

_____ feet

Problem Solving • Real World

6. Phil measured the height of the door in his room. It is 80 inches high. What is this height renamed as feet and inches?

_____

7. **H.O.T.** Jaime has 1 yard of string. She cut it into 1-foot lengths. Then she cuts each foot in half.

How many pieces of string does Jaime have? _____

How long is each piece in inches? _____

Draw a picture to show your work.

8. Esther bought a painting. It is 2 feet wide. How many inches wide is the painting?

_____

9. Jack found a rope that was 3 feet 4 inches long. How long was the rope in inches?

_____

10. ⭐ **Test Prep** Aaron has a rope that is 4 yards long. How many feet long is the rope?

Ⓐ 4 feet

Ⓑ 12 feet

Ⓒ 36 feet

Ⓓ 48 feet

11. ⭐ **Test Prep** Jennifer's height is 64 inches. How can she rename her height using feet and inches?

Ⓐ 6 feet 4 inches

Ⓑ 5 feet 4 inches

Ⓒ 5 feet

Ⓓ 4 feet 6 inches

Name _____

Find a Pattern · Perimeter

Solve.

Shape	Number of Tiles	Perimeter (in units)
1	1	4
2	3	8
3	5	12

Each side is 1 unit.

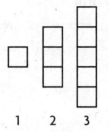

1   2   3

1. What pattern do you see for the number of tiles?

Each shape has 2 more tiles than the one before it.

2. What pattern do you see for the perimeters?

_____

3. How many tiles will be used to make Shape 5?

_____

4. What will the perimeter of Shape 5 be?

_____

5. **What if** the length of each side of the tiles above is 2 feet? What would the perimeter of the fourth shape be?

_____

6. Kevin has a pet-sitting business. The first week he saves $2. The second week he saves $4. The third week he saves $8. If the pattern continues, what will Kevin save in the fifth week?

_____

Lesson Check

1. Dan made the pattern. The first four shapes in the pattern are shown. If Dan continues the pattern, what is the perimeter of the sixth shape? Each side is 1 unit.

Ⓐ 4 units

Ⓑ 6 units

Ⓒ 8 units

Ⓓ 10 units

2. Wesley made this pattern. The first three shapes in the pattern are shown. If he continues the pattern, what is the perimeter of the fifth shape? Each side is 1 unit.

Ⓐ 5 units

Ⓑ 8 units

Ⓒ 10 units

Ⓓ 12 units

Spiral Review

3. Which shape is a polygon? (Lesson 11.3)

Ⓐ   Ⓒ

Ⓑ   Ⓓ

4. How many sides make up the polygon? (Lesson 11.3)

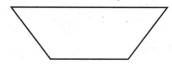

Ⓐ 3   Ⓒ 5

Ⓑ 4   Ⓓ 6

5. Which number completes the fact family? (Lesson 7.9)

$6 \times \blacksquare = 24$

$\blacksquare \times 6 = 24$

$24 \div 6 = \blacksquare$

$24 \div \blacksquare = 6$

Ⓐ 4   Ⓒ 6

Ⓑ 5   Ⓓ 30

6. Steven has 30 pencils. He placed two-fifths of them in his backpack. How many pencils are in his backpack? (Lesson 9.7)

Ⓐ 5

Ⓑ 6

Ⓒ 10

Ⓓ 12

Name _____

Investigate: Find Area

Count to find the area of the shape.

1.

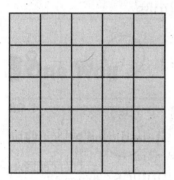

1	4		9	
2	5	7	10	12
3	6	8	11	13

14 square units

2.

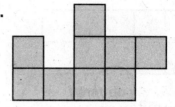

_____ square units

Multiply to find the area of the shape.

3.

_____ square units

4.

_____ square units

5.

_____ square units

6.

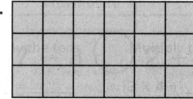

_____ square units

Problem Solving

7. Sasha covers a table with 9 rows of square tiles. There are 6 tiles in each row. What is the area Sasha covered?

_____

8. Zoe makes a design with 3 rows of 7 square tiles. If each tile costs $2, how much does Zoe spend?

_____

Lesson Check

1. What is the area of this rectangle?

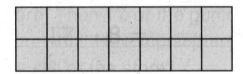

- (A) 2 square units
- (B) 7 square units
- (C) 14 square units
- (D) 16 square units

2. Martin makes 3 designs with square tiles. Each design has 4 rows of 2 tiles. What is the total area of the tiles?

- (A) 24 square units
- (B) 12 square units
- (C) 9 square units
- (D) 8 square units

Spiral Review

3. There are 9 tables in a cafeteria. Each table has 6 chairs. Which expression shows the number of chairs? (Lesson 8.9)

- (A) 9 + 6
- (C) 9 ÷ 6
- (B) 9 × 6
- (D) 9 − 6

4. Ahmed baked 16 muffins. One-fourth of the muffins are blueberry. How many muffins are blueberry muffins? (Lesson 9.7)

- (A) 2
- (C) 6
- (B) 4
- (D) 8

5. What is the length of the ribbon to the nearest half inch? (Lesson 13.2)

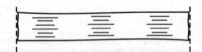

- (A) 1 inch
- (B) $1\frac{1}{2}$ inches
- (C) 2 inches
- (D) $2\frac{1}{2}$ inches

6. Kara makes this pattern with tiles. If she continues the pattern, how many tiles should she place in the fifth row? (Lesson 12.7)

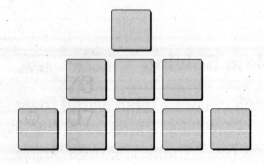

- (A) 6
- (C) 8
- (B) 7
- (D) 9

Name _____

Relate Perimeter and Area

Find the perimeter and the area.
Tell which rectangle has a greater area.

1.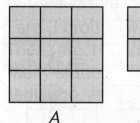

A   *B*

2.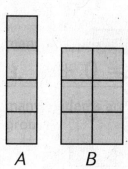

A   *B*

Rectangle *A*:

perimeter = __12__ units

area = __9__ square units

Rectangle *B*:

perimeter = _____ units

area = _____ square units

Rectangle _____ has a greater area.

Rectangle *A*:

perimeter = _____ units

area = _____ square units

Rectangle *B*:

perimeter = _____ units

area = _____ square units

Rectangle _____ has a greater area.

Problem Solving

3. Tara's bedroom is shaped like a rectangle. It is 9 feet long and 8 feet wide. What is the perimeter and area of her bedroom?

_____

_____

4. Mr. Sanchez has 16 feet of fencing to put around a garden that is shaped like a rectangle. He wants the garden to have the greatest possible area. How long should he make the sides of the garden?

_____

_____

Lesson Check

1. Which shape has a perimeter of 12 units and an area of 8 square units?

Ⓐ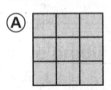

Ⓑ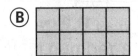

Ⓒ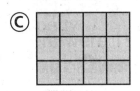

Ⓓ

2. All four of the rectangles below have the same perimeter. Which rectangle has the greatest area?

Ⓐ

Ⓑ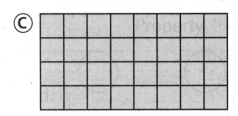

Ⓒ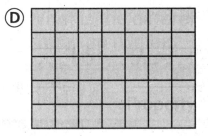

Ⓓ

Spiral Review

3. Kerrie covers a table with 8 rows of square tiles. There are 7 tiles in each row. What is the area that Kerrie covered in square units? (Lesson 13.8)

Ⓐ 15 square units

Ⓑ 35 square units

Ⓒ 42 square units

Ⓓ 56 square units

4. If the pattern continues, what are the next two shapes? (Lesson 12.5)

○△○○△○○△○○△

Ⓐ ○△

Ⓑ □○

Ⓒ ○○

Ⓓ △○

Name _____

Solve Perimeter and Area Problems

Essential Question How can you find the unknown length of a side in a plane shape when you know its perimeter or area?

Real World Chen has 27 feet of fencing to put around his garden. He has already used the lengths of fencing shown below. How much fencing does he have left for the last side?

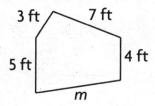

Write an equation for the perimeter.

$5 + 3 +$ ____ $+$ ____ $+ m = 27$

Think: if I knew the length of m, I would add all the side lengths to find the perimeter.

Add the lengths of the sides you know.

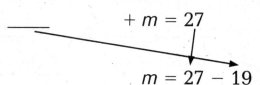

$5 + 3 + 7 + 4 + m = 27$

____ $+ m = 27$

$m = 27 - 19$

Write a related number sentence.

Think: addition and subtraction are inverse operations.

So, Chen has _____ feet of fencing left.

____ $= 27 - 19$

Try This! Find the length of one side of a square.

The square has a perimeter of 20 inches.
What is the length of each side of the square?

Remember

A square has 4 equal sides.

Write a multiplication equation for the perimeter.

$4 \times s = 20$

$4 \times$ _____ $= 20$

Use a multiplication fact you know to solve.

Math Talk **Explain** why you can use multiplication to find the perimeter of a square.

So, the length of each side is _____ inches.

© Houghton Mifflin Harcourt Publishing Company

Area and Unknown Lengths

Lauren has a rectangular rug. The area of her rug is 45 square feet. The width of the rug is 5 feet. What is the length of the rug?

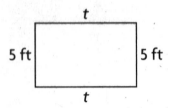

Write an equation for the area.

$t \times$ _____ $=$ _____

Use a multiplication fact you know to solve.

_____ $\times 5 = 45$

So, the length of the rug is _____ feet.

Think About It

1. The perimeter of the shape at the right is 24 yards. **Explain** how you would find the unknown side length. Then find the unknown side length, w.

   _____

   _____

   _____

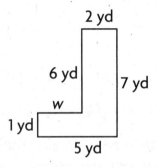

2. The perimeter of the square at the right is 16 centimeters. Would you use an addition or multiplication equation to find the length of one side? **Explain**. Find the side length, b.

   _____

   _____

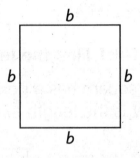

3. **Justify** why you can use an addition equation or a multiplication equation to find the perimeter of a square.

   _____

   _____

   _____

Math Talk **Explain** how you could use division to find the length of a side of a square.

Name _____

Practice

4. Find the unknown side length, n.

Perimeter = 25 centimeters

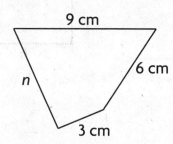

9 cm

n

6 cm

3 cm

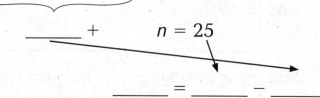

$9 + \underline{\hspace{1cm}} + \underline{\hspace{1cm}} + n = 25$

$\underline{\hspace{1cm}} + \qquad n = 25$

$\underline{\hspace{1cm}} = \underline{\hspace{1cm}} - \underline{\hspace{1cm}}$

$n = \underline{\hspace{1cm}}$ centimeters.

Find the unknown side length.

5.

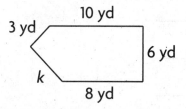

3 yd   10 yd

6 yd

k

8 yd

Perimeter = 32 yards

$k = \underline{\hspace{1cm}}$ yards

6.

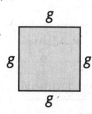

g

g g

g

Area = 81 square inches

$g = \underline{\hspace{1cm}}$ inches

7. H.O.T.

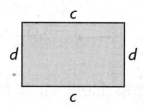

c

d d

c

Area = 8 square feet

Perimeter = 12 feet

$c = \underline{\hspace{1cm}}$ feet $d = \underline{\hspace{1cm}}$ feet

8. **Explain** how you found the unknown side lengths in Exercise 7.

_____

_____

_____

_____

Problem Solving • Real World

9. Latesha wants to make a border with ribbon around a shape she made and sketched at the right. She will use 44 centimeters of ribbon for the border. What is the unknown side length?

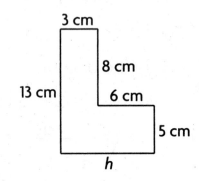

_____

10. Makumi is designing a rectangular rabbit pen. She wants the pen to have an area of 20 square feet. Each side is a whole number of feet. What is the greatest possible perimeter the pen could have? **Explain**.

_____

_____

_____

_____

11. ⭐ **H.O.T.** Each side of the rug at the right is the same length. The perimeter of the rug is 42 feet. How long is each side of the rug?

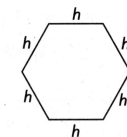

_____

12. ⭐ **Test Prep** Drew's garden is shaped like a rectangle. The area of his garden is 54 square yards. What is the width, p, of his garden?

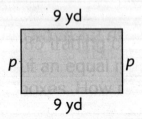

9 yd

p   p

9 yd

(A) 4 yards   (C) 6 yards

(B) 5 yards   (D) 18 yards

13. ⭐ **Test Prep** Eleni wants to put up a fence around her square garden. The garden has a perimeter of 28 meters. How long will each side of the fence be?

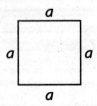

a

a   a

a

(A) 6 meters   (C) 8 meters

(B) 7 meters   (D) 14 meters

Investigate: Customary Units for Capacity

Choose the unit you would use to measure the capacity.
Write *cup*, *pint*, *quart*, or *gallon*.

1.

2.

3.

4.

___cup___   _____   _____   _____

Circle the groups that equal the unit named.
Then, describe the amount using the unit shown.

5.

8 pints in _____ quarts

6.

10 cups in _____ pints

Problem Solving

7. Frankie makes fruit punch. He uses 8 quarts of juice. How many gallons of juice did Frankie use?

_____

8. Miss Kimura uses 20 cups of water to make soup. How many quarts of water does she use?

_____

Lesson Check

1. Which names the same amount as shown in the picture?

(A) 8 cups   (C) 12 pints

(B) 4 pints   (D) 1 gallon

2. A large pot holds 16 pints of water. Which names the same amount as 16 pints?

(A) 2 gallons

(B) 8 pints

(C) 12 pints

(D) 16 cups

Spiral Review

3. The table shows the distance each student lives from school. Which student lives the *greatest* distance from school? (Lesson 10.4)

Distance from School

Student	Distance
Deanna	$\frac{1}{2}$ mile
Lee-Ann	$\frac{3}{8}$ mile
Aaron	$\frac{4}{10}$ mile
Kareem	$\frac{5}{6}$ mile

(A) Deanna   (C) Aaron

(B) Lee-Ann   (D) Kareem

4. Which shape has a perimeter of 10 units and an area of 4 square units? (Lesson 13.9)

(A)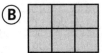

(B)

(C)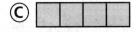

(D)

5. Marcus has 415 baseball cards. Jasmine has 187 baseball cards. How many more cards does Marcus have than Jasmine? (Lesson 2.5)

(A) 602   (C) 238

(B) 328   (D) 228

6. Which number sentence is in the same fact family as $24 \div 6 = 4$?

(Lesson 7.9)

(A) $3 \times 8 = 24$ (C) $6 \times 4 = 24$

(B) $24 - 6 = 18$ (D) $24 - 4 = 20$

Name _____

Change Customary Units for Capacity

Essential Question How can you change a customary unit for capacity to a smaller or larger unit?

Real World Ty measured how much water a jar can hold. He found it can hold 3 cups. He wants to rename the measurement as pints and cups. How many pints and cups can the jar hold?

Remember

2 cups = 1 pint

STEP 1 Draw a picture of the cups.

STEP 2 Circle groups of 2 cups to show pints.

2 cups = _____ pint

There is _____ group of 2 cups, or 1 pint.

There is _____ left over.

So, the jar can hold _____ pint _____ cup.

____ pint   ____ cup

Activity Materials ▪ pint and quart containers ▪ rice

Fill the pint container with rice. Pour the rice into the quart container. Repeat until the container is full. Record how many pints you poured.

_____ pints = 1 quart

Try This! Rename 5 pints using quarts and pints.

Draw 5 pints and circle groups of 2 to show quarts.

There are _____ quarts with _____ pint left over.

So, 5 pints is _____ quarts _____ pint.

Math Talk **Explain** how you could check your work.

Change to Smaller Units

When you rename 2 cups as 1 pint or rename 2 pints as 1 quart, you change from smaller units to larger units. You can also change from larger units to smaller units.

The yogurt at Sunny Foods is sold in cups. Dija needs to buy 2 quarts of yogurt. How many cups of yogurt should Dija buy?

STEP 1 Each box represents 1 quart of yogurt that Dija needs to buy. Write the number of quarts for each box.

STEP 2 There are 4 cups in 1 quart. Draw lines on each box to show 4 cups.

Label the number of cups in each box.

STEP 3 Add the number of cups to find the total. Write the amount on the shopping list.

So, Dija needs to buy _____ cups of yogurt.

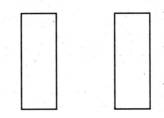

Shopping List

Total Amount of Yogurt: _____ cups

_____ quart   _____ quart

_____ cups   _____ cups

_____ cups + _____ cups = _____ cups

Think About It

1. **Apply** The drawing at the right shows 1 pint. Draw a line or lines on the box to show cups.
   Think: How many cups are in a pint?

   1 pint = _____ cups

1 pint

_____

2. **Compare** How does the capacity of a quart container compare to the capacity of a pint container? **Explain** how you know.

   _____

   _____

   _____

Math Talk **Explain** why it is helpful to know how to change from pints to cups.

Name _____

Practice

Circle groups to rename the capacity using the units named.

3. 5 cups, using pints and cups

_____ pint   _____ pint

5 cups = _____ pints _____ cup

4. 7 cups, using pints and cups

7 cups = _____ pints _____ cup

5. 9 pints, using quarts and pints

9 pints = _____ quarts _____ pint

Draw lines on the boxes to show cups. Then write the capacity using cups.

6. 3 quarts = _____ cups

1 quart   1 quart   1 quart

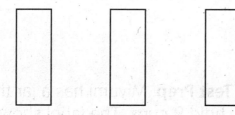

____ cups   ____ cups   ____ cups

7. 2 pints = _____ cups

1 pint   1 pint

____ cups   ____ cups

8. ⟨ Write Math ⟩ When you change from a smaller unit to a larger unit, are there more of the larger units or fewer of the larger units? **Explain**.

_____

_____

Problem Solving • Real World

9. Macy needs 6 cups of juice for a punch recipe. She has only a pint measure. How many pints of juice should she measure?

_____

10. Mr. Ross needs 11 pints of milk. How can he buy that amount in quart and pint containers?

_____

11. **H.O.T.** Hassan has 1 quart of soup. He pours the soup into pint containers. Then he pours half of each pint of soup into bowls. How many bowls of soup does Hassan fill? What amount of soup is in each bowl? Draw a picture to show your work.

_____ bowls of soup

_____ of soup in each bowl

12. ⭐ **Test Prep** Rosie makes 6 quarts of lemonade. She wants to store the lemonade in pint containers. How many pint containers does she need?

Ⓐ 2

Ⓑ 3

Ⓒ 6

Ⓓ 12

13. ⭐ **Test Prep** Miyumi has a jar that can hold 9 cups. The label shows how much the jar can hold using pints and cups. Which measurement does the label show?

Ⓐ 2 pints 1 cup

Ⓑ 2 pints 2 cups

Ⓒ 4 pints 1 cup

Ⓓ 4 pints 2 cups

Name _____

Customary Units for Weight

Choose the unit you would use to measure the weight.
Write *ounce* or *pound*.

1.

2.

3.

4.

pound _____

_____

_____

_____

5.

6.

7.

8.

_____

_____

_____

_____

Find an object in the classroom to match each description.
Draw and label the object.

9. weighs more than 10 pounds

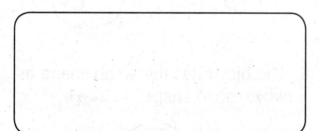

10. weighs less than 8 ounces

Problem Solving

11. Gina bought four 8-ounce bags
of walnuts. How many pounds of
walnuts did Gina buy?

_____

12. Ms. Mott uses some sugar to make
a batch of muffins. Did the sugar she
used weigh 4 ounces or 4 pounds?

_____

Lesson Check

1. Serena buys a bag of apples that weigh 32 ounces. How many pounds does her bag of apples weigh?

  Ⓐ 1 pound   Ⓒ 3 pounds

  Ⓑ 2 pounds   Ⓓ 4 pounds

2. Haley buys 4 bags of trail mix. Each bag weighs 4 ounces. How much does the trail mix weigh in all?

  Ⓐ 4 ounces   Ⓒ 1 pound

  Ⓑ 8 ounces   Ⓓ 2 pounds

Spiral Review

3. What is the missing numerator? (Lesson 10.7)

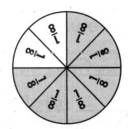

$$\frac{6}{8} = \frac{\blacksquare}{4}$$

  Ⓐ 2   Ⓒ 4

  Ⓑ 3   Ⓓ 5

4. Frankie uses 4 pints of milk to make milk shakes. Which shows the same amount? (Lesson 13.10)

Ⓐ  Ⓒ

Ⓑ  Ⓓ

5. Which solid shape could have the view shown? (Lesson 12.4)

  Ⓐ cube

  Ⓑ cylinder

  Ⓒ square pyramid

  Ⓓ rectangular prism

6. The block has the same shape as which solid shape? (Lesson 12.1)

  Ⓐ cube

  Ⓑ cylinder

  Ⓒ square pyramid

  Ⓓ triangular prism

Name _____

Change Customary Units for Weight

Essential Question How can you change ounces to pounds or pounds to ounces?

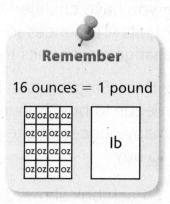

Remember

16 ounces = 1 pound

Real World Matt's puppy weighs 23 ounces. Matt wants to find the weight of the puppy in pounds and ounces. How many pounds and ounces does the puppy weigh?

Shade the boxes to show 23 ounces.

There is _____ group of 16 ounces, or

_____ pound. There are _____ ounces left over.

So, Matt's puppy weighs

_____ pound _____ ounces.

_____ ounces

_____ pound _____ ounces

Try This! Draw a picture to help you rename 19 ounces as pounds and ounces.

So, 19 ounces = _____ pound _____ ounces.

Math Talk **Explain** how you can write the weight in pounds as a fraction greater than 1.

Change to Smaller Units

So far, you have changed smaller units to larger units (16 ounces to 1 pound). You can also change larger units to smaller units.

At the Dairy Stop, cheese is sold in ounces. Tania needs to buy 2 pounds of cheese. How many ounces of cheese does Tania need to buy?

STEP 1 Each box shows 1 pound of cheese that Tania needs to buy. Write the number of pounds for each box.

STEP 2 There are 16 ounces in 1 pound. Draw lines on each box to show 16 ounces.

Label the number of ounces in each box.

STEP 3 Add the weights to find the total number of ounces. Write the weight on the shopping list.

_____ ounces + _____ ounces = _____ ounces

So, Tania needs to buy _____ ounces of cheese.

Shopping List

Total Weight of Cheese: _____ ounces

_____ pound   _____ pound

_____ ounces   _____ ounces

Think About It

1. **Apply** The box at the right shows half of a 1-pound package of cheese. Draw lines on the box to show ounces. How many ounces are there in the package of cheese?

$\frac{1}{2}$-pound package of cheese

_____

2. **Compare** How does a weight of 1 pound compare to a weight of 8 ounces? **Explain** how you know.

_____

_____

Math Talk How is changing ounces to pounds different from changing pounds to ounces?

© Houghton Mifflin Harcourt Publishing Company

Name _____

Practice

3. Rename 20 ounces using pounds and ounces.
Shade the boxes to show 20 ounces.

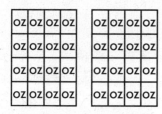

_____ pound _____ ounces

4. Rename 35 ounces using pounds and ounces.

oz|oz|oz|oz oz|oz|oz|oz oz|oz|oz|oz
oz|oz|oz|oz oz|oz|oz|oz oz|oz|oz|oz
oz|oz|oz|oz oz|oz|oz|oz oz|oz|oz|oz
oz|oz|oz|oz oz|oz|oz|oz oz|oz|oz|oz

_____ pounds _____ ounces

Draw lines in each box to show ounces.
Then, write the weight as ounces.

5. 2 pounds = _____ ounces

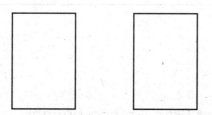

_____ ounces   _____ ounces

6. 3 pounds = _____ ounces

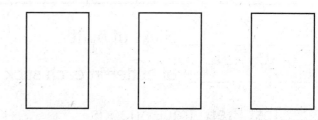

_____ ounces   _____ ounces   _____ ounces

7. **Write Math** ▶ When you change from pounds to ounces, are there more or fewer ounces? **Explain**.

_____

_____

_____

Problem Solving • Real World

8. Lois bought 24 ounces of walnuts. What is this weight in pounds and ounces?

_____

9. Jamal needs 4 pounds of carrots for a recipe. His scale measures in ounces only. How many ounces of carrots does Jamal need?

_____

10. H.O.T. There are 4 sticks of butter in a 1-pound package. How many ounces does each stick of butter weigh? Draw a picture to show your work.

_____ sticks of butter

_____ of butter in each stick

11. ⭐ Test Prep Tracey needs 3 pounds of oatmeal. At the store, oatmeal is sold in ounces. How many ounces of oatmeal does Tracey need?

Ⓐ 14 ounces

Ⓑ 40 ounces

Ⓒ 48 ounces

Ⓓ 64 ounces

12. ⭐ Test Prep Franco bought 38 ounces of nails. How many pounds and ounces of nails did he buy?

Ⓐ 1 pound 18 ounces

Ⓑ 2 pounds 4 ounces

Ⓒ 2 pounds 6 ounces

Ⓓ 3 pounds 8 ounces

Name _____

Metric Units for Capacity and Mass

Choose the unit you would use to measure the
capacity. Write *milliliters* or *liters*.

1.    **2.**    **3.**    **4.**

milliliters _____   _____   _____

Choose the unit you would use to measure the mass.
Write *gram* or *kilogram*.

5.    **6.** 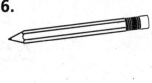   **7.**    **8.**

_____   _____   _____   _____

9. Find a container that has a capacity
less than 1 liter. Draw the container
in the space at the right.

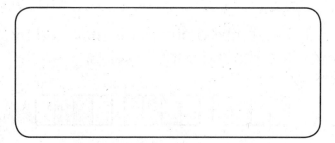

Problem Solving

10. Marty is measuring the mass of a
large table. Should Marty use grams
or kilograms to measure?

_____

11. Tina is measuring the mass of a
dragonfly. Should Tina use grams
or kilograms to measure?

_____

Lesson Check

TEST PREP

1. Milliliters would be the best unit for measuring the capacity of which object?

   Ⓐ pitcher of ice water

   Ⓑ bathtub

   Ⓒ large bottle of soda

   Ⓓ eye dropper

2. Which unit would be used to measure the mass of a hippopotamus?

   Ⓐ liter

   Ⓑ kilogram

   Ⓒ gram

   Ⓓ meter

Spiral Review

3. Which unit would you use to measure the distance between two cities? (Lesson 13.3)

   Ⓐ centimeter

   Ⓑ decimeter

   Ⓒ meter

   Ⓓ kilometer

4. Find the product. (Lesson 5.4)

   $$\begin{array}{r} 8 \\ \times\, 4 \\ \hline \end{array}$$

   Ⓐ 40   Ⓒ 24

   Ⓑ 32   Ⓓ 12

5. What mixed number is modeled by the shaded parts? (Lesson 9.5)

   Ⓐ $\frac{3}{4}$

   Ⓑ $1\frac{3}{4}$

   Ⓒ $2\frac{1}{3}$

   Ⓓ $2\frac{3}{4}$

6. Jennifer's bedroom is 30 decimeters long. How many meters is this? (Lesson 13.4)

   Ⓐ 3,000 meters

   Ⓑ 300 meters

   Ⓒ 3 meters

   Ⓓ 1 meter

Name _____

Chapter 13 Extra Practice

Lessons 13.1, 13.3

Choose the customary and metric unit you would use to measure the length. Write *inch*, *foot*, *yard*, or *mile*. Then write *millimeter*, *centimeter*, *meter*, or *kilometer*.

1.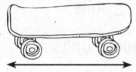

2.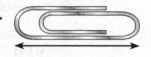

3.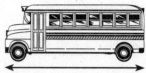

_____   _____   _____

_____   _____   _____

Lessons 13.2, 13.4

Measure the length to the nearest half inch.

1.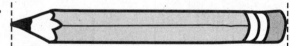

2.

_____   _____

Use a ruler. Draw a line for the length.

3. 6 centimeters

Lessons 13.5 – 13.7

Find the perimeter.

1. A rectangle has sides that are 7 centimeters long and 2 centimeters wide.

Use an inch ruler to find the perimeter.

2.

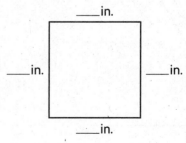

____in.

____in.   ____in.

____in.

_____ centimeters   _____ inches

© Houghton Mifflin Harcourt Publishing Company

Lessons 13.8 – 13.9

Find the perimeter of the shape. Count or multiply
to find the area of the shape.

1.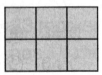

Perimeter = _____ units

Area = _____ square units

2.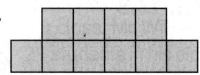

Perimeter = _____ units

Area = _____ square units

Lesson 13.10

Circle the groups that equal the unit named. Then, rename
the capacity using the unit shown.

1.

8 cups in _____ quarts

2.

6 cups in _____ pints

Lessons 13.11 – 13.12

Choose the unit you would use to measure the weight.
Write *ounce* or *pound*. Then choose the unit you would
use to measure the mass. Write *gram* or *kilogram*.

1.

_____

_____

2.

_____

_____

3.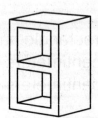

_____

_____

Name _____

Read and Write Numbers Through Ten Thousands

Essential Question What are some ways you can read and write 4- and 5-digit numbers?

🔓 UNLOCK the Problem REAL WORLD

A sign at the Mountain State Fair shows the number of visitors. How can you write the number of visitors to the fair in three ways?

- What is the greatest place-value position in a 5-digit number?

  _____

Mountain State Fair • Number of Visitors				
TEN THOUSANDS	THOUSANDS	HUNDREDS	TENS	ONES
4	9,	5	1	3

🔑 **Read and write numbers.**

Word form is a way to write a number using words.

Word Form: forty-nine thousand, five hundred thirteen

Expanded form is a way to write a number by showing the value of each digit.

Expanded Form: $40,000 + 9,000 + 500 + 10 + 3$

Standard form is a way to write a number using the digits 0 to 9, with each digit having a place value.

Standard Form: 49,513

So, three ways you can write the number of visitors are

_____ form, _____ form,

and _____ form.

Math Talk **Explain** why you can write 4 ten thousands as 40 thousands or 400 hundreds.

Share and Show

1. Complete the expanded form for 17,598.

   10,000 + _____ + 500 + 90 + _____

Write the number in standard form.

2. 4,000 + 600 + 70 + 4   _____

3. seventy-eight thousand, two hundred sixty-one _____

4. 70,000 + 2,000 + 100 + 80   _____

Write the value of the underlined digit two ways.

5. <u>6</u>7,920   6. <u>8</u>,063

_____   _____

On Your Own . . . .

Write the number in standard form.

7. 5,000 + 600 + 90 + 7   _____

8. twenty thousand, three hundred fifty-nine _____

9. ninety-one thousand, three hundred two _____

Write the value of the underlined digit two ways.

10. 6,<u>8</u>18   11. <u>9</u>1,342

_____   _____

12. Rename 43,290 as thousands and tens.

    _____ thousands _____ tens

13. Rename 2,934 as tens and ones.

    _____ tens _____ ones

Problem Solving REAL WORLD

14. The number of children who attended the fair on opening day is 4,351 more than the value of 2 ten thousands. How many children attended the fair on opening day?

    _____

Name _____

Compare 4- and 5-Digit Numbers

Essential Question What are some ways you can compare 4- and 5-digit numbers?

🔓 UNLOCK the Problem REAL WORLD

Cody collected 2,365 pennies. Jasmine collected 1,876 pennies. Who collected more pennies?

You can compare numbers in different ways to find which number is greater.

- What do you need to find?

_____

_____

🔑 ONE WAY Use a number line.

The numbers on a number line are in order from least to greatest.

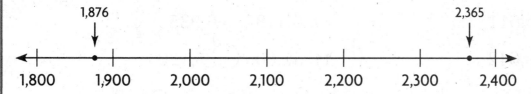

2,365 is to the right of 1,876. So, 2,365 ◯ 1,876.

So, Cody collected more pennies.

🔑 ANOTHER WAY Use place value.

Compare 27,376 and 27,513.

Compare digits in the same place-value position from left to right.

TEN THOUSANDS	THOUSANDS	HUNDREDS	TENS	ONES
2	7,	3	7	6
2	7,	5	1	3

STEP 1: Compare the ten thousands. The digits are the same.

STEP 2: Compare the thousands. The digits are the same.

STEP 3: Compare the hundreds. 3 ◯ 5

So, 27,376 ◯ 27,513.

Read Math

Read < as *is less than.*
Read > as *is greater than.*
Read = as *is equal to.*

Math Talk **Explain** how you know that 568 is less than 4,786.

© Houghton Mifflin Harcourt Publishing Company

Share and Show

1. Compare 2,351 and 3,018. Which number has more thousands? Which number is greater?

_____

Compare the numbers. Write <, >, or = in the ◯.

2. 1,481 ◯ 4,001

3. 7,891 ◯ 7,891

4. 29,314 ◯ 36,495

5. 35,421 ◯ 6,925

On Your Own

Compare the numbers. Write <, >, or = in the ◯.

6. 9,481 ◯ 10,005

7. 27,891 ◯ 23,450

8. 45,611 ◯ 45,611

9. 7,418 ◯ 6,935

10. 39,314 ◯ 39,642

11. 51,000 ◯ 5,120

Problem Solving REAL WORLD

12. Nina has a dictionary with 1,680 pages. Trey has a dictionary with 1,490 pages. Use <, >, or = to compare the number of pages in the dictionaries.

_____

13. The odometer in Ed's car shows it has been driven 28,946 miles. The odometer in Beth's car shows it has been driven 35,042 miles. Which car has been driven more miles?

_____

14. Avery said that she is 3,652 days old. Tamika said that she is 3,377 days old. Who is younger?

_____

Add More than Two Addends

Essential Question How can you add more than two addends?

🔑 UNLOCK the Problem REAL WORLD

Mrs. Gomez sold 23 cucumbers, 38 tomatoes, and 42 peppers at the Farmer's Market. How many vegetables did she sell in all?

You can use the Commutative and Associative Properties of Addition to help you add.

- What operation will you use to solve the problem?

  _____

Remember

Commutative Property of Addition: you can add in any order and get the same sum.

Associative Property of Addition: you can group addends in different ways and get the same sum.

🔑 Look for an easy way to add 23 + 38 + 42.

STEP 1 Line up the numbers by place value.	**STEP 2** Group the ones to make them easy to add.	**STEP 3** Group the tens to make them easy to add.
	Think: Make a ten.	**Think:** Make doubles.
2 3 3 8 + 4 2	1 2 3 3 8 ⟩10 + 4 2 ‾‾‾‾ 3	1 5 ⟨ 5 ⟨ 2 3 3 8 + 4 2 ‾‾‾‾ 1 0 3

So, Mrs. Gomez sold 103 vegetables in all.

Math Talk **Describe** an easy way to add 18 + 45 + 28.

🔑 Example Use properties to add 136 + 37 + 51.

STEP 1 Line up the numbers by place value.	**STEP 2** Change the grouping.	**STEP 3** Add.
	Think: Adding 37 + 51 first would be easy because there is no regrouping needed.	
1 3 6 3 7 + 5 1	1 3 6 3 7 ⟩88 + 5 1	1 1 1 3 6 + 8 8 ‾‾‾‾ 2 2 4

So, 136 + 37 + 51 = _____.

Share and Show

1. Find the sum. **Explain** how you can use
   properties to add.

$$\begin{array}{r} 113 \\ 26 \\ +\ 54 \\ \hline \end{array}$$

_____

_____

Find the sum.

2. $$\begin{array}{r} 81 \\ 73 \\ +\ 19 \\ \hline \end{array}$$

3. $$\begin{array}{r} 215 \\ 76 \\ +\ 125 \\ \hline \end{array}$$

4. $$\begin{array}{r} 57 \\ 62 \\ 356 \\ +\ 43 \\ \hline \end{array}$$

On Your Own

Find the sum.

5. $$\begin{array}{r} 103 \\ 349 \\ +\ 87 \\ \hline \end{array}$$

6. $$\begin{array}{r} 218 \\ 18 \\ +\ 302 \\ \hline \end{array}$$

7. $$\begin{array}{r} 333 \\ 471 \\ 56 \\ +\ 29 \\ \hline \end{array}$$

8. $176 + 195 + 24 =$ _____

9. $106 + 41 + 41 + 134 =$ _____

Problem Solving REAL WORLD

10. The customers at a video store rented 326 comedies,
    119 dramas, 93 thrillers, and 41 cartoons on Friday
    night. How many movies were rented in all on
    Friday night?

    _____

Name _____

Addition and Subtraction Expressions

Essential Question How can you use expressions to model situations with numbers?

🔓 UNLOCK the Problem REAL WORLD

There are 11 girls and 14 boys taking art lessons. What expression can you write to represent the total number of students taking art lessons?

An expression is part of an equation. It combines numbers and operation signs, but does not have an equal sign.

- **What information is given?**

  _____

  _____

  _____

🔑 **Write an expression to match the words.**

- Read the words carefully to find the important information.

- Think about whether the situation is joining, separating, or comparing groups.

- Decide what operation sign to use in the expression.

Math Talk How can you change an expression into an equation?

Think: There are 11 girls. There are 14 boys.
Add to join the boys and girls.

11   +   14

So, the expression that matches the words is 11 + 14.

🔑 Examples Write an expression to match the words.

A Mr. Nelson's students collected 168 cans of food. They gave away 79 cans on Saturday.

_____

B There are 54 students in the cafeteria. They are joined by 62 students.

_____

Share and Show

1. Write an expression for 25 students in the classroom and 7 more students joining.

   Think: Choose the operation to join groups of different sizes.

   _____

Write an expression to match the words.

2. Mandy's book has 49 pages. She has read 36 pages so far.

   _____

3. Ms. Cooper has 20 packages to deliver today. She delivered 8 packages before lunch.

   _____

On Your Own
Write an expression to match the words.

4. Jessica has 245 stamps. Alex has 379 stamps. Alex wants to know how many more stamps he has than Jessica.

   _____

5. Mario used 6 apples, 5 oranges, and 12 strawberries for the fruit salad. Mario wants to know how many pieces of fruit he used.

   _____

6. Mr. Levy ordered 29 tiles for the kitchen floor. Then he ordered 31 more tiles.

   _____

7. Gina practices the piano for 60 minutes every day. So far, she has practiced for 45 minutes.

   _____

Problem Solving

Use the table for 8–9. Write an expression to match the words.

8. Glue is on sale for 15¢ less than the regular cost.

   _____

9. Tim bought a box of crayons and glitter. He wants to know how much he spent.

   _____

Art Supplies	
Item	Cost
Box of Crayons	98¢
Glue	72¢
Glitter	55¢

Name _____

Addition and Subtraction Equations

Essential Question How can you use equations to model situations with numbers?

UNLOCK the Problem REAL WORLD

There are 11 students on the bus. After some students get off, 6 students are left. How many students got off the bus?

What equation can you write for the problem?

An equation is a number sentence that uses the equal sign to show that two amounts are equal.

🔑 **Write an equation for the problem.**

- Identify the known and unknown amounts.

- Think about whether the situation is joining, separating, or comparing groups.

Think: You separate the group because some students are getting off.

- Decide what operation sign to use in the equation.

students on the bus		students who get off		students left
11	−	s	=	6

So, the equation for the problem is $11 - s = 6$.

- What information is known?
  _____
  _____
- What is unknown?
  _____

Math Idea

You can use a variable to stand for an unknown amount.

Math Talk **Explain** why you use the subtraction sign.

Try This! **Write an equation for the problem.**

Jenna has some dimes, d. After she finds 3 more dimes she has 15 dimes in all. How many dimes did Jenna have to start?

dimes to start		dimes found		dimes in all
d	+	_____	=	_____

Share and Show

1. Write an equation for the problem. There are 187 animals at the zoo. Alan saw some of the animals, *a*. He has 109 more animals to see. How many animals did Alan see?

_____

- Circle the information you know.
- Underline what is unknown.
- What symbol or letter will you use?

_____

- What operation can you use?

_____

Write an equation for the problem.

2. The Outdoor Club plants 45 trees. The club plants 18 oak trees. The rest are elm trees, *e*. How many elm trees does the club plant?

_____

3. Julia has some stamps, *s*. She gets 15 more stamps. She now has 237 stamps. How many stamps did Julia have to start?

_____

On Your Own

Write an equation for the problem.

4. Jin takes 138 pictures. Lucy also takes some pictures, *p*. They take 309 pictures in all. How many pictures does Lucy take?

_____

5. Carl buys a shirt for $18. He then buys a pair of jeans. He spends $41 in all. How much did the jeans, *j*, cost?

_____

Problem Solving  REAL WORLD

Use the table. Write an equation for the problem.

6. Football got 16 more votes than baseball. How many votes did football, *f*, get?

_____

Favorite Sport	
Sport	**Votes**
Baseball	41
Basketball	52
Soccer	37

Name _____

Concepts and Skills

Write the number in standard form. (pp. P283–P284)

1. $3,000 + 700 + 80 + 6$ _____

2. eighty-nine thousand, four hundred six _____

Compare the numbers. Write <, >, or = in the ◯**.** (pp. P285–P286)

3. 5,410 ◯ 5,063   **4.** 6,138 ◯ 6,138

5. 8,542 ◯ 70,204   **6.** 94,326 ◯ 62,857

Find the sum. (pp. P287–P288)

7.
$$\begin{array}{r} 82 \\ 65 \\ +\ 45 \\ \hline \end{array}$$

8.
$$\begin{array}{r} 70 \\ 109 \\ +\ 70 \\ \hline \end{array}$$

9.
$$\begin{array}{r} 237 \\ 54 \\ 391 \\ +\ 13 \\ \hline \end{array}$$

Write an expression to match the words. (pp. P289–P290)

10. Ed has 52 tiles to paint. So far, he has painted 28 tiles.

11. Ms. Lee ordered 81 shirts for the school. Then she ordered 47 more shirts.

_____   _____

Problem Solving REAL WORLD

Write an equation for the problem. (pp. P291–P292)

12. Ty has some shells, *s*. After he finds 4 more shells, he has 16 shells in all. How many shells did Ty have to start?

13. A shirt is on sale for $3 off. Rita pays $9 for the shirt. What was the original price, *p*, of the shirt?

_____   _____

Fill in the bubble completely to show your answer.

14. The car odometer showed 47,693 miles. What is the value of the digit 7 in 47,693? (pp. P283–P284)

Ⓐ   7

Ⓑ   70

Ⓒ   700

Ⓓ 7,000

15. A movie theater showed a movie four times in one day. There were 59 people at the first show. There were 40 people, 465 people, and 215 people at the next three shows. How many people were at the four shows in all? (pp. P287–P288)

Ⓐ 779

Ⓑ 769

Ⓒ 679

Ⓓ 669

16. Muffins are on sale for 8¢ less than the regular price. The regular price is 56¢ each. Which expression can be used to find the sale price? (pp. P289–P290)

Ⓐ 56¢ + 8¢

Ⓑ 56¢ − 8¢

Ⓒ 56¢ × 8¢

Ⓓ 56¢ ÷ 8¢

17. Sal sold 24 hats on Monday and Tuesday. On Tuesday, he sold 8 hats. How many hats did he sell on Monday? Which equation can be used to solve the problem?

(pp. P291–P292)

Ⓐ $24 + 8 = h$

Ⓑ $h - 24 = 8$

Ⓒ $h + 8 = 24$

Ⓓ $h - 8 = 24$

Name _____

Multiplication with 11 and 12

Essential Question What strategies can you use to multiply with 11 and 12?

🔑 UNLOCK the Problem REAL WORLD

It takes Bobby 11 minutes to walk to school each morning. How many minutes will Bobby spend walking to school in 5 days?

- What are the groups in this problem?

_____

_____

Multiply. $5 \times 11 = $ ▨

🔑 ONE WAY Break apart an array.

Make 5 rows of 11. Use the 10s facts and the 1s facts to multiply with 11.

$5 \times 10 = $ _____ $5 \times 1 = $ _____

$5 \times 11 = $ _____ $+$ _____

$5 \times 11 = $ _____

🔑 ANOTHER WAY Find a pattern.

Look at the list.

Notice the product has the same factor in the tens and ones places.

To find 5×11, write the first factor in the tens and ones places.

$5 \times 11 = 55$

$1 \times 11 = 11$
$2 \times 11 = 22$
$3 \times 11 = 33$
$4 \times 11 = 44$

$5 \times 11 = $ _____
$6 \times 11 = 66$
$7 \times 11 = 77$
$8 \times 11 = 88$
$9 \times 11 = 99$

So, Bobby will spend _____ minutes walking to school.

Try This! **What if** it took Bobby 12 minutes to walk to school? How many minutes will he spend walking to school in 5 days?

Break apart the factor 12.

$5 \times (10 + 2)$

$5 \times 10 = 50$ $5 \times 2 = 10$

$5 \times 12 = $ _____ $+$ _____ $= $ _____

Double a 6s fact.

Find the 6s product. $5 \times 6 = 30$

Double that product. _____ $+$ _____ $= $ _____

So, $5 \times 12 = $ _____. Bobby will spend _____ minutes walking to school.

Share and Show

1. How can you use the 10s facts and the
   2s facts to find 4 × 12?

   _____

   _____

Find the product.

2. 9 × 11 = _____

3. 7 × 12 = _____

4. _____ = 4 × 11

On Your Own

Find the product.

5. _____ = 11 × 6

6. _____ = 12 × 2

7. 0 × 11 = _____

8. _____ = 6 × 12

9. 8 × 12 = _____

10. 7 × 11 = _____

11. _____ = 12 × 9

12. 3 × 12 = _____

13. 1 × 12 = _____

Problem Solving REAL WORLD

Use the graph for 14–15.

14. The graph shows the number of
    miles some students travel to school
    each day. How many miles will
    Carlos travel to school in 5 days?

    _____

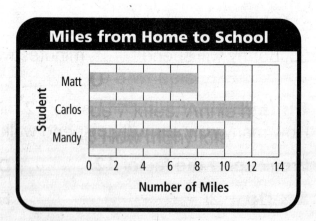

15. Suppose that Mandy takes 9 trips to school, and Matt takes
    11 trips to school. Who travels more miles? **Explain**.

    _____

    _____

Name _____

Division with 11 and 12

Essential Question What strategies can you use to divide with 11 and 12?

🔓 UNLOCK the Problem · REAL WORLD

Tara collects 60 postcards. She arranges them in 12 equal stacks. How many postcards are in each stack?

Divide. $60 \div 12 = $ ▪

> • Do you need to find the number of groups or the number in each group?
>
> _____
>
> _____

🔑 One Way Use a multiplication table.

Since division is the inverse of multiplication, you can use a multiplication table to find a quotient.

Think of a related multiplication fact.

$$12 \times ▪ = 60$$

• Find the row for the factor 12.
• Look across to find the product, 60.
• Look up to find the missing factor.
• The missing factor is 5.

Since $12 \times 5 = 60$, then $60 \div 12 = $ _____.

×	0	1	2	3	4	5	6	7	8	9	10	11	12
0	0	0	0	0	0	0	0	0	0	0	0	0	0
1	0	1	2	3	4	5	6	7	8	9	10	11	12
2	0	2	4	6	8	10	12	14	16	18	20	22	24
3	0	3	6	9	12	15	18	21	24	27	30	33	36
4	0	4	8	12	16	20	24	28	32	36	40	44	48
5	0	5	10	15	20	25	30	35	40	45	50	55	60
6	0	6	12	18	24	30	36	42	48	54	60	66	72
7	0	7	14	21	28	35	42	49	56	63	70	77	84
8	0	8	16	24	32	40	48	56	64	72	80	88	96
9	0	9	18	27	36	45	54	63	72	81	90	99	108
10	0	10	20	30	40	50	60	70	80	90	100	110	120
11	0	11	22	33	44	55	66	77	88	99	110	121	132
12	0	12	24	36	48	60	72	84	96	108	120	132	144

🔑 Another Way Use repeated subtraction.

• Start with 60.
• Subtract 12 until you reach 0.
• Count the number of times you subtract 12.

$$\begin{array}{r} 60 \\ -12 \\ \hline 48 \end{array} \quad \begin{array}{r} 48 \\ -12 \\ \hline 36 \end{array} \quad \begin{array}{r} 36 \\ -12 \\ \hline 24 \end{array} \quad \begin{array}{r} 24 \\ -12 \\ \hline 12 \end{array} \quad \begin{array}{r} 12 \\ -12 \\ \hline 0 \end{array}$$

You subtract 12 five times.

$60 \div 12 = $ _____

So, there are 5 postcards in each stack.

Math Talk What other strategies can you use to divide?

Share and Show

1. Use the multiplication table on page P297 to find $99 \div 11$.

   Think: What is a related multiplication fact?

   _____

Find the missing factor and quotient.

2. $11 \times \blacksquare = 66$ $66 \div 11 = \blacksquare$ 3. $12 \times \blacksquare = 24$ $24 \div 12 = \blacksquare$

   $\blacksquare = $ _____ $\blacksquare = $ _____ $\blacksquare = $ _____ $\blacksquare = $ _____

4. $11 \times \blacksquare = 33$ $33 \div 11 = \blacksquare$ 5. $12 \times \blacksquare = 72$ $72 \div 12 = \blacksquare$

   $\blacksquare = $ _____ $\blacksquare = $ _____ $\blacksquare = $ _____ $\blacksquare = $ _____

On Your Own

Find the missing factor and quotient.

6. $11 \times \blacksquare = 55$ $55 \div 11 = \blacksquare$ 7. $12 \times \blacksquare = 48$ $48 \div 12 = \blacksquare$

   $\blacksquare = $ _____ $\blacksquare = $ _____ $\blacksquare = $ _____ $\blacksquare = $ _____

8. $12 \times \blacksquare = 96$ $96 \div 12 = \blacksquare$ 9. $8 \times \blacksquare = 88$ $88 \div 8 = \blacksquare$

   $\blacksquare = $ _____ $\blacksquare = $ _____ $\blacksquare = $ _____ $\blacksquare = $ _____

Find the quotient.

10. $11 \div 11 = $ _____   11. $77 \div 11 = $ _____   12. _____ $= 60 \div 12$

13. _____ $= 22 \div 11$ 14. $72 \div 12 = $ _____   15. $84 \div 12 = $ _____

16. $36 \div 12 = $ _____   17. _____ $= 108 \div 12$ 18. $12 \div 12 = $ _____

Compare. Write <, >, or = for each $\bigcirc$.

19. $96 \div 8 \bigcirc 96 \div 12$ 20. $77 \div 11 \bigcirc 84 \div 12$ 21. $99 \div 11 \bigcirc 84 \div 7$

Problem Solving REAL WORLD

22. Justin printed 44 posters to advertise the garage sale. He gave 11 friends the same number of posters to display around the neighborhood. How many posters did Justin give each friend?

    _____

Name _____

Multiplication and Division Relationships

Essential Question How can you write related multiplication and division equations for 2-digit factors?

Multiplication and division are inverse operations.

🔓 UNLOCK the Problem · REAL WORLD

Megan has a rose garden with the same number of bushes planted in each of 4 rows. There are 48 bushes in the garden. How many bushes are in each row of Megan's garden?

- What do you need to find?

_____

_____

🔑 One Way

Make an array.

48 ÷ 4 =

Count 48 tiles. Make 4 rows by placing 1 tile in each row.

Continue placing 1 tile in each of the 4 rows until all the tiles are used.

Draw the array you made.

☐
☐
☐
☐

There are _____ tiles in each row.

_____ ÷ _____ = _____

So, there are _____ rose bushes in each row of Megan's garden.

🔑 Another Way

Write related equations.

48 ÷ 4 =

Think: 4 times what number equals 48?

4 × 12 = _____

You can check your answer using repeated addition.

_____ + _____ + _____ + _____ = _____

Write related equations.

_____ × _____ = 48

48 ÷ _____ = _____

Math Talk How can you tell if two equations are related?

Share and Show

1. Complete the related equations for this array.

    $3 \times 11 = 33$ $33 \div 3 = 11$

    _____   _____

Write the related multiplication and division equations
for the set of numbers.

2. 1, 11, 11

    _____

    _____

    _____

    _____

3. 5, 12, 60

    _____

    _____

    _____

    _____

4. 7, 11, 77

    _____

    _____

    _____

    _____

On Your Own

Write the related multiplication and division equations
for the set of numbers.

5. 7, 12, 84

    _____

    _____

    _____

    _____

6. 6, 11, 66

    _____

    _____

    _____

    _____

7. 12, 9, 108

    _____

    _____

    _____

    _____

Problem Solving  REAL WORLD

8. Megan cut 96 roses to make
   flower arrangements. She made
   12 equal arrangements. How many
   roses were in each arrangement?

   _____

9. Megan put 22 roses in a vase.
   She cut the same number of roses
   from each of 11 different bushes.
   How many roses did she cut from
   each bush?

   _____

Name _____

Multiplication and Division Expressions and Equations

Essential Question How can you use expressions and equations to represent multiplication and division situations?

🔓 UNLOCK the Problem REAL WORLD

There are 8 floats in the parade. There are 6 people on each float. What expression can you write to represent the total number of people on all the floats?

- What information is given?

  _____

  _____

🔑 Write an expression to match the words.

- Read the words and decide what operation to use in the expression.

Think: 8 floats with 6 people on each float means 8 groups of 6.
Multiply to find the total number of people.

8×6

So, an expression to match the words is 8×6.

Math Idea

- Multiply to join equal groups.
- Divide to find the number of equal groups or the number in each group.

Example Write an equation for the problem.

There are 35 people in a marching band. Each row has 5 people. How many rows are there?

Think: There are 35 people in equal rows of 5 people. I don't know the number of rows.

number of people in band		number in each row		number of equal rows
↓		↓		↓
_____	÷	_____	=	r

Math Talk How can you write an equation to find the total number of people on the floats in the parade?

So, an equation for the problem is _____.

© Houghton Mifflin Harcourt Publishing Company

Share and Show

1. Write an expression for 3 students sharing $18 equally.

   Think: The problem is about equal sharing, so divide.

   _____

Write an equation for the problem.

2. There are 4 equal groups of students. There are 12 students in all. How many students, *s*, are in each group?

   _____

3. Two friends share 16 grapes equally. How many grapes, *g*, does each friend have?

   _____

On Your Own

Write an expression to match the words.

4. Each vase has 10 flowers. There are 4 vases.

   _____

5. The parking lot holds 72 cars. There are 9 equal rows.

   _____

Write an equation for the problem.

6. A ranger sees the same number of deer each day for 5 days. He sees 25 deer in all. How many deer, *d*, does he see each day?

   _____

7. There are seats for 6 people on each park tour. There are 5 tours each day. How many people, *p*, can go on park tours each day?

   _____

Problem Solving

Use the table for 8–9.

8. Write an equation to show how many yogurt cups, *y*, you can buy for 90¢.

   _____

Snack Bar	
Snack	Price
Granola bars	20¢
Pretzels	15¢
Yogurt cup	30¢

9. There are 2 granola bars in each pack. Write an expression to show the cost of 1 granola bar.

   _____

Name _____

Use Multiplication Patterns

Essential Question How can you multiply with 10, 100, and 1,000?

🔓 UNLOCK the Problem REAL WORLD

Mrs. Goldman ordered 4 boxes of yo-yos for her toy store. Each box had 100 yo-yos. How many yo-yos did Mrs. Goldman order?

- Circle the numbers you need to use.
- What operation can you use to find the total when you have equal groups?

  _____

🔑 Use a basic fact and a pattern to multiply.

Factors	Products
4×1	= 4
4×10	= 40
4×100	= 400

Think: Use the basic fact $4 \times 1 = 4$. Look for a pattern of zeros.

So, Mrs. Goldman ordered 400 yo-yos.

Math Idea

As the number of zeros in a factor increases, the number of zeros in the product increases.

Try This! Use a basic fact and a pattern to find the products.

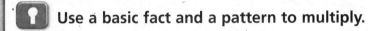

A. $1 \times 3 = 3$

$10 \times 3 =$ _____

B. $5 \times 1 \quad = 5$

$5 \times 10 \quad = 50$

$5 \times 100 \quad =$ _____

$5 \times 1,000 =$ _____

Math Talk When multiplying $9 \times 1,000$, how many zeros will be in the product? **Explain.**

Share and Show

1. **Explain** how to use a basic fact and a pattern to find 6×100.

_____

_____

Use a basic fact and a pattern to find the products.

2. $7 \times 10 =$ _____	3. $10 \times 5 =$ _____	4. $3 \times 10 =$ _____
$7 \times 100 =$ _____	$100 \times 5 =$ _____	$3 \times 100 =$ _____
$7 \times 1{,}000 =$ _____	$1{,}000 \times 5 =$ _____	$3 \times 1{,}000 =$ _____

On Your Own

Use a basic fact and a pattern to find the products.

5. $2 \times 10 =$ _____	6. $10 \times 8 =$ _____	7. $9 \times 10 =$ _____
$2 \times 100 =$ _____	$100 \times 8 =$ _____	$9 \times 100 =$ _____
$2 \times 1{,}000 =$ _____	$1{,}000 \times 8 =$ _____	$9 \times 1{,}000 =$ _____

Find the product.

8. $10 \times 8 =$ _____   9. $6 \times 100 =$ _____   10. _____ $= 4 \times 100$

11. $1{,}000 \times 4 =$ _____   12. _____ $= 1{,}000 \times 3$ 13. $9 \times 100 =$ _____

Problem Solving

Use the pictograph.

14. Patty has 20 fewer yo-yos in her collection than Chuck. Draw yo-yos in the pictograph to show the number of yo-yos in Patty's collection. **Explain** your answer.

_____

_____

Yo-Yo Collections	
Name	**Number of Yo-Yos**
Max	◯ ◯ ◯
Chuck	◯ ◯ ◯ ◯
Patty	

Key: Each ◯ = 10 Yo-Yos.

Name _____

✓ Checkpoint

Concepts and Skills

Find the product. (pp. P295–P296)

1. $4 \times 11 =$ _____

2. $11 \times 8 =$ _____

3. _____ $= 3 \times 12$

Find the quotient. (pp. P297–P298)

4. $72 \div 12 =$ _____

5. _____ $= 33 \div 11$

6. $108 \div 12 =$ _____

**Write the related multiplication and division equations
for the set of numbers.** (pp. P299–P300)

7. 9, 11, 99

_____

_____

_____

_____

8. 8, 12, 96

_____

_____

_____

_____

9. 5, 12, 60

_____

_____

_____

_____

Write an expression to match the words. (pp. P301–P302)

10. There are 20 slices of bread. Toshi eats 4 slices of bread each day.

_____

11. Each boat can hold 7 riders. There are 5 boats.

_____

Find the product. (pp. P303–P304)

12. $8 \times 100 =$ _____

13. _____ $= 7 \times 10$

14. $1,000 \times 6 =$ _____

Problem Solving REAL WORLD

Solve. (pp. P295–P296)

15. There are 11 oranges in each bag. How many oranges are in 6 bags?

_____

16. There are 12 eggs in one dozen. How many eggs are in 4 dozen?

_____

© Houghton Mifflin Harcourt Publishing Company

Getting Ready for Grade 4   P305

Fill in the bubble completely to show your answer.

17. Steven reads 11 pages of his book each day. How many pages will he read in 7 days? (pp. P295–P296)

   (A) 77

   (B) 72

   (C) 18

   (D) 4

18. A florist has 84 roses to arrange in vases. She wants each vase to hold 12 roses. How many vases does the florist need? (pp. P297–P298)

   (A) 96

   (B) 72

   (C) 8

   (D) 7

19. Mr. Davis drives 55 miles to and from work each week. If he drives to work 5 days each week, how many miles does Mr. Davis drive to and from work each day? (pp. P299–P300)

   (A) 5

   (B) 11

   (C) 50

   (D) 60

20. Three families each donated 12 cans of soup for the food drive. Which equation could be used to find how many cans, c, the families donated in all?
   (pp. P301–P302)

   (A) $3 + 12 = c$

   (B) $3 \times 12 = c$

   (C) $12 - 3 = c$

   (D) $12 \div 3 = c$

Name _____

Use Models to Multiply Tens and Ones

Essential Question How can you use base-ten blocks and area models to model multiplication with a 2-digit factor?

🔓 UNLOCK the Problem 〉REAL WORLD

Three groups of 14 students toured the state capitol in Columbus, Ohio. How many students toured the capitol in all?

Multiply. $3 \times 14 = $ ▪

- What do you need to find?

  _____

  _____

- Circle the numbers you need to use.

🔑 One Way

STEP 1

Model 3×14 with base-ten blocks.

3 rows of 10   3 rows of 4

STEP 2

Multiply the tens and ones. Record each product.

$3 \times 10 = $ _____ $3 \times 4 = $ _____

STEP 3

Add the products.
30 + 12 = 42
$3 \times 14 = 42$

So, 42 students toured the capitol.

🔑 Another Way

STEP 1

Model 3×14 with an area model.

3 rows of 10   3 rows of 4

STEP 2

Multiply the tens.   Multiply the ones.

$3 \times 10 = $ _____ $3 \times 4 = $ _____

STEP 3

Add the products.
30 + 12 = 42
$3 \times 14 = 42$

Math Talk How are the two ways to find a product alike?

Share and Show

1. One way to model 18 is 1 ten 8 ones.
   How can knowing this help you
   find 4 × 18?

   _____

   _____

Find the product. Show your multiplication and addition.

2.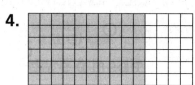

   3 × 16 = ▣

   _____

   _____

   _____

3. 5 × 13 = ▣

   _____

   _____

   _____

4. 6 × 14 = ▣

   _____

   _____

   _____

On Your Own

Find the product. Show your multiplication and addition.

5. 4 × 13 = ▣

   _____

   _____

   _____

6. 5 × 15 = ▣

   _____

   _____

   _____

7. 3 × 17 = ▣

   _____

   _____

   _____

Problem Solving REAL WORLD

8. Randy is 5 feet tall. How many inches tall is he?

   Remember: 1 foot = 12 inches

   _____

Name _____

Use Multiplication Properties

Essential Question How can you use multiplication properties to find a product with a 2-digit factor?

🎀 UNLOCK the Problem 〉REAL WORLD 〉

There are 3 groups working on the school play. There are 14 students in each group. How many students are working on the school play?

Multiply. 3×14

You can use multiplication properties to find products.

- How many groups are there?

  _____

- How many students are in each group?

  _____

🔓 **One Way** Use the Associative Property of Multiplication.

The Associative Property of Multiplication states that when the grouping of the factors is changed, the product is the same.

You can write $3 \times (2 \times \underline{})$.

Think: $14 = 2 \times 7$

Change the grouping of the factors to use a fact you know.

$(3 \times 2) \times 7 = \underline{} \times \underline{}$

Then multiply the fact you know.

$\underline{} \times \underline{} = \underline{}$

🔓 **Another Way** Use the Distributive Property.

The Distributive Property states that multiplying a sum by a number is the same as multiplying each addend by the number and then adding the products.

You can write $3 \times (10 + 4)$.

Think: $14 = 10 + 4$

Multiply each addend by 3.

$(3 \times 10) + (3 \times 4)$

Then add the products.

$\underline{} + \underline{} = \underline{}$

So, _____ students are working on the school play.

Math Talk Which method do you prefer? **Explain** why.

Share and Show

1. Use the Associative Property of Multiplication to find 4×16.

   Think: $16 = 2 \times 8$
   Group the factors to
   multiply facts you know.

   $4 \times \underline{\hspace{1cm}} \times \underline{\hspace{1cm}} = 4 \times \underline{\hspace{1cm}} \times \underline{\hspace{1cm}}$

   $4 \times 16 = \underline{\hspace{1cm}}$

Find the product. Name the property you used.

2. $5 \times 13 = 5 \times (10 + 3)$

   $\underline{\hspace{3cm}}$

   $\underline{\hspace{3cm}}$

   Property

3. $17 \times 4 = (10 + 7) \times 4$

   $\underline{\hspace{3cm}}$

   $\underline{\hspace{3cm}}$

   Property

4. $21 \times 2 = (7 \times 3) \times 2$

   $\underline{\hspace{3cm}}$

   $\underline{\hspace{3cm}}$

   Property

On Your Own

Find the product. Name the property you used.

5. $4 \times 18 = 4 \times (2 \times 9)$

   $\underline{\hspace{3cm}}$

   $\underline{\hspace{3cm}}$

   Property

6. $15 \times 7 = (10 + 5) \times 7$

   $\underline{\hspace{3cm}}$

   $\underline{\hspace{3cm}}$

   Property

7. $3 \times 16 = 3 \times (2 \times 8)$

   $\underline{\hspace{3cm}}$

   $\underline{\hspace{3cm}}$

   Property

Find the product.

8. 2×19

   $\underline{\hspace{3cm}}$

9. 4×22

   $\underline{\hspace{3cm}}$

10. 18×3

   $\underline{\hspace{3cm}}$

Find the missing number.

11. $5 \times 18 = 5 \times (\underline{\hspace{1cm}} \times 9)$

12. $19 \times 7 = (10 + \underline{\hspace{1cm}}) \times 7$

Problem Solving

13. Lacey pasted 4 pictures on each page of her photo album. There are 19 pages in the album. How many pictures did Lacey paste in all?

    $\underline{\hspace{5cm}}$

14. Mrs. Carney bought 18 packages of cupcakes for a party. There are 5 cupcakes in each package. How many cupcakes did Mrs. Carney buy?

    $\underline{\hspace{5cm}}$

Name _____

Model Division with Remainders

Essential Question How can you use counters to model division with remainders?

🔓 UNLOCK the Problem REAL WORLD

Madison has 13 seeds. She wants to put the same number of seeds in each of 3 pots. How many seeds can Madison put into each pot?

- How do you know how many groups to make?

_____

🔑 Activity Materials ▪ counters

Use counters to find 13 ÷ 3.

STEP 1 Use 13 counters. Draw 3 circles for the 3 pots.

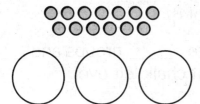

STEP 2 Place one counter in each group until there are not enough to put 1 more in each of the groups.

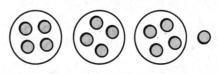

There are _____ counters in each circle.

There is _____ counter left over.

13 ÷ 3 is 4 with 1 left over.

The quotient is 4.

The remainder is 1.

So, Madison can put 4 seeds in each pot. There is 1 seed left over.

After dividing a group of objects into equal groups as large as possible, there may be some left over. The amount left over is called the remainder.

Math Talk **Explain** why you cannot have a remainder of 3 when you divide by 3.

Try This! **What if** Madison wants to put 4 seeds in each pot. How many pots will Madison need? How many seeds will be left over?

_____

Share and Show

1. Divide 13 counters into 2 equal groups.

    There are _____ counters in each group,

    and _____ counter left over.

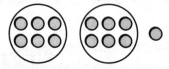

Complete.

2. April divided 17 counters into 4 equal groups.

    There were _____ counters in each

    group and _____ counter left over.

3. Divide 20 counters into groups of 6.

    There are _____ groups and _____ counters left over.

On Your Own

Complete.

4. Divide 14 pencils into 3 equal groups.

    There are _____ pencils in each

    group and _____ pencils left over.

5. Divide 60 pieces of chalk into groups of 8.

    There are _____ groups and _____ pieces of chalk left over.

Find the total number of objects.

6. There are 2 shoes in each of 6 groups and 1 shoe left over.

    There are _____ shoes in all.

7. There are 4 apples in each of 3 groups and 3 apples left over.

    There are _____ apples in all.

Problem Solving REAL WORLD

Use the bar graph for 8.

8. If Hector divides the oak leaves evenly into 4 display boxes, how many leaves will be in each box? How many leaves will be left over?

    _____

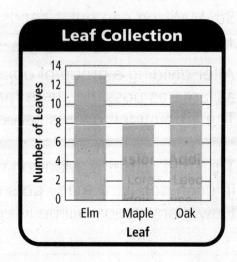

Model and Record Division

Essential Question How can you model and record division with a 2-digit quotient?

 UNLOCK the Problem REAL WORLD

Emma baked 54 muffins. She wants to put an equal number of muffins on each of 4 plates. How many muffins can she put on each plate? How many muffins will be left over?

- Circle the numbers you need to use.
- How many equal groups are there?

_____

🔑 **Find 54 ÷ 4.**

STEP 1 Use base-ten blocks to model the problem. Draw circles to represent the 4 equal groups.

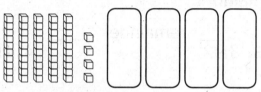

Number of muffins on each plate ←
Number of muffins ←
$4\overline{)54}$
↑
Number of plates

STEP 2 Place 1 ten in a each group until there are not enough to put 1 more in each group.

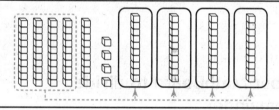

$\begin{array}{r} 1 \\ 4\overline{)54} \\ -4 \end{array}$

← Record the tens in each group.
← Subtract the tens put in the groups.

STEP 3 Regroup the remaining ten as ones.

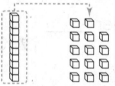

$\begin{array}{r} 1 \\ 4\overline{)54} \\ -4 \\ \hline 14 \end{array}$

← Record the ones after regrouping.

STEP 4 Place 1 one in each group until there are not enough to put 1 more in each group.

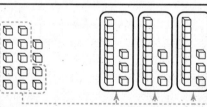

$\begin{array}{r} 13 \\ 4\overline{)54} \\ -4 \\ \hline 14 \\ -12 \end{array}$

← Record the ones in each group.
← Subtract the ones put into groups.

STEP 5 Count the ones that are left over and record the remainder.

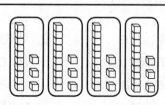

$\begin{array}{r} 13 \\ 4\overline{)54} \\ -4 \\ \hline 14 \\ -12 \\ \hline 2 \end{array}$

← quotient
← remainder

So, Emma can put _____ muffins on each plate.

There will be _____ muffins left over.

Math Talk How can you check your answer when there is a remainder?

Share and Show

1. Find 43 ÷ 2.

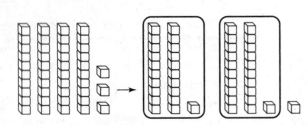

- How many equal groups are there? _____
- How many tens go in each group? _____
- How many ones go in each group? _____
- How many ones are left over? _____
- The quotient is _____.
- The remainder is _____.

**Use base-ten blocks and your MathBoard to divide.
Record the quotient and remainder.**

2. 5)64   remainder _____   3. 3)92   remainder _____   4. 4)88   remainder _____

On Your Own

**Use base-ten blocks and your MathBoard to divide.
Record the quotient and remainder.**

5. 2)72   remainder _____   6. 6)69   remainder _____   7. 3)52   remainder _____

Problem Solving

8. Roger has 85 trading cards. He wants to put an equal number in each of 3 boxes. How many cards will he put into each box? How many cards will be left over?

_____

9. Riley has 47 postcards. She wants to put 6 postcards on each poster board. How many poster boards will she need? How many postcards will be left over?

_____

Name _____

Use Division Patterns

Essential Question How can you use basic facts and patterns to divide by 10, 100, and 1,000?

UNLOCK the Problem REAL WORLD

Mr. Sanchez needs to order 6,000 marbles. There are 1,000 marbles in each box. How many boxes will he need?

- Circle the numbers you need to use.
- What operation can you use to find the number of equal groups?

_____

Use a basic fact and a pattern to divide.

Dividend		Divisor	Quotient
6	÷	1	= 6
60	÷	10	= 6
600	÷	100	= 6
6,000	÷	1,000	= 6

Think:
Use the basic fact $6 ÷ 1 = 6$.
Look for a pattern of zeros.

So, Mr. Sanchez will need 6 boxes.

Example

Divide. 8,000 ÷ 100

8,000	÷	1	= 8,000
8,000	÷	10	= 800
8,000	÷	100	= 80

So, $8,000 ÷ 100 =$ _____.

Math Idea

As the number of zeros in the divisor increases, the number of zeros in the quotient decreases.

Math Talk When dividing $5,000 ÷ 10$, how many zeros will be in the quotient? **Explain.**

© Houghton Mifflin Harcourt Publishing Company

Lesson 15

Share and Show

1. **Explain** how to use a basic fact and a pattern to find

   7,000 ÷ 1,000. _____

   _____

   _____

Use a basic fact and a pattern to divide.

2. 5,000 ÷ 1 = _____	3. 300 ÷ 1 = _____	4. 9 ÷ 1 = _____
5,000 ÷ 10 = _____	300 ÷ 10 = _____	90 ÷ 10 = _____
5,000 ÷ 100 = _____	300 ÷ 100 = _____	900 ÷ 100 = _____
5,000 ÷ 1,000 = _____		9,000 ÷ 1,000 = _____

On Your Own

Use a basic fact and a pattern to divide.

5. 4 ÷ 1 = _____	6. 2,000 ÷ 1 = _____	7. 800 ÷ 1 = _____
40 ÷ 10 = _____	2,000 ÷ 10 = _____	800 ÷ 10 = _____
400 ÷ 100 = _____	2,000 ÷ 100 = _____	800 ÷ 100 = _____
4,000 ÷ 1,000 = _____	2,000 ÷ 1,000 = _____	

Find the quotient.

8. 30 ÷ 10 = _____   9. 6,000 ÷ 10 = _____   10. 700 ÷ 10 = _____

11. 900 ÷ 100 = _____   12. 500 ÷ 100 = _____   13. 4,000 ÷ 100 = _____

Problem Solving REAL WORLD

14. Can each student put his baseball cards into boxes of 100 cards with none left over? **Explain**.

    _____

    _____

Baseball Card Collections	
Name	**Number of Cards**
Justin	800
Liam	700
Mark	650

Name _____

Concepts and Skills

Find the product. Show your multiplication and addition. (pp. P307–P308)

1.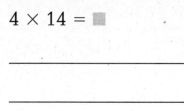

$4 \times 14 = \blacksquare$

_____

_____

_____

2.

$3 \times 18 = \blacksquare$

_____

_____

_____

3.

$5 \times 17 = \blacksquare$

_____

_____

_____

Find the product. Name the property you used. (pp. P309–P310)

4. $4 \times 16 = 4 \times (2 \times 8)$

_____

_____

Property

5. $15 \times 6 = (10 + 5) \times 6$

_____

_____

Property

6. $5 \times 14 = 5 \times (2 \times 7)$

_____

_____

Property

Divide. Use counters or base-ten blocks to help. (pp. P313–P314, P315–P316)

remainder _____

7. $6\overline{)70}$

remainder _____

8. $5\overline{)66}$

remainder _____

9. $4\overline{)84}$

10. $400 \div 10 =$ _____

11. $800 \div 100 =$ _____

12. $3,000 \div 1,000 =$ _____

Problem Solving REAL WORLD

Use the bar graph for 13. (pp. P311–P312)

13. Eli divides the blue marbles evenly into 4 bags. How many marbles are in each bag? How many marbles are left over?

_____

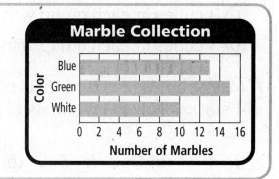

Marble Collection

Getting Ready for Grade 4   P317

Fill in the bubble completely to show your answer.

14. Marilyn is 4 feet tall. How many inches
    tall is she? Remember: 1 foot = 12 inches
    (pp. P307–P308)

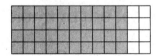

   Ⓐ 16 inches

   Ⓑ 42 inches

   Ⓒ 48 inches

   Ⓓ 60 inches

15. Mr. Randall bought 17 packages of tape. There are
    3 rolls of tape in each package. How many rolls of
    tape did Mr. Randall buy? (pp. P309–P310)

   Ⓐ 14

   Ⓑ 20

   Ⓒ 40

   Ⓓ 51

16. Keung put 23 cubes into 6 equal groups. How
    many cubes are in each group? How many cubes
    are left over? (pp. P311–P312)

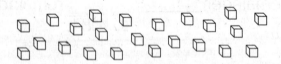

   Ⓐ 2 cubes in each group with 1 cube left over

   Ⓑ 2 cubes in each group with 5 cubes left over

   Ⓒ 3 cubes in each group with 1 cube left over

   Ⓓ 3 cubes in each group with 5 cubes left over

17. Ms. Webb divides 67 sheets of paper equally into
    4 stacks. How many sheets of paper are left over?
    (pp. P313–P314)

   Ⓐ 1   Ⓑ 3   Ⓒ 5   Ⓓ 9

Name _____

Lesson 16

Fahrenheit Temperature

Essential Question How can you read Fahrenheit temperature on a thermometer?

Temperature is a measure of how hot or cold something is. **Degrees Fahrenheit (°F)** are customary units of temperature.

CONNECT You know how to read numbers on a number line. Reading a thermometer scale is like reading a number line.

🔓 UNLOCK the Problem   REAL WORLD

How can you read Fahrenheit temperature on a thermometer?

🔑 **Read the Fahrenheit thermometer.**

STEP 1 Find the top of the gray bar. Look at the scale.

The bar is between 60 and 70.

It is at _____.
_____

STEP 2 Write and read the temperature.

Write: _____°F

Read: sixty-eight degrees Fahrenheit

So, the temperature is 68°F.

Water boils at 212°F.

Normal body temperature is about 98°F.

Normal room temperature is 72°F.

Water freezes at 32°F.

Try This! Estimate a temperature for the activity outdoors. Explain.

• ice skating _____

_____

• playing soccer _____

_____

Math Talk Why do you think outdoor thermometers usually do not show the boiling point of water?

© Houghton Mifflin Harcourt Publishing Company

Getting Ready for Grade 4   P319

Share and Show

1. Complete the sentences to read the temperature. The top of the gray bar is between the numbers

   _____ and _____ . It is 2 marks above 100.

   It is at _____ .

   Temperature: _____

Circle the better estimate for the temperature.

2. a cold, snowy day	3. a warm, sunny day	4. room temperature
26°F 66°F	80°F 30°F	20°F 68°F

On Your Own

Write the temperature in °F.

5.

   Temperature: _____

6.

   Temperature: _____

7.

   Temperature: _____

Circle the better estimate for the temperature.

8. water in a fish bowl	9. hot soup	10. inside a refrigerator
71°F 21°F	45°F 150°F	38°F 18°F

Problem Solving REAL WORLD

11. Name an activity you might do outdoors when the temperature is 85°F. **Explain.**

_____

_____

Name _____

Celsius Temperature

Essential Question How can you read Celsius temperature on a thermometer?

Degrees Celsius (°C) are metric units of temperature. Metric units are often used for scientific measurement. When scientists record observations of temperature, they often use degrees Celsius.

🔑 UNLOCK the Problem REAL WORLD

You can read Celsius temperature like you read Fahrenheit temperature. What is the temperature shown on this thermometer?

🔑 **Read the Celsius thermometer.**

STEP 1 Find the top of the gray bar. Look at the scale.

The bar is between 20 and 30.

It is at _____.

_____

STEP 2 Write and read the temperature.

Write: _____ °C

Read: twenty-six degrees Celsius

So, the temperature is 26°C.

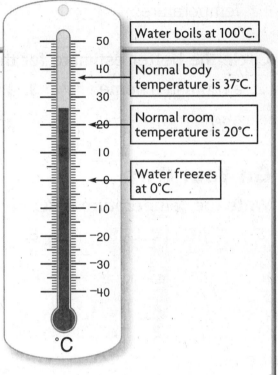

Water boils at 100°C.

Normal body temperature is 37°C.

Normal room temperature is 20°C.

Water freezes at 0°C.

°C

Try This! Estimate a temperature for the activity outdoors. Explain.

• raking leaves _____

_____

• flying a kite _____

_____

Math Talk Would you expect an outdoor temperature to reach 100°C? **Explain.**

Share and Show

1. Complete the sentences to read the temperature. The top of the gray bar is between the numbers

   _____ and _____. It is 3 marks above 10.

   It is at _____.

   Temperature: _____

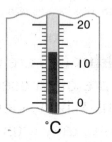

Circle the better estimate for the temperature.

2. a room in a home	3. a warm day	4. heated milk
22°C 4°C	28°C 1°C	15°C 45°C

On Your Own

Write the temperature in °C.

5.

°C

Temperature: _____

6.

°C

Temperature: _____

7.

°C

Temperature: _____

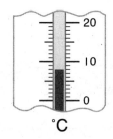
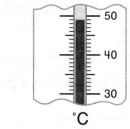

Circle the better estimate for the temperature.

8. water in a swimming pool	9. a bubbling pot of pasta	10. a snowy night
5°C 25°C	100°C 10°C	32°C 0°C

Problem Solving REAL WORLD

11. How might you dress to go outdoors when the temperature is 0°C? **Explain**.

_____

_____

Name _____

Change Units for Length

Essential Question How can you change a unit for length to a smaller or larger unit?

CONNECT You have learned about different customary and metric units of length. In this lesson, you will use relationships to change units.

UNLOCK the Problem · REAL WORLD

Gina needs a piece of wood that is 4 feet long to make a bench. How many inches of wood does Gina need?

• What do you need to do to answer the question?

_____

🔑 **Complete a table to find how the units are related.**

STEP 1   Look for a pattern to complete the table. Describe the relationship.

Feet	1	2	3	4	5
Inches	12	24	36		

Remember

1 foot = 12 inches
1 yard = 3 feet, or 36 inches

1 meter = 100 centimeters
1 kilometer = 1,000 meters

To find the number of inches, add _____ inches for each foot.
_____

STEP 2   Use the relationship to find the number of inches in 4 feet.

4 feet = _____ inches

So, Gina needs _____ inches of wood to make a bench.

Examples

A. Change 5 feet to inches.

Use the relationship:

Add _____ to 48 inches.

So, 5 feet = _____ inches.

B. Change 200 centimeters to meters.

Think: 100 centimeters = _____ meter

So, 200 centimeters = _____ meters.

 What do you need to know in order to change from one unit of length to another?

Share and Show

1. How can you change 3 meters to centimeters?
   Complete the table to show how the units are related.

Meters	1	2	3	
Centimeters	100	200		400

To find the number of centimeters,
add _____ centimeters for each meter.

So, 3 meters = _____ centimeters.

Find the missing number.

2. 400 centimeters = _____ meters

3. 5 meters = _____ centimeters

On Your Own

Complete the table.

4.

Yards	1	2	3	4	
Feet	3	6	9		15

5.

Kilometers	1	2	
Meters	1,000		3,000

Find the missing number.

6. 18 feet = _____ yards

7. 3 feet = _____ inches

8. 2 kilometers = _____ meters

9. 700 centimeters = _____ meters

Problem Solving

10. Jorge needs 800 centimeters of wire for a garden fence. The wire is sold in meters. How many meters of wire does Jorge need?

11. Wanda needs 14 feet of fabric to make curtains. She has 5 yards of fabric. Does Wanda have enough fabric to make the curtains? **Explain.**

Name _____

Change Units for Capacity

Essential Question How can you change a unit for capacity to a smaller or larger unit?

Capacity is the amount a container will hold. Cups (c), pints (pt), quarts (qt), and gallons (gal) are customary units used to measure capacity. Liters (L) and milliliters (mL) are metric units used to measure capacity.

🔑 UNLOCK the Problem  REAL WORLD

Marcus needs 3 liters of juice to make punch. How many milliliters of juice does he need?

> • What do you need to find?
>
> _____
>
> _____

🔑 **Complete a table to find how the units are related.**

STEP 1 Look for a pattern to complete the table. Describe the relationship.

Liters	1	2	3	
Milliliters	1,000	2,000		4,000

> **Remember**
>
> 1 liter = 1,000 milliliters
>
> 1 pint = 2 cups
> 1 quart = 2 pints, or 4 cups
> 1 gallon = 4 quarts, 8 pints, or 16 cups

To find the number of milliliters, add _____ milliliters for each liter.

STEP 2 Use the relationship to find the number of milliliters in 3 liters.

3 liters = _____ milliliters

So, Marcus needs _____ milliliters of juice.

Try This! Change 4,000 milliliters to liters.

Think: 1,000 milliliters = 1 liter

▨ × 1,000 = 4,000

_____ × 1,000 = 4,000

So, 4,000 milliliters = _____ liters.

 Which amount is greater, 2 liters or 1,500 milliliters? **Explain**.

Share and Show

1. How can you change 4 pints to cups?
Complete the table to find how the units are related.

Pints	1	2	3	4	5
Cups	2	4	6		

To find the number of pints, add

_____ cups for each pint.

So, 4 pints = _____ cups.

Find the missing number.

2. 10 cups = _____ pints

3. 6 pints = _____ cups

On Your Own

Complete the table.

4.

Quarts	1	2	3	4	5
Cups	4	8	12		

5.

Gallons	1	2	3	4	
Pints	8	16	24		40

Find the missing number.

6. 4 quarts = _____ cups

7. 5 gallons = _____ pints

8. 14 cups = _____ pints

9. 6,000 milliliters = _____ liters

Problem Solving REAL WORLD

10. Irina needs 5 gallons of paint for her house. The paint is sold in quarts. She knows that 1 gallon is equal to 4 quarts. How many quarts of paint does Irina need?

_____

11. Dan needs 4 liters of juice to make punch. He has 3,200 milliliters of juice. Does Dan have enough juice to make punch? **Explain.**

_____

_____

Name _____

Change Units for Weight and Mass

Essential Question How can you change a unit for weight or mass to a smaller or larger unit?

Weight is the measure of how heavy an object is. Ounces (oz) and pounds (lb) are customary units for measuring weight.

Mass is the amount of matter in an object. Grams (g) and kilograms (kg) are metric units for measuring mass.

UNLOCK the Problem REAL WORLD

Eva needs 4 pounds of tomatoes to make sauce. How many ounces of tomatoes does she need?

- How are ounces related to pounds?
_____
_____

Complete a table to find how the units are related.

STEP 1 Look for a pattern to complete the table. Describe the relationship.

Pounds	1	2	3	4	5
Ounces	16	32	48		

Remember

1 pound = 16 ounces

1 kilogram = 1,000 grams

To find the number of ounces, add _____ ounces for each pound.
_____

STEP 2 Use the relationship to find the number of ounces in 4 pounds.

4 pounds = _____ ounces

So, Eva needs _____ ounces of tomatoes.

Try This! **Change 80 ounces to pounds.**

Think: Subtract 16 ounces for each pound until you reach 0. Count the number of times you subtracted 0.

80 ounces = _____ pounds

Math Talk Which amount is greater, 10 pounds or 150 ounces? **Explain.**

Share and Show

1. How can you change 4 kilograms to grams?
   Complete the table to find how the units are related.

Kilograms	1	2	3	4	5
Grams	1,000	2,000	3,000		

To find the number of grams, add _____ grams for each kilogram.

So, 4 kilograms = _____ grams.

Find the missing number.

2. 5 kilograms = _____ grams

3. 6,000 grams = _____ kilograms

On Your Own

Complete the table.

4.

Ounces	16	32		64
Pounds	1	2	3	

5.

Grams	1,000	2,000		4,000
Kilograms	1	2	3	

Find the missing number.

6. _____ ounces = 3 pounds

7. 4,000 grams = _____ kilograms

8. 64 ounces = _____ pounds

9. 7 kilograms = _____ grams

Problem Solving

10. Walt needs 2 kilograms of rice for a recipe. One bag of rice contains 1,000 grams. How many bags of rice does Walt need?

11. Kim needs 3 pounds of carrots to make soup. She has 36 ounces of carrots. Does Kim have enough carrots to make soup? **Explain.**

_____

_____

Name _____

✓ Checkpoint

Concepts and Skills

Write the temperature in °F or °C. (pp. P319–P320, P321–P322)

1.

   Temperature: _____

2.

   Temperature: _____

3.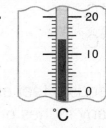

   Temperature: _____

Circle the better estimate for the temperature. (pp. P319–P320, P321–P322)

4. a classroom	5. a hot day	6. cold milk
34°F 74°F	3°C 33°C	6°C 48°C

Complete the table. Then find the missing number.

(pp. P323–P324, P325–P326, P327–P328)

7.

Feet	1	2	3	4	5
Inches	12	24	36		

5 feet = _____ inches

8.

Meters	1	2	
Centimeters	100		300

300 centimeters = _____ meters

9.

Quarts	1	2	3	4	5
Cups	4	8	12		

5 quarts = _____ cups

10.

Kilograms	1	2	3
Grams	1,000	2,000	

3 kilograms = _____ grams

Problem Solving REAL WORLD

11. Use the table at the right. Al needs 4 gallons of paste. The paste is sold in pints. How many pints of paste does Al need? (pp. P325–P326)

Gallons	1	2	3	4
Pints	8	16	24	

_____

Fill in the bubble completely to show your answer.

12. Sasha is drinking iced tea. Which is the best estimate of the temperature of her iced tea? (pp. P321–P322)

   Ⓐ   4°C

   Ⓑ   34°C

   Ⓒ   64°C

   Ⓓ 104°C

13. Theo needs 6 feet of rope to decorate a frame. How many inches of rope does Theo need?

   (pp. P323–P324)

   Ⓐ   3 inches

   Ⓑ 16 inches

   Ⓒ 60 inches

   Ⓓ 72 inches

14. Mariko needs 5 liters of apple juice to make fruit punch. How many milliliters of apple juice does Mariko need? (pp. P325–P326)

   Ⓐ   80 milliliters

   Ⓑ   500 milliliters

   Ⓒ 1,000 milliliters

   Ⓓ 5,000 milliliters

15. Chet needs 5 pounds of walnuts to make a cereal mix. The walnut packages at the store are labeled in ounces. How many ounces of walnuts does Chet need? (pp. P327–P328)

   Ⓐ 50 ounces

   Ⓑ 60 ounces

   Ⓒ 80 ounces

   Ⓓ 500 ounces